BE A GREAT SWIMMING TEACHER – REVIEWS:

I was lucky. The good teaching I received when first learning to swim laid the foundations for me to develop my skills further, eventually gaining a Bronze Medal at the 2004 Olympic Games. If those first steps on the ladder had not been so positive, I feel sure I would not have achieved the success I did.

Be A Great Swimming Teacher is going to be a valuable resource for helping the trainee teacher to develop the skills required to lay down these good foundations. Its focus throughout is not just on **what** to teach but on **how** to teach and to **best present** the material to the class. The qualities of a good teacher and how to plan a lesson steer the teacher along the road of good practice.

Throughout the book, the attention and understanding of the reader is enhanced by the identification of key points, the highlighting of material with colour or boxes and the extensive use of photographs and drawings. The **building block programme** gives the new teacher a framework to follow, clearly emphasising the main teaching points and how to demonstrate what is required.

The authors use their experience to explain clearly what works and why. I feel sure this text will help us develop better teachers of swimming, setting more youngsters on the road to further success... and who knows, the gaining of future Olympic Medals.

Stephen Parry
Olympic Medallist

*   *   *

I got into swimming as an excitable seven year old with a huge desire to win. I was never the biggest or strongest but I did have what I now realise was a better than average desire to listen and learn. I was lucky enough as a 12 year old to get to work with Colin Stripe. I turned up to every session morning and evening and so did he. I continued to listen and work on the drills and sessions Colin coached. We developed a large respect and trust for each other over the next six years up to and including the 2008 Olympics. I improved every year and won numerous national and international titles. I put this down to the disciplines of sensible hard work and commitment to basic skills that Colin always taught.

Colin kept it fun, interesting and refused to compromise my well being as a person and an athlete. Together with his co-author Patricia Parkes, many of the qualities he displayed as a coach have been applied to the training of teachers. I believe that the quality of any learn to swim programme is determined by the quality of the teaching. My experiences as an athlete have taught me that it is so very important to lay the best foundations as early as possible in a swimmers career. That is exactly what this book does. It lays the best foundations to become **a great swimming teacher**.

Francesca Halsall
Olympic Games Finalist 2008 & 2012,
European Champion and Commonwealth Games Silver Medallist

The most important element to laying the best foundations for any swimming programme is the training of high quality and effective swimming teachers. The better we can train our teachers, the better our learning to swim programmes will be.

In this book the authors take a number of unique approaches to the subject. Throughout, their descriptions, discussions and key points are based on their extensive teaching and coaching experience. The **building block programme** for each stroke guides the teacher along a structured pathway and shows the teacher how to demonstrate their teaching points in a clear and effective way. Few books (if any) have focused in such detail on how the teacher should demonstrate the stroke to a class of pupils, yet this is such a very important part of teaching swimming. Stroke problems, their causes and effect are identified and solutions given while the **improvement circle** concept gives the teacher a flexible and adaptable framework upon which to develop a stroke further.

The extensive use of photographs and drawings help to focus the teacher's attention and bring the subject to life. This book makes a valuable contribution to the existing literature on teaching swimming and is a must for any trainee teacher or practising teacher wanting to take a fresh approach.

Rosa Gallop
ASA Talent Development Officer for London and the South East

* * *

Be A Great Swimming Teacher takes an innovative and creative approach to teaching swimming. It encourages the trainee teacher to think openly (rather than in a more closed manner) about their approach to teaching and promotes a style which caters for individual differences ... teach **The Person** rather than **Teach the Syllabus**.

Throughout there is an emphasis on methodical planning and preparation and a focus on purposeful activities to create an enjoyable learning environment. The text also addresses the areas of balance, connection, poise, rhythm and timing, all of which are essential key components to develop early in a learn to swim programme.

The authors frequently revisit these components during the developmental stages. The better these foundations are first taught, the greater the chance that one day some may develop into **World Class Swimmers**.

Ian Armiger
Director of Swimming, Loughborough University

* * *

Be A Great

Swimming Teacher

What every swimming teacher should know

Colin Stripe and Patricia Parkes

Wizard Publishing

ISBN: 9780955021053

The Authors and Publishers have made all reasonable efforts to clarify source or ownership of any quoted content or copyright and have acknowledged accordingly. However, if errors have been unintentionally made, owners are invited to contact the publishers so that acknowledgement can be given

The publishers are grateful to:
Barbara James and John Baines for editing and proofreading
Cover design by ©Patricia Parkes
Images and diagrams design and management by ©Colin Stripe

Typeset by Hope Services (Abingdon) Ltd.
Printed on acid free paper by Butler Tanner & Dennis. Tel +44(0)1373 451500

Published by:

Wizard Publishing
An imprint of Gilbert Massara Publishing
17 Tovey Close
London Colney
Hertfordshire, AL2 1LF, UK

www.gmpub.co.uk

Contents

About the Authors

Colin Stripe:

After competing as a young swimmer, Colin studied for his degree in Physical Education at Loughborough College. He taught for two years in Basingstoke before continuing his studies at the University of Western Ontario, Canada, where in 1980 he gained a Master's degree in Physical Education. In 1981 he was appointed the Swimming Development Officer for the London Borough of Barking and Dagenham and Chief Coach for Barking Swimming Club.

In 1992 Colin moved to Liverpool where he took up the position of Chief Swimming Coach for the City Council, later combining this with the additional responsibility for the overall Swimming Development in Liverpool.

Colin has been an active past member of the British Swimming Coaches and Teachers Association, serving as their president in 1989/90 and as their Secretary in 1992/95 and again 1999/2000. During his career he was appointed coach to a number of GB and English National teams. He coached a number of International Swimmers during their junior development years including Olympic bronze medallist Stephen Parry, Michael Rock and 2010 European Champion Francesca Halsall.

In 2008 he stopped coaching to manage the newly created "Swim Liverpool" programme. He retired in April 2011 and now works as a self employed Management Consultant.

Patricia Parkes:

Pat has been involved in swimming almost all her life. As a former Essex County Champion, she naturally progressed into teaching and coaching all aspects of swimming. She worked for 17 years as a specialist swimming teacher at Coopers Coborn School, Upminster and tutored ASA teachers and coaches training courses throughout Essex and the East London Area.

In 1984, Pat was awarded the Royal Life Saving Society President's Commendation for her work at Coopers Coborn School and was appointed an ASA Senior Staff Tutor in 1986. On leaving Coopers Coborn School, she worked as a Swimming Consultant, running a variety of courses for Local Authorities, Schools and Swimming Clubs and represented Essex on the ASA Education Committee and the Southern Counties ASA Education Committee.

In 1994 Pat moved with her husband Brian to Dorset and continued her work as a Swimming Consultant in the local area. She now assists people with health problems and coaches a tri-athlete.

Acknowledgements

We would like to thank Gilbert Massara and colleagues at Wizard Publishing for the unending support, patience and guidance they have given us.

We would also like to thank the managers, teachers and swimmers of the City of Liverpool Swimming Development Programme for their co-operation during the many photographic sessions. In particular, special thanks are given to Jo Dunn, Jane Babes, Ian Ingman, Sarah Jones and Richard Easton for their teacher demonstrations and to Liam Owens for his underwater photography.

A final thank you must be given to our respective spouses, Joan Stripe and Brian Parkes who have supported and encouraged us from the start to the finish of this project.

Colin Stripe and Patricia Parkes
September 2013

Foreword

This book is the result of many years listening to cries of help from students and novice teachers. As joint authors, we have combined our knowledge and experience of teaching, coaching and tutoring to blend theory and application into a unique, progressive way to teach swimming.

When we first decided to write this book, we wanted it to be a swimming book with a difference. While we realised that many people had written books on swimming, some repetitive of old ways and thoughts, we believed we could bring a fresh "attack" to the subject by taking a strong "teacher centred" approach. This is therefore a book written for teachers of swimming, be them novice or experienced.

For each stroke, a detailed description and discussion is enhanced through in-depth drawings and photographs. A "building block" programme is then presented focusing on a new framework for teaching. Main problems are clearly identified and solutions given. This is then followed by a unique "improvement circle" concept to help the teacher take their pupils beyond the learner stage.

Throughout the focus is on teaching the teacher not just what to teach (knowledge and understanding) but also on how to best present and deliver this knowledge to the class through the use of clear demonstrations, good teaching practices and key teaching points. Our aim is to encourage teachers to put in place the right "building blocks" to teach a child to swim and develop them into a strong skilful swimmer who could move into a local community club programme to progress their skills further.

We have been able to write freely, without the constraints of candidates having to pass examinations at the end of a training course. It is not our intention, however that this book be used as a substitute for the ASA's own excellent publications but we would hope that candidates would find the text of some value as an additional source to which they may refer. We also hope this book will prove a useful text for both the novice and experienced teacher either preparing for a swimming lesson or as a manual on the poolside to which reference can be made.

Our enthusiasm for the sport has been the driving force behind writing this book and we simply hope to encourage other teachers to learn more and make a commitment to become *A Great Swimming Teacher.*

Colin Stripe and Patricia Parkes
September 2013

Chapter 1

First Things First

Main Focus:

- Who is the book for?

- What is our starting point?

- What is our style of presentation?

- Our search for a better way

- A new framework for teaching

- A system of **building blocks**

- The concept of **rhythm**

- Techniques to give the swimmer **time**

- The need to make learning **fun**

- Beyond the learner

- A concept of **improvement circles**

- The use of progressive sequences

- Assessing a stroke

- What are the main responsibilities of the teacher?

- A summary poem by Patricia Parkes

Chapter 1

First Things First

INTRODUCTION

Who is the book for?

This book is written for people who wish to teach swimming well.

People who become hooked on teaching swimming vary enormously in their age, background and reasons for their involvement. For some, it is their profession but for many, it is still a voluntary pastime. Often swimming teachers start life as either:

- An **ex-swimmer** who does not want to give up the sport entirely.
- A **pupil** studying swimming as part of their school Physical Education curriculum.
- A **higher education student teacher** who is looking for a further qualification.
- A **parent** who is drawn from the balcony to help on the pool side.

Whatever their background, once they experience that 'buzz' a teacher gets when a student struggles across the width for the first time, they usually become hooked for many years, if not for life.

Why is this book needed?

We, as experienced swimming teachers, are conscious that we do not want to re-invent the wheel. There are many books on teaching swimming, in particular several quality volumes from the governing body of the sport. This literature is, however, primarily concerned with knowledge, theory and with getting candidates through their examination at the end of a certification course.

Our review of literature has highlighted a lack of written material where the main focus is on **the swimming teacher** and this is something we hope to address. This manual is free from the restraints of an examination syllabus and the primary focus is to instruct teachers to open their minds to a variety of ways to deliver and achieve a set of outcomes from their teaching. In addition we want to encourage teachers to experiment and think about how they can make their own teaching as effective as possible.

What are our objectives?

Our aim is to provide the swimming teacher with a working manual for use in the management of their swimming programme. The objectives are to:

- **Provide a guide to the many enthusiasts** in the sport who simply teach swimming for the enjoyment it brings them. The focus is to show them not only what to teach, but also how to best demonstrate and present this to a class of children.

- **Stimulate the already practising professional** into new and exciting ways of thinking about their teaching.

- **Show how the various stages of stroke development can be effectively linked together** in a clear and constructive way to lay the foundations for a learner to develop into a strong, skilful swimmer.

How are these objectives achieved?

These objectives are achieved by:

- **Presenting a clear and concise view** of swimming theory and how this specifically relates to teaching swimming.

- **Showing how the teacher** can best present and deliver this knowledge to pupils.

- **Outlining a framework of building blocks** in which the skills required to swim are developed in a progressive way.

- **Introducing a concept of improvement circles** to take a pupil beyond the learner stage to being ready to move into a local community club programme to progress their skills further.

What is our starting point?

Teaching swimming is an art. An artist creates a picture by first deciding on the composition, then choosing and mixing the colours before building the picture slowly using a variety of skills and techniques to eventually produce a finished work. In the same way, a swimming teacher assesses the pupil, chooses a variety of skills, drills, practices and techniques to build up a programme of instruction to produce a finished outcome; a pupil who can swim.

The choices the teacher makes in terms of what to teach and how to teach is a **creative process** and this determines the nature of the programme of instruction. It is a skill that develops over time and is the **true art of teaching swimming**.

⊶ The more skilful a teacher is at this process, the more successful they are likely to be as a teacher.

The art of teaching is more than just knowledge and understanding. Great teaching requires the teacher to communicate, motivate and engage pupils in the activity of learning to swim in a way that they enjoy the experience and have fun.

⊶ How a swimming teacher creates this environment, is also part of the true art of teaching.

The ideal stroke

Teachers must remember that the ideal stroke is not always possible. Many descriptions can be found of how each stroke should be performed. While it is useful to form a mental picture of the ideal stroke, teachers must never lose sight of the fact that the learner is not a 'mini version' of an Olympic swimmer.

⊶ Part of the skill of teaching is recognising that beginners cannot always match ideals.

When teaching beginners, be aware that:

What should happen and what actually does happen are not always the same.

This may be due to a lack of skill or to physical limitations such as size, strength, flexibility or buoyancy. The teacher must learn to recognise these and at times tolerate a certain level of deviation from the ideal.

⊶ The ability to be able to adapt skills and practices and knowing what is acceptable and what is not, comes with experience and is a vital element in the art of teaching.

OUR STYLE OF PRESENTATION

In presenting our material, we took our starting point to be from when a pupil has gained a level of confidence and water competency and is ready to start learning the strokes. The very beginning stages of introducing a child to the water and working through a collection of exercises to build water confidence is well documented by other authors and the governing body's learn to swim literature. We felt there was little to add to this body of knowledge.

The driving force behind this book has been our own open-mindedness and willingness to question whether things can be done better. In our search for a better way, we have taken great care to show how the current knowledge on the teaching of swimming is best presented, for as with all teaching, the style of presentation is vital. The style has to be of practical use to the teacher, with the emphasis on the word 'practical'.

The material also needs to be presented in a way that not only provides the first time teacher with a useful guide, but also stimulates the already practising professional. To achieve this, the following features are used in this book:

- **Descriptions for each stroke** are broken down into sections and each is followed by a discussion.

- **Key words and statements** are written in bold.

- **Key points** are highlighted by the symbol 🗝

- **Special notes and technical information** are highlighted by the symbol

- **Key questions** are highlighted throughout; many are presented as section headings.

- **A building programme** is presented in 'blocks' with progressive practices, reasons and teaching points clearly shown.

- **Photographs and diagrams** are used extensively throughout, to show the teacher *what to look for* when the stroke is performed and *how to best demonstrate* what is required.

- **The recognition of stroke problems** is discussed and solutions given.

- **A concept of improvement circles** is presented as a model to further develop the stroke beyond the learner stage.

Throughout, special attention is given to the order in which practices are put together to ensure the sequence is effective.

OUR SEARCH FOR A BETTER WAY

How original can you be when teaching a child to swim? After all *'a front crawl leg kick is a front crawl leg kick'* and *'swimming is swimming'*.

As we have said, our intention is not to reinvent the wheel but more to redesign the vehicle upon which the wheel is attached.

🗝 Our vehicle is a framework in which the skills needed to swim are developed in a progressive way.

The framework for our teaching programme is based on four main principles:

- **A system of building blocks.**
- **A concept of rhythm.**
- **Techniques to give the swimmer time.**
- **The need for learning to be fun.**

Principle 1: A system of building blocks

Most books on teaching swimming follow a similar format. They look at the four swimming strokes, (front crawl, backstroke, breaststroke and butterfly) and describe each using the following key headings:

- Body position
- Leg kick
- Arm pull
- Breathing
- Co-ordination.

These form the basic components of any stroke. Then under each heading, it is usual to list a series of practices that the teacher can use to develop that particular component of the stroke.

The result is a very neat and orderly presentation. Given this format, however, it is understandable that teachers often only ever think of a stroke in terms of its component parts and adopt a style of teaching that develops a stroke in the following way:

- First, they develop the leg kick, working faithfully through the practices shown.
- Next they move onto the arm pull, again working through the practices listed.
- It is likely that much of the work so far has been done within the confines of breath holding because the skill of breathing has not yet been taught.
- Once the breathing has been tried, the teacher stands back as their pupil attempts the complete stroke, hoping that all the pieces of the 'jigsaw' fit together.

The problem is the sum of all the parts, never quite seem to match up to the whole and the stroke easily breaks down.

It is as if all the pieces of the jigsaw do not fit together very well. This has led us to conclude that teaching the basic components of each stroke in isolation from one another and then hoping they fit together, may not be the most effective approach.

Is there a better way?

The fitting together of all the components must be part of a systematic plan which:

builds up the skills required to swim in a progressive way.

The term 'build' is used very deliberately here, for this is exactly how the teacher should think of developing a stroke; much the same way a builder builds a house.

Building a house needs the skills of a number of different tradesmen like a bricklayer, a plumber, a carpenter and an electrician. It is likely that two or three of these tradesmen will be working on the house at any one time. Furthermore, these tradesmen come and go at various stages in the building of the house. It is not possible for example, for all the electrical jobs to be carried out in one go as some of the work depends on the other tradesmen having reached certain stages in their own work. The electrician for example, will be called back on several occasions adding a little bit more each time until the house is completed.

In much the same way, the swimming teacher needs to build up a stroke from the different basic components, namely body position, leg kick, arm pull, breathing and co-ordination. These too should be used on a 'come and go' basis, gradually feeding into the programme at various stages until the whole stroke is built up.

All the kicking practices for example, should not be carried out in one go as some of the work depends on elements of the other basic components having already been taught, such as breathing.

Teachers should avoid thinking about developing each of the basic components of a stroke in isolation; it is more helpful to think in terms of stages referred to as 'building blocks'. A diagram of this concept is presented in Figure 1.1.

The main features of the building programme

These are:

- Each building block is made up of a **number of skills** drawn from any one or more of the five basic components that make up the complete stroke.
- Skills are woven together to form a **central pathway** along which the pupil is taken.
- The stroke is **gradually built up in a sequential way.**
- The **sequence is progressive**, so the skills in each building block need to be mastered before the pupil progresses onto the next one.

The stroke is built up gradually with teaching practices that encourage the pupil to develop the correct timing and rhythm of the stroke.

By the end of the building programme the complete stroke can be attempted in a more confident way without it quickly breaking down.

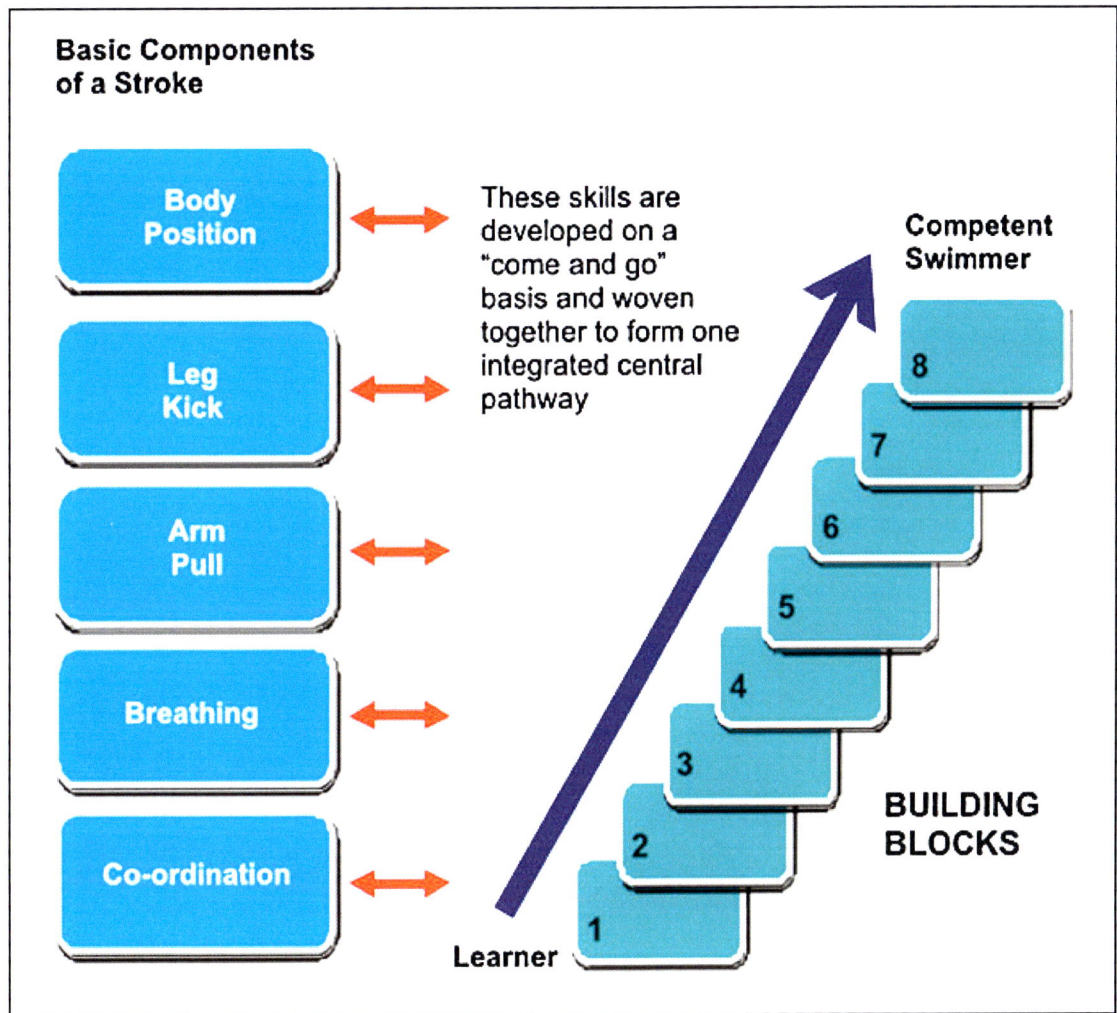

Figure 1.1
A diagram of the 'building block concept'

Principle 2: The concept of rhythm

What do we mean by the **rhythm** of the stroke? When you watch a skilled swimmer, you see what can be described as a very rhythmic type of activity. It consists of many stroke cycles, repeated over and over again, with each cycle lasting only a short time, less than two or three seconds.

A rhythm is defined as:

> **A continuous series of repeated cycles, each one very much like the last.**

If you look at the stroke patterns for the leg and arm movements in all strokes, you begin to appreciate just how rhythmical the activity of swimming really is.

For example, Figures 1.2 and 1.3 show the stroke patterns for the leg and arm actions for the front crawl. You can see that the same overall pattern is constantly repeated over and over again.

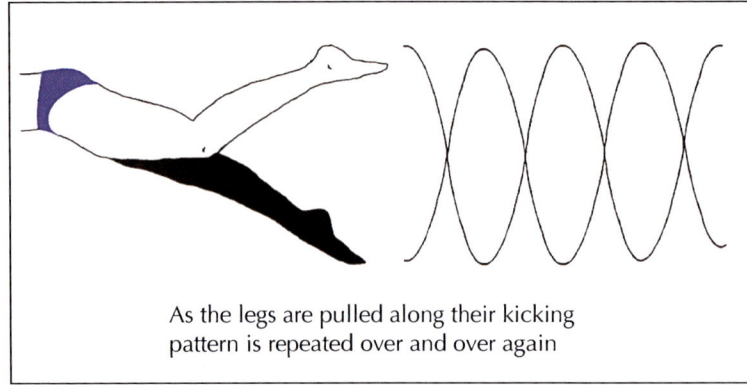

Figure 1.2
Repeated kicking patterns in front crawl

As the legs are pulled along their kicking pattern is repeated over and over again

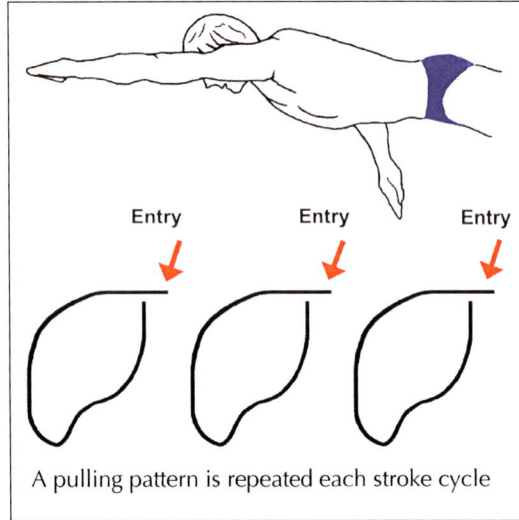

Figure 1.3
Repeated pulling patterns in front crawl

A pulling pattern is repeated each stroke cycle

Variations in rhythm

Individuals performing the same stroke will vary. If you look closely at six swimmers racing down the pool on front crawl, your perception would be that each swimmer's stroke is slightly different, resulting in a rhythm which is unique to their own stroke. Why is this?

- **Physical factors** such as the swimmer's size, strength, flexibility and buoyancy all play a large part in shaping their stroke.
- **Skill factors** such as variations in the way each phase of the stroke is executed will affect the timing, co-ordination and consequently the rhythm of the stroke.

Each individual stroke cycle is made up of a number of easily definable phases. In its simplest form, an arm movement can be broken down into:

- A p**ropulsive** phase
- A **recovery** phase.

The propulsive phase in turn is often broken down into a number of much smaller phases, (entry, stretch, catch, down-sweep, in-sweep and up-sweep).

⚷— It is the small variations in the way each phase is executed, which gives the individual swimmer a unique appearance.

How can the concept of rhythm help our teaching?

By first identifying the rhythm and then applying it to the practices, the pupils are encouraged early in their learning to develop a 'feel' for the correct timing and co-ordination. Then by concentrating on maintaining a set rhythm, the stroke is less likely to break down when the complete stroke is attempted.

Above all, working to a rhythm forces the pupil to slow everything down and gives them . . . **time**. This is the third principle upon which our teaching programme is based and time is needed to learn the different phases of the stroke correctly.

Principle 3: The need for time

The trouble with beginners is that they are often in a mad rush to do things. When the whole stroke is attempted, especially for the first time, their instinct to survive becomes stronger than all the previously practised skills. The stroke generates into little more than thrashing the water and because they have invariably forgotten to breathe, the stroke breaks down as they gasp for air.

If only the stroke could be slowed down enough to allow the swimmer time to attempt the skills properly.

It was this aim, namely to find a way of slowing everything down, which gave rise to our thinking on rhythm. The two are very much linked. We theorised that if the learner could work to a pre-determined rhythm, it would be easier to slow them down enough to give them time to do all the things necessary to perform the stroke effectively. In turn, this must result in more effective teaching.

⚷— It is important for the teacher to continually check whether the pupils simply have enough time to perform the practices and skills correctly.

Too often this is not the case. The movement is not slowed down enough and the learner does not have time to:

- **Think** about what they are doing.
- **Perform** the movement correctly.

 Techniques to give pupils more time often involve giving the learner plenty of support in the water. It should not be considered a step backwards for example, to use two floats instead of one or even use arm bands if necessary at any time during the building programme. Giving plenty of support and working a number of practices to a specific rhythm, helps give the learner the time they need during the early stages of learning.

Principle 4: Learning needs to be fun

This is the fourth and final principle on which our learners' programme is based. The idea that learning to swim should be fun is something that some people may scorn and others accept. Yet if you were to ask children at the end of a lesson *'so did you have fun?'*, how many of them would say *'Yes'*?

Too often teachers are in danger of not giving serious thought to this aspect of their teaching. It is all too easy to become predictable, even regimented, which leaves little room for flair, imagination and originality. It is important for teachers to realise that the best learning occurs when the pupil is also having fun.

🔑 Fun needs to be planned, it does not occur automatically.

Learning to swim should be a pleasurable experience, something that the pupils enjoy and would like to do again because it made them happy.

Avoiding boredom

On the other hand, a dilemma arises because skills have to be practised over and over again before the pupil becomes proficient enough to move on to the next stage of the programme. This regular exposure to repeated practice is the way we learn new skills and ingrain them to become deep-seated habits. Care must be taken however, to avoid this becoming boring.

The danger is that to solve this dilemma, teachers invariably try one of two things:

- **They try to rush everything and teach too much too soon**. The aim of the lesson is set at teaching the complete front crawl in thirty minutes, so they work through a range of practices covering legs, arms, breathing and co-ordination skills.

You cannot hope to cover such a large amount in one lesson and yet, it has been our experience that teachers often attempt this in their efforts to make the lesson interesting and fun.

- **They use the last five or ten minutes of a lesson to give the pupils free time** to do what they want. The fun coming from simply being allowed to 'do your own thing'.

We question this approach. If you were to watch a group of children who have just been given ten minutes free time in a pool, their initial response is one of excitement, but after three or four minutes this usually dies down and they are left wondering what to do.

Increasing the fun element of a lesson

Children need to be continually directed and stimulated but this does not mean it cannot be fun.

Fun is the result of creating the right atmosphere.

With children, this is achieved by using their imagination. Skills and games can be devised which use children's imagination and at the same time provide a useful learning experience.

Free fall parachuting

The skill of floating on your front can be brought to life by taking a little time to encourage the pupils to imagine they are all 'free fall parachuting'. You want them to look down at the 'ground' (bottom of the pool) and float face down with the arms and legs apart.

As they are falling towards the ground, you can also ask them in small groups of two, three or four to join hands and fall as a team holding the same position. This takes the practice from an individual one to a group activity.

Team try to
join hands

Figure 1.4
Free-fall parachuting as a group while practising the star float.

In terms of skill development, the pupils are practising:

- Floating.
- Putting their faces in the water.
- Opening their eyes underwater.

At the same time the teacher has turned an ordinary situation into an exciting and daring game.

Using your imagination

There are many ways of getting children to repeat skills over and over again. Stories that relate to current television programmes are always good for creating the right atmosphere. Teachers are only limited by their own imagination. However this does take some thought and preparation on the part of the teacher. Do not underestimate the value of the fun element for:

 A few moments of the lesson spent creating the right atmosphere can improve greatly the learning environment.

IMPROVERS' PROGRAMMES: BEYOND A LEARNER

Once the basic building blocks have been mastered, the student begins to move into the stages of **improver**. The focus is on practising skills to establish a good rhythm, correct co-ordination and the ability to maintain an effective stroke over an ever-increasing distance.

 The longer a pupil is allowed to perform a skill poorly, the more difficult it is to correct.

It takes time and patience for **good skills** to become **good habits**. Practice, practice and more practice are required before the stroke can become smooth, co-ordinated and effective.

 To perform a movement, the body first has to learn to select the correct nervous pathways to be used. If these pathways are used frequently, they turn into a habit enabling the stroke to be performed in a smooth and co-ordinated manner.

When bad habits are learnt, the wrong nervous pathways are used and it takes a great deal of effort to correct a fault and re-train the body to select new nervous pathways so the stroke is performed effectively.

This is why it is vital that the right building blocks are laid down and good skills are learnt right from the start. If this occurs, it makes the progression to the improver stage much easier.

Improvement circles

Once the building block programme of the learner has been completed, an improver programme is gradually introduced built around a number of **core improvement skills** that together form an **improvement circle**. The concept is shown in Figure 1.5.

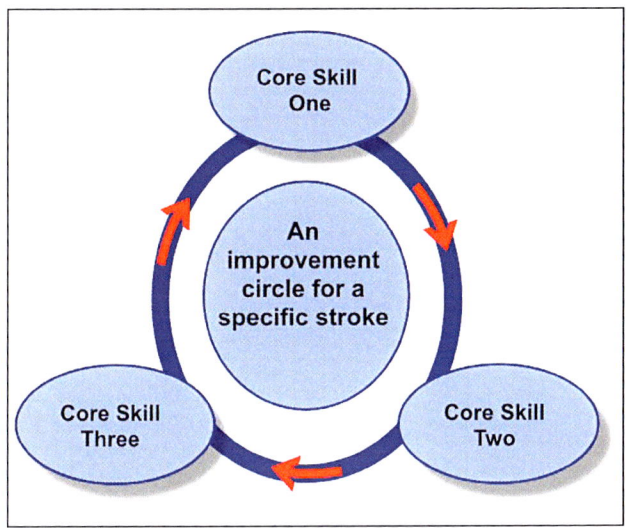

Figure 1.5
The improvement circle model

The term 'circle' is used quite deliberately here, because the core skills are repeated over and over many times in various ways. For each of the strokes (Chapters 5, 6, 7 and 8), we will show how this can be achieved.

The concept of improver circles gives the teacher a model to follow when planning their improver programme. It helps the less experienced teacher to focus on a repeated sequence of skills to improve the stroke. Like all models, they can be adapted. The more experienced teacher for example, may choose to use different core skills to those outlined in the stroke chapters. This is fine, as long as the teacher remembers:

 There is no short cut to developing a skill into a habit. Repeated practice is essential.

The teacher must therefore become adept at disguising this repetitive practice in a way that is still fun and so the pupils remain motivated.

At first, the teacher may revert back to practising the core skills with support. This helps give the pupils time to focus on what is required. Once a competent level of proficiency is achieved, the same core skills are further developed without support.

It is important that the teacher does not ignore all other practices and activities and concentrate *only* on the core improver skills. A wide range of practices, activities and challenges are still required to improve water competence and add variety and enjoyment to the lesson. Nevertheless, the core improvement skills must be practised over and over again to develop the full stroke effectively.

 The challenge for the teacher is to weave these core improvement skills many times into their improver programme by delivering a wide range of practices to achieve the same result.

This is a case where the 'wheel' does have to be re-invented continually for the teacher cannot just keep repeating the same practice. The pupils will very soon become bored so the teacher must be prepared to find many different ways of practising and establishing the same skill. This is where the teacher must use their imagination and flair to keep pupils motivated.

To deliver an effective improver programme it is also important that the teacher becomes proficient at two further skills:

- **Designing progressive sequences** to effectively establish good habits and skills.
- **Assessing a stroke**.

Progressive sequences

As the pupil becomes more proficient it is not only the practices used which are important, but also the **order** in which they are put together. If they are in a sequence which is progressive and where the skills are linked and continually re-enforced, their effectiveness is increased considerably.

The importance of designing sequences of a progressive nature where each one builds on the one before cannot be underestimated. It allows the swimmer to build up the stroke gradually while concentrating on one or two key teaching points. A number of examples are given in this book but with practice the teacher can become skilled at designing and putting together their own progressive sequences to establish and ingrain good technique.

Assessing a stroke

The ability to assess a stroke requires the teacher to:

- Look at a stroke.
- Assess its effectiveness.
- Identify any faults.
- Prioritise what needs to be corrected.
- Plan how this is to be done and the practices needed.

A skilled teacher can run quickly through this sequence in their mind for several pupils in their lesson. This results in a snapshot assessment that is effective during the early stages of learning.

As the pupil becomes more proficient, a more detailed assessment of the stroke is required. This involves the teacher watching a pupil swim a number of widths or lengths of the pool, usually with several rest periods, while they record key elements of the stroke.

THE TEACHER'S RESPONSIBILITIES

What are the main responsibilities of the teacher? As we conclude this first chapter, it is useful to be clear as to what they are. There are three main responsibilities:

- To teach a skill which could **save or extend life**.
- To encourage the development of this skill to enable **participation in a wide range of other aquatic activities** for fun and enjoyment and as part of a healthy lifestyle.
- To **keep an open mind** throughout their teaching career.

Teaching a skill which could save or extend life

Whether teaching swimming is a profession or a pastime, it is essential to bear in mind that parents are entrusting the teacher with a very special responsibility; the responsibility of teaching their child to swim.

The teacher is also taking on the responsibility for teaching a life-skill which may help to extend or even save life. In the current drive for improved health and fitness and a healthier lifestyle for both children and adults, swimming has an important part to play. It is truly a sport for all and one which can be pursued throughout a lifetime by both the able-bodied and people with disabilities.

Teaching a skill which enables participation in a wide range of other aquatic activities

As a skill, swimming opens up the opportunity to take part in a wide range of exciting aquatic activities including canoeing, sailing, wind surfing and sub-aqua. These are in addition to the more regular aquatic activities like diving, water polo, synchronised swimming and competitive swimming. To be responsible for developing a skill, which opens up such a wide range of possibilities, is worthwhile in itself.

Throughout the learning experience the teacher also has the responsibility to ensure this is achieved in an enjoyable, fun and safe environment.

Keeping an open mind

The very best teachers have the most open minds.

Teachers also have a responsibility to keep an open mind. They must continually think about, question and evaluate their own teaching methods and be prepared to review and try new approaches. This is achieved by constantly updating knowledge through reading, attending courses and conferences and through sharing information with other teachers.

If teachers frequently ask themselves:

What can I do differently to teach a particular skill more successfully?

they eliminate the risk of their teaching becoming routine, predictable and consequently boring.

    Never become a teacher who sits on a pile of floats or leans on a wall giving an appearance of being totally disinterested.

WHERE DO WE GO FROM HERE?

Before using the ideas, principles and concepts presented in this chapter to look at each of the four strokes, we must first:

- Discuss what make a **good teacher**?
- Outline how to best **manage and plan a lesson** effectively.
- Gain some insight as to **why things happen in water**.

These topics form the basis of Chapters 2, 3 and 4.

FIRST THINGS FIRST

We want you to know what's inside this book
Turn the pages, read, learn and look.
Building blocks, circles, drawings and stuff
Start at the beginning, there's more than enough
Of methods, techniques all in detail
Lessons to prepare, before you set sail
Onto the poolside, dressed in the right gear
Where anxious kids wait, your words to hear,
So turn the pages and see how we feature
The ways to become a Great Swimming Teacher

Pat Parkes

Chapter 2

What Makes A Good Teacher?

Main Focus:

- A range of good communication skills
- The ability to be able to plan a lesson carefully
- The organisational skills to manage the risk factors and create a safe environment in which to learn
- A thorough knowledge of the sport
- The ability to motivate pupils
- The skill to demonstrate to the pupils correctly
- The competency to observe and assess a stroke quickly and accurately
- A professional image by adopting a suitable dress code on the poolside
- A professional manner in dealing with the customer
- Adaptability in order to deal with the unusual and unexpected
- The skills and confidence to control a class and deal with misbehaviour
- A summary poem by Patricia Parkes

Chapter 2

What Makes A Good Teacher?

🔑 **Good teachers are successful teachers.**

The list of factors that help a teacher to be successful is endless, but three form the basis of all good teaching. These are:

- **The use of good communication skills.**
- **The careful planning of the lesson.**
- **The creation of a safe environment in which to learn.**

GOOD COMMUNICATION SKILLS

Over the last ten years, the terminology used to describe the theory of swimming has changed. The pull/push descriptions based on the action/reaction principle of Newton's Third Law of Motion have been replaced by a greater emphasis on sculling and the idea of moving the limbs in 'sweeps, circles and curved patterns'.

These new descriptions have, however, been mostly confined to books on coaching the competitive swimmer. The swimming community has been slow to adopt this new terminology for teaching. Consequently, a gap has developed between coaching and teaching in terms of the 'jargon' that each uses. This causes misunderstanding and confusion for the teacher trying to come to terms with swimming theory. Part of our aim is to help bridge this gap.

To achieve this we are concerned with two clear but different lines of communication:

- **Understanding the theory** – from the written page to the teacher.
- **Putting the theory into practice** – from the teacher to the pupil.

Figure 2.1 shows this as a simple input/output diagram.

Figure 2.1
An input/output diagram of communication

The problem is that many teachers have not been properly guided as to how to put the theory into practice.

 It is important that what the teacher tells the child produces the correct results so they must give considerable thought to the language used when giving instructions. It is not just a case of using the same terminology found in the swimming theory. This terminology has to be adapted and changed so the pupils understand clearly what is required of them. This is a vital skill for the teacher to acquire and is a major focus throughout this book.

For example:

In the front crawl stroke, the theory describes the first part of the hand motion as:

'A sweep downwards and slightly outwards followed by a sweep inwards'.

This terminology could be difficult for a child to understand. The desired movement is more likely to be achieved by asking the pupils to:

'Press the hand down to a point under the chin'

 Not only is it vital the teacher understands the theory, but it is also equally important they communicate this to their pupils. Communication is a skill in its own right and is a major factor in the art of teaching.

The fundamentals of good communication

The line of communication
The line of communication is shown in Figure 2.2.

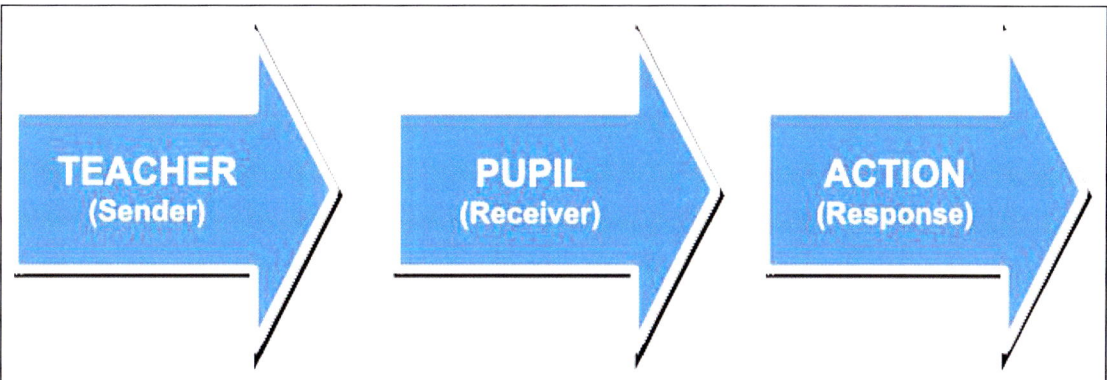

Figure 2.2
The line of communication

- The teacher *sends* the message to the pupil. This may be verbal or non-verbal (like a gesture or an expression).
- The pupil *receives* the message and interprets it.
- The pupil then *responds* with some action or change in behaviour.

⌛ For communication to be successful the action (*response*) has to be what the teacher (the *sender*) intended.

Giving effective messages

What can the teacher do to ensure their message is sent effectively?

1. Use language appropriate to the pupil.

2. Keep instructions short, clear and concise.

3. Use positive communication.

4. Select the correct teaching position.

5. Use their voice effectively.

1. Language appropriate to the pupils

The teacher must be careful to give instructions and explanations in a language and at the level the pupils understand. The terminology used for very young children is very different to that used for older children and this is different again if teaching teenagers or adults.

2. Short, clear concise instructions

Most instructions should only last fifteen to thirty seconds. The teacher needs to be concise and sure of exactly what they want to say before they say it. A good rule to follow is:

🔑 K.I.S.S. – Keep It Straight-forward and Simple

3. Keep communication positive

Positive points tell the pupil what the teacher wants them to do. They emphasise the correct movements. Negative points only tell the pupil what not to do, without giving information of what is needed.

For example, in breaststroke a beginner may experience some difficulty in turning the feet out.

- A positive teaching point would be: *'trace circles with your heels'*.
- A negative teaching point would be: *'you are not turning your feet out'*.

🔑 Using positive communication is a more effective way of developing and strengthening skills.

Also, do not underestimate the value of non-verbal messages as an effective communication tool.

Hand signals are a swimming teacher's greatest asset.

Often the pupils cannot hear when their ears are under the water but they can see. Eye contact, a nod or a smile works wonders with a nervous pupil. Use an interesting voice, varying the tones and pitch and **don't be afraid to laugh**. The lesson needs to be a happy one.

4. Teaching position

The teacher should always be in a position where every pupil can be seen and where everyone in the class can hear their voice. This is normally at the end of a line as shown in Figure 2.3.

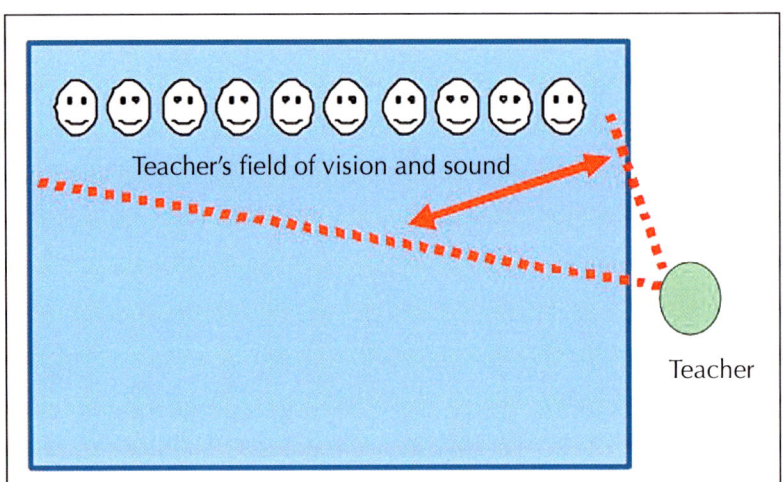

Figure 2.3
The correct teaching position for effectively communicating with a group

In Figure 2.3 the key factors are:

- The teacher can see all the pupils.
- The pupils can easily see the teacher.
- The teacher can project their voice to the whole group.

A central position is not advisable because the voice is projected only to the pupils immediately in front of the teacher and not to the ones at either end.

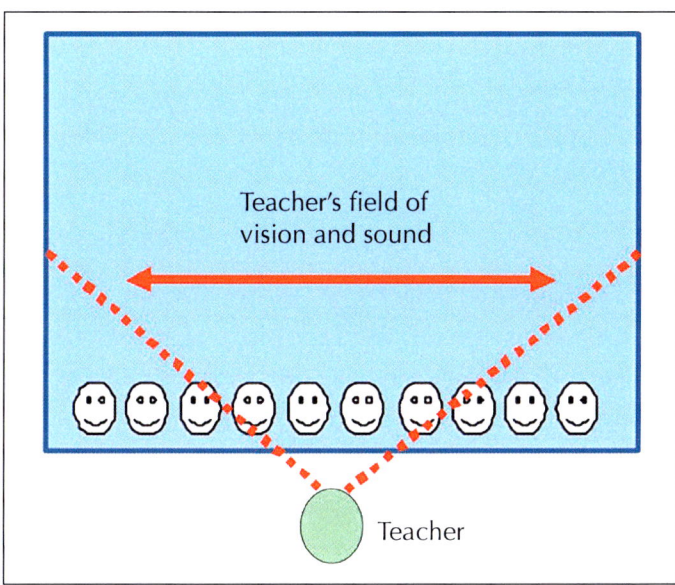

Figure 2.4
The limitations of a central position when teaching a group

In Figure 2.4 the key factors are:

- The teacher cannot see every child all of the time.
- The pupils at either end of the line will have difficulty hearing the teacher.

A central position may be used if the teacher is standing on the opposite side of the pool.

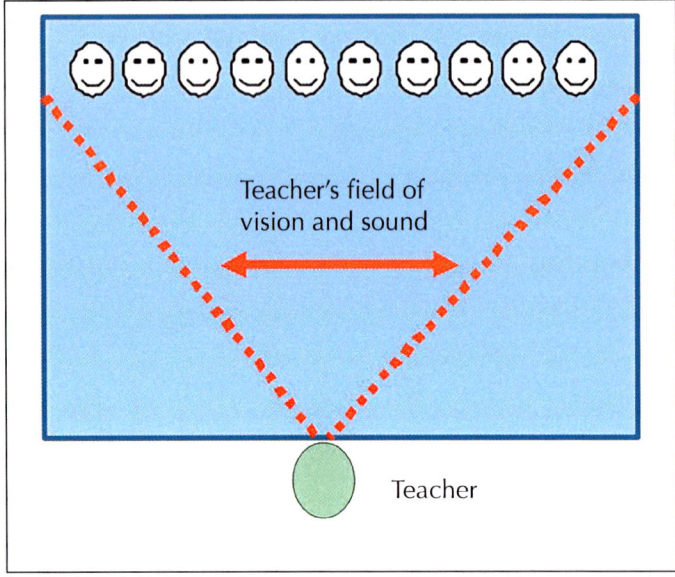

Figure 2.5
Using a central teaching position to work with a group from the opposite side of the pool

In Figure 2.5 the key factors are:

* The teacher is far enough away for each pupil to be seen.
* If the teacher projects their voice effectively all pupils will hear them.

A central position may also be used if the class is broken down into smaller ability groups and instructions are given to each group separately.

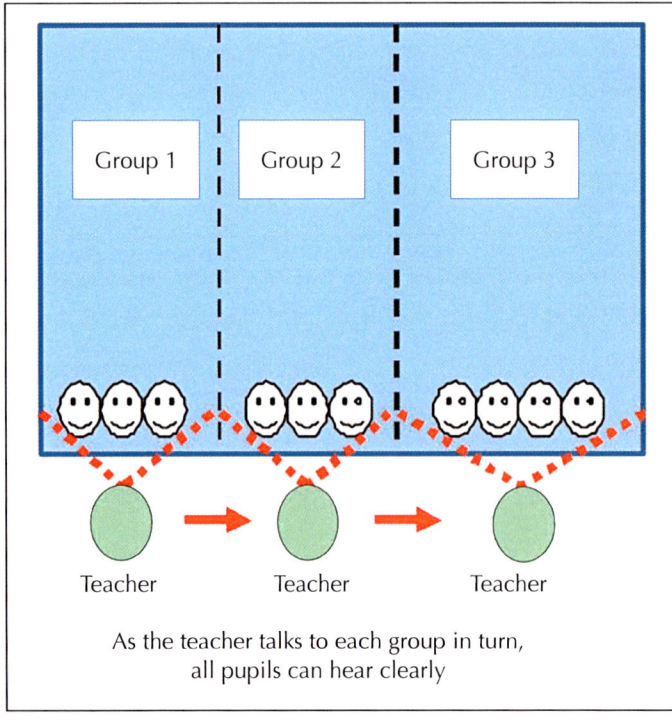

Figure 2.6
Using a central teaching position to work with mixed ability groups

> **In Figure 2.6 the key factors are:**
>
> - Three ability groups are shown.
> - Each group can follow its own individual lesson plan.
> - Instructions are given to each group in turn.

5. Use of voice

🔑 The voice is a teacher's greatest tool.

A teacher's voice and especially the ability to **project their voice** are key components in determining the quality of a lesson. When teaching a group it is an essential skill to master. In a swimming pool environment, where the noise levels may be high, pupils must be able to hear the teacher at all times. The teacher must project their voice to:

- Control the class.
- Deal with any misbehaviour.
- Ensure the safety of the children.

It is a skill that develops with practice.

The **tone** of the voice can:

- **Calm and reassure a nervous child**. A first swimming lesson can be very daunting for some children. It is a new experience, a new environment and maybe a cause of great fear. A teacher who appears calm and friendly soon erases those fears and forms a bond of trust.

- **Set the mood of the lesson**. A teacher who uses their voice to show enthusiasm is halfway towards making the lesson interesting and fun for the pupils. Vary the pitch and tone of the voice throughout a lesson: to pass on instructions; to give positive reinforcement; or to encourage pupils to reach new goals. Being polite, friendly and welcoming is an essential style to adopt.

 A useful tip to avoid voice strain, if teaching non-stop for several lessons, is to deliberately lower the pitch of the voice. This helps to protect the vocal chords.

CAREFUL PLANNING OF THE LESSON

The second requirement for good teaching is careful planning.

🔑 Good teaching does not just happen, it has to be planned.

Unfortunately, some teachers often fail to plan, finding it either too time-consuming or believing it to be an unnecessary part of their job. The danger is that such teachers are likely to:

- Use an unbalanced programme of work, spending too much time on some components and not enough time on others.
- Try to teach too much, but then end up teaching very little.

☛ The teacher needs to set some time aside to carefully prepare a plan before the start of each lesson. It is not difficult and is time well spent.

The two stages of planning

Stage 1:

The first stage is to produce an overall plan for a programme of work covering a number of lessons over several weeks. This involves the following steps:

- List the major areas to be covered.
- Then breakdown these areas into smaller components.
- Decide on the specific order these components will be taught.

Stage 2:

Once Stage 1 has been completed, detailed plans can be prepared before the start of each lesson. They involve asking two key questions:

- What is it I want to achieve? This is the **objective**.
- How do I go about it? This is the **method**.

As soon as possible after the lesson, a review of what has been achieved must also be carried out. This is the **evaluation**.

☛ Objective, method and evaluation form the three cornerstones when planning a lesson.

This is shown in Figure 2.7.

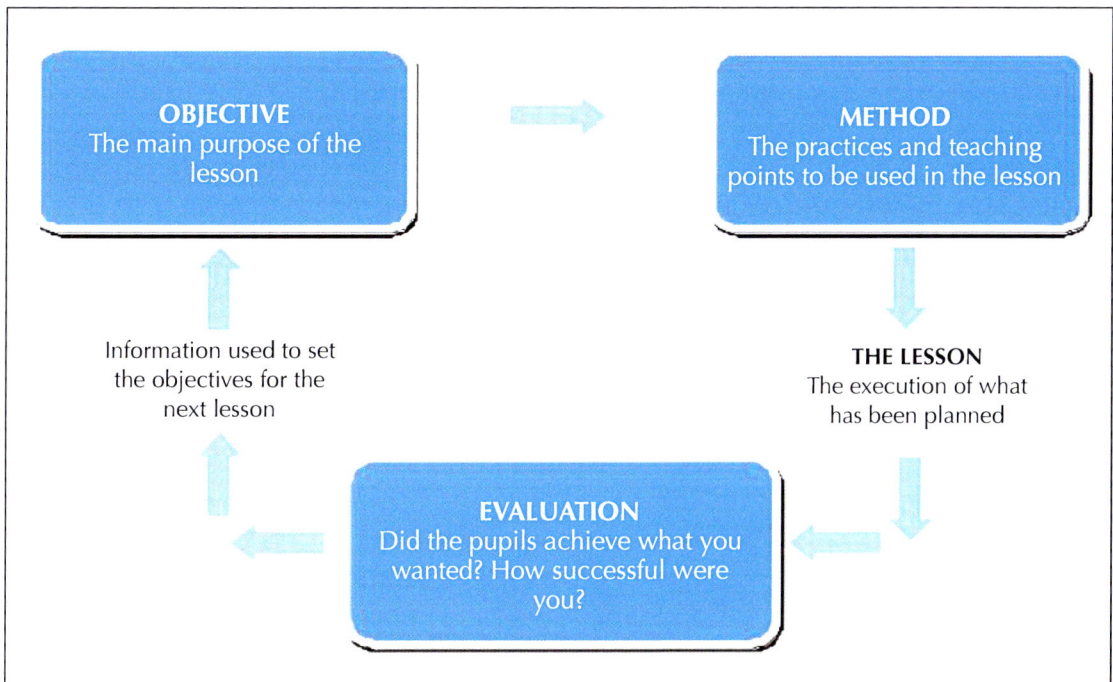

Figure 2.7
The cornerstones for planning a lesson

Individual lesson plans and the planning of a scheme of work are covered in detail in Chapter 3.

RISK MANAGEMENT: CREATING A SAFE ENVIRONMENT

A fundamental part of teaching swimming is to create a safe environment in which the lesson can take place. The potential **risk** has to also be managed and planned.

Water is a dangerous element and so the teacher has a responsibility to ensure that:

- The class is taught within their capability.
- The pupils stay within a depth they can cope with.
- The class is safe at all times.

To manage the risk, the teacher must:

- Be aware of the pool Operating Procedures and Emergency Action Plan.
- Manage the risk factors that are under their direct control.

The pool Operating Procedures and Emergency Action Plan

These are documents produced by the facility management and are usually kept by the pool manager or supervisor. Each pool is different. It may not be necessary for the teacher to have a complete copy of these documents because they are often very detailed but they should be familiar with those areas which may impact on them in a teaching situation. For example, they need to be aware of the location of:

- The emergency exits.
- The panic buttons on the poolside.
- The ropes, buoyancy aids and poles for a reach and rescue.
- The fire extinguishers.

It is a good idea for a teacher who is going to teach for the first time in a pool, to walk around beforehand with a plan of the poolside and mark down where safety items are situated. Also, it is important to note the depth of the pool and where the depth may change. It is also important for the teacher to know:

- What is the procedure if the fire alarm goes off?
- What is the procedure to administer first aid?

Teachers and pupils must all be familiar with the sound of the pool fire alarm and the action they must take if it goes off. The specific roles and responsibilities of the teacher and the pool lifeguards should be clearly understood.

During the inspection of the poolside the teacher should also note any specific hazards that may affect the teaching environment. For example:

- Lane lines stored on the poolside.
- Canoes stored in racks on the wall.
- The position of any tall lifeguard seats.

Managing the risk factors that are under a teacher's direct control

The teacher controls any risk factors through the planning and organisation of their lesson. To manage these factors, the teacher needs to ask themselves the key questions outlined in Figure 2.8.

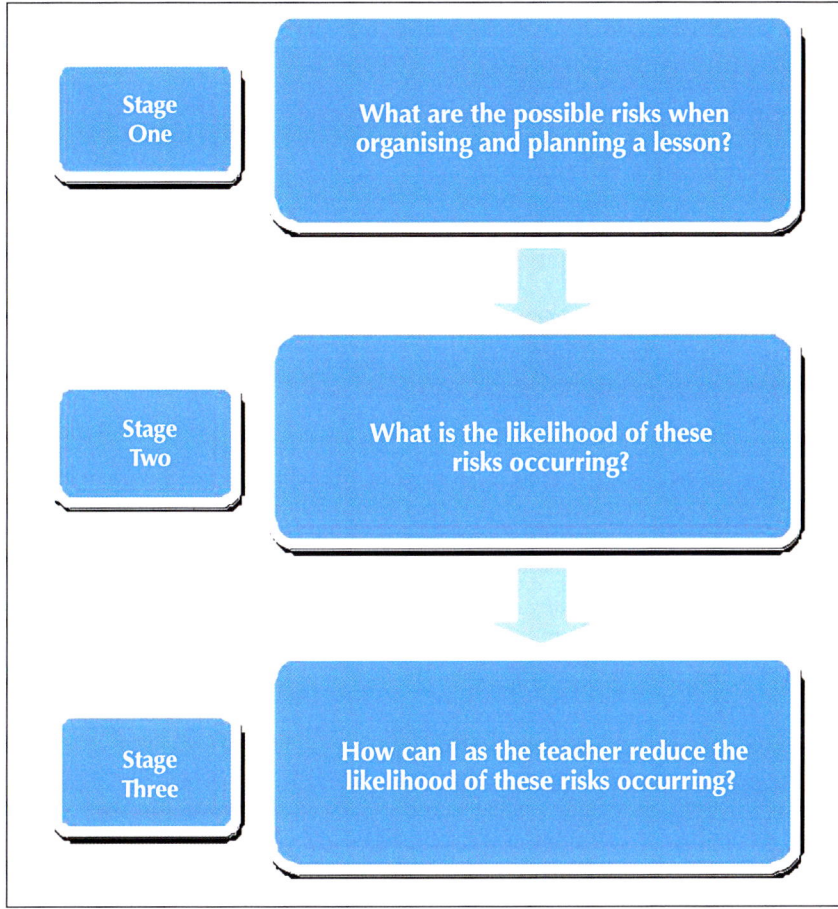

Figure 2.8
The risk management process for teaching a lesson

During Stage 2, each risk identified can be given a 'high, medium or low' grading as to their likelihood. Those factors receiving a high grading can then be prioritised.

Having identified what to do in Stage 3, the teacher then needs to design and implement a **risk management plan** to eliminate or reduce the risks as much as possible. This plan should be documented by completing a **Risk Assessment Sheet** shown in Figure 2.9.

Basic safety rules

From a safety and discipline point of view, teachers should ensure the following basic safety rules are implemented:

- Pupils should not enter the water or leave the water without the teacher's permission.

- The teacher must control the environment by insisting that pool rules are followed, for example, no running on the poolside and no pushing in.

- When the teacher asks the pupils to stop what they are doing, they must do so and listen carefully to the teacher.

- The teacher is in charge of the lesson and should not teach in the water. If necessary use additional water assistants.

- Ensure that no pupil entering the water is chewing.

- The pupils should not wear any jewellery.

- If goggles are worn, check that they are not too tight and that the pupils are instructed how to put them on and remove them safely.

- If a pupil is attempting to swim a length of the pool for the first time, they should always swim from deep water to shallow water keeping close to the side of the pool. Ideally, a competent swimmer should be swimming by the pupil's side.

- Check that all equipment to be used is safe and in good order. The equipment should not be left lying around for the teacher to trip over.

Risk Assessment Sheet for a swimming lesson

Hazards/risks	Who is at risk?	Risk rating	Existing measures to control the risk	Additional actions to reduce the risk
1 Slipping on wet surfaces	Pupils Teacher	Medium	Safety notices and guidelines displayed on poolside. High level of supervision from lifeguards.	Ensure pupils are briefed regularly on appropriate behaviour. Ensure pupils walk at all times. Ensure pupils sit down when waiting on the poolside.
2 Tripping over equipment	Pupils Teacher	Low	Use of mobile equipment boxes on poolside. All equipment put away after lesson.	Keep pool edge clear of equipment. Equipment in use kept tidy on poolside. Ensure poolside is free of all obstructions.
3 Collision in the water with other pupils or the poolside	Pupils	Medium	Instruction given in a very controlled environment.	Ensure pupils listen to all instructions. Make sure pupils have enough space to practise. Be extra vigilant when swimming on the back. Where possible, make sure pupils move in the same direction.

Hazards/risks	Who is at risk?	Risk rating	Existing measures to control the risk	Additional actions to reduce the risk
4 Drowning	Pupils	Low	Instruction provided by qualified teachers. Qualified lifeguard present at all times. Lifeguards are positioned so they can observe the pupils at all times.	Take registers at the start of every lesson. Regular head counting during and after lesson. Regularly raise pupils' awareness of where the pool changes to deep water.

Figure 2.9
A Risk Assessment Sheet for a swimming lesson

ADDITIONAL QUALITIES OF A GOOD TEACHER

As well as good communication skills and careful planning of the lesson, four additional factors also contribute to all good teaching. These are:

- **A thorough knowledge of the sport.**
- **The ability to motivate pupils.**
- **The skill to demonstrate to the pupils correctly.**
- **The competency to observe and assess a stroke quickly and accurately.**

Knowledge of the sport

The more a teacher knows about the basic skills of swimming and how to teach and present them, the more successful they are likely to be as a teacher. Good teachers need to:

- Practise their teaching skills regularly.
- Continually evaluate what they teach and how they teach it so they can distinguish between:
  – What works well for them and should be repeated.
  – What could be done differently to be more successful.
- Read and re-read books to keep up-to-date with current thinking in the sport.
- Take the time to observe other teachers in action.
- Be prepared to attend conferences and talk to other teachers in the sport.

Remember that education is a life-long experience.

The moment you close your mind to new ideas or stop thinking, analysing and evaluating your experiences, is the moment you cease to become a good teacher. Some swimming teachers may claim to have ten years' experience, but in fact they have little more than one years' experience ten times. They learn very little after the first year because they refuse to change old ways or keep their minds open to new ideas and be flexible in their approach.

The ability to motivate

All teachers should aim to be good motivators.

🔑 Great teachers inspire children to learn.

To best achieve this, it is important to:

- Create a teaching environment that is **fun**.
- Create a teaching situation in which the pupil is likely to experience meaningful **success**.

It is useful to remember motivation as the following formula:

FUN + SUCCESS = MOTIVATION

The need for fun and enthusiasm

The ability to inspire children by making an ordinary exercise or practice seemingly special, is part of the art of making a lesson fun. The teacher needs to fire the pupils' imaginations to make them *want* to do it. If learning to swim is made an enjoyable activity the teacher can stimulate the pupil's inner desire to want to learn.

The need for fun does not only apply to the pupils . . . but also to the teacher as well:

A bored teacher will result in a boring lesson.

🔑 It is important that the teacher enjoys what they are doing and that they find teaching a fulfilling experience.

The teacher must sell the sport by their enthusiasm.

How is this achieved?

- **Keep the lesson stimulating** by using a wide variety of practices, drills and activities. When skills have to be repeated, find ways of wrapping the same exercise up in a different parcel.

- **Offer plenty of praise** and positive feedback during the early stages of learning.
- **Present skills to be learned at the level of the pupils**. The practices should stretch them but should not be so difficult that they see no chance of success.
- Use a competent swimmer to **demonstrate**.
- **Set realistic goals and targets** that can be attained with practice.
- Make use of **award schemes**.

The need for success

There is nothing like success to breed more success. If a pupil can experience success on a regular basis, it reinforces their desire to continue and heightens their motivation.

The measure of success need not necessarily be the whole stroke. A pupil suddenly able to achieve a push and glide feels a measure of success and this stimulates them to progress to learn the leg action. By carefully planning a learn-to-swim programme, a measure of success can be gained in a series of small steps until the whole stroke is attempted and achieved.

The achievement of a task gives the pupil a direct measure of how well they are performing. The teacher must ensure, however, that any tasks set are:

- **Realistic** for the level being taught.
- **Progressive** by nature so practices are built upon previously taught skills.

If the targets are too easy, the pupils can soon become bored and if they are too hard, frustration and loss of interest can occur. The targets can come from a reputable organisation that has a progressive award scheme where certificates and badges are used as a direct measure of success.

 A word of warning on badge schemes! This is not an easy option. Take care not to develop a programme around a 'badge-itis' concept. For a swimming programme to be truly progressive, the teacher needs to look carefully at the awards available and selectively 'pick and mix' from a number of different schemes.

The need for feedback

One of the key roles for the teacher must be to feedback information to the pupils about their performance. The pupils need to know:

- When they perform the skills correctly.
- When they perform the skills incorrectly.

When the skill is performed correctly, praise is required.

When learning a new skill, praise should be frequent and should be based on rewarding effort just as much as success.

🔑 Praise is one of the most important stimuli for the learner.

When the skills are performed incorrectly, it is necessary to try to encourage some change.

The teacher's approach will differ, depending on the age of the pupils they are teaching.

With young pupils (aged six to twelve years) this is best achieved by emphasising what is required of the pupil after praising them in some way. Therefore:

- **Praise** them for their effort.

- Follow this by **outlining the correct movement** you want them to perform

 Notice there is no dwelling on what they are doing wrong; rather use praise and positive encouragement to achieve the goals.

With older pupils and adults the teacher needs to give more explanation. After some praise, tell them what they are doing wrong and give them a reason for the problem. Any criticism must be constructive and be followed by emphasising what correction they need to make.

The ability to demonstrate skills correctly

This is often an area that teachers do not consider.

🔑 Any demonstration must be done with the thought of how it will look to the pupil.

This means that it has to be done:

- First and foremost **accurately**.
- Secondly, **at the right angle to the class** so they can see it clearly.

For example:
When demonstrating the breaststroke leg action, very little is gained by doing the demonstration standing on one leg while working the other. Pupils invariably copy the teacher literally and end up performing a 'one legged' action in the water. It is far better to either:

- Sit on the side or on a stool and show the legs working together.
- Use a pair of trainers on the hands to imitate feet.

Backstroke arm action is another area that often presents difficulties for the teacher. A teacher's own lack of flexibility may result in a poor demonstration. A teacher must recognise this and use an alternative method. This may involve the use of pictures and photographs or using a pupil lying on a bench to demonstrate so the teacher can manipulate the arm action to show the correct pathway.

It is a very good idea for the teacher to practise in front of a mirror before presenting the demonstration to the class.

The competency to observe and assess a stroke

The competency to assess and analyse a stroke both quickly and confidently is a vital skill to master. It is something however, which the novice teacher often struggles with. There are two kinds of assessment:

- **A snapshot assessment** where a teacher observes a pupil and makes a quick evaluation about a stroke problem and instantly gives feedback to the pupil about the corrections required. A teacher carries out this kind of assessment many times in a lesson. The process of observing and evaluating a stroke and then implementing the correction is something the teacher needs to master.

- A second kind of assessment is **a more formal observation** which involves watching one swimmer perform over several widths or lengths of the pool while the teacher records what they observe on a **Stroke Assessment Sheet**. However, this is something that the teacher rarely has an opportunity to do, as it is a time- consuming exercise working with only one swimmer at a time. Nevertheless it is a useful skill to perfect as it often features on many teacher training courses.

The analysis of a stroke involves three stages:

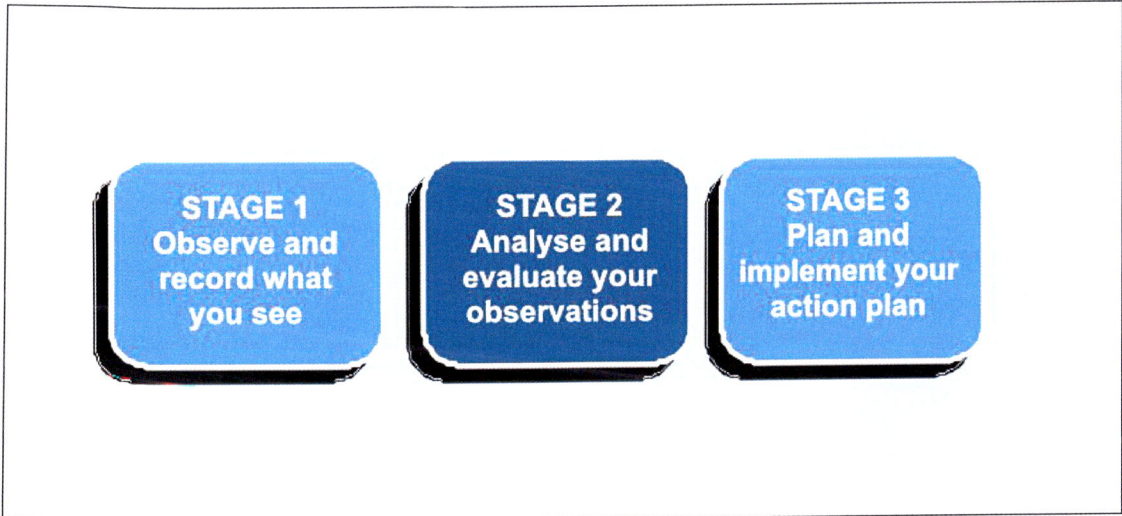

Figure 2.10
The three stages of assessing and analysing a stroke

Of the three stages outlined above, the ability to observe accurately is a vital skill for good teaching.

The skill of observation

Whether it is a snapshot assessment where the observations are memorised or a more formal assessment where the observations are recorded, it is important that:

🔑 The teacher memorises or records what they *actually* see and not what they think they should see according to the textbook descriptions of the strokes.

This is the main weakness of the novice teacher. They learn the textbook theory of the strokes and then fall into the trap of simply repeating it when they observe a swimmer. They fail to observe a swimmer and record what they actually see. To guide the teacher in this process we have included a sample of a Stroke Assessment Sheet at the end of this chapter.

To make accurate observations, it is important for the teacher to view the stroke from various positions including:

- From the side.
- From the front (swimmer moving towards you).
- From behind (swimmer moving away from you).
- From above or elevated position.
- From below the water (using underwater viewing windows or cameras).

When making observations, remember that there are difficulties seeing underwater, particularly if the water surface is very disturbed. Also be aware that water refracts light so the image below the surface may be distorted.

The recording process

The recording process should involve the identification of both strengths and weaknesses for an individual pupil. These are recorded on the Stroke Assessment Sheet (an example is presented at the end of this chapter). The process usually involves breaking the stroke down into the following components:

- General impressions of the stroke.
- Body position.
- Leg action.
- Arm action.
- Breathing.
- Timing and co-ordination.
- Future improvements.

The evaluation

Following this, an evaluation of the assessment is made. The teacher must prioritise any faults and develop a plan of practices to correct any problems. These are added to the Stroke Assessment Sheet in the 'Future improvements'section.

To analyse and evaluate observations, a thorough knowledge of the strokes (outlined in Chapters 5, 6, 7 and 8) is needed so the teacher can identify any problems or areas that need improvement. During this process, the teacher must remember to be tolerant of individual differences and decide what to change and what to leave alone.

Having identified what needs to be changed, the teacher can use the building block programme together with the problems and solutions sections in the stroke chapters to produce a plan to correct faults and build on the fundamentals of the stroke.

There should then follow a period of time to allow the corrective practices to take place before a re-assessment is carried out which hopefully will show some improvement.

Some final considerations for quality teaching

There are some final considerations that are important for quality teaching. These are:

- **Adopt a suitable dress code** when on the poolside.
- **Be adaptable** when handling the unusual and unexpected.
- **Learn how to deal with misbehaviour** .

Dress code on poolside

The following are guidelines for a good dress code:

- The teacher should be dressed appropriately. It is not suitable, for example, to teach in a swimsuit. A teacher's clothes should present a professional image to the pupils, parents and pool management.
- The teacher should be easily be identifiable and should not wear the same uniform as the lifeguards.
- Teaching assistants in the water should wear a tee-shirt to cover a swimsuit.

Being adaptable

Sometimes teachers are presented with difficulties such as:

- Diving boards placed in the deep end restricting movement around the pool.
- Oddly-shaped pools such as free-form fun pools, so there are no rails or immediate sides.

- The sudden closure of certain areas of the pool resulting in having to teach in either very shallow or deep water.

It is important that the teacher does not become upset by such difficulties. A teacher who is prepared to be adaptable can also be highly successful even when the teaching environment is not ideal.

For example:
If the water is very shallow then use the depth to advantage. The pupils can put their hands on the bottom of the pool and practise the leg movements of the various strokes.

Dealing with misbehaviour

All children are not angels! How the teacher handles misbehaviour varies enormously depending on the age of the pupils but the teacher must deal with problems of misbehaviour **fairly and consistently**.

When a pupil's behaviour is likely to cause danger to themselves or others or disrupts the lesson then the teacher must take some immediate action:

- Initially, a firm warning is required, telling the offender that the behaviour must stop or punishment will follow.

- One of the most effect punishments at the hands of the teacher is to remove the pupil from the class and have them sit on the side of the pool for a short period of time. In this way, the teacher is enforcing the idea that to take part in the class is a reward for good behaviour.

- Another strategy is to pretend not to see it. Some pupils see misbehaving as a way of getting recognition. Therefore punishing their behaviour only encourages them to misbehave even more. By ignoring their behaviour the teacher is sending them the message that it is not worthy of attention.

When administering a punishment, the teacher must:

- Be consistent in its administration.

- Impose the punishment in an impersonal way.

- Once the punishment is complete, do not make the pupil feel guilty; make them feel they are a valued member of the group again.

 Some educators say we should never punish young people but should only reinforce their positive behaviour. Teachers must however, always be aware that they teach in an environment where class control is paramount for children's safety. Teachers cannot therefore, allow their control of the class to get 'out of hand'.

But remember . . .

There is a fine balance between being in control and being too authoritarian, repressing the opportunity for fun and enjoyment.

STROKE ASSESSMENT SHEET

Stroke:	
Name of swimmer:	

		Age of pupil:	
Date:			
Name of assessor:			

General impressions of the stroke

Observations

Body Position

Observations

Observations

Leg Action

Arm Action

Observations

Breathing

Observations

Timing / Coordination

Observations

Future Improvements

Observations

WHAT MAKES A GOOD TEACHER

Someone who knows how to get the job done,
To make the work hard but yet seem like fun.
To watch over the class with a very keen eye,
Teach all the strokes . . . including the 'fly',
Make use of the time to the very last minute,
Plan a lesson, with all segments in it.
Demonstrate strokes with a great deal of care
Avoid lifting arms and flailing the air!
Speak slowly and clearly, so everyone hears,
Smile and reassure gently, to take away fears.
Enjoy teaching others to jump in and swim
Keep lessons interesting and full to the brim,
Success is gained by a lot of hard work
Analysis and assessment are points not to shirk,
Know when to give work and when to give rest
All these qualities will make you the best!

Pat Parkes

Planning A Lesson

Main Focus

- What is the planning process?

- How is a lesson structured?

- The importance of having a clear aim for the lesson

- Using an Introductory activity to start the lesson

- Designing a main theme which is progressive and interesting

- Concluding the lesson with directed choice activities and specific challenges

- Using a clear framework to review and evaluate the lesson

- Sample lesson plans

- A programmed lesson

- Managing assistants

- Planning a course / scheme of work

- A summary poem by Patricia Parkes

Chapter 3

Planning A Lesson

LESSON PLANS

🔑 Good swimming lesson management is achieved by planning, observing and evaluating each individual lesson.

The planning process for each lesson follows the framework shown in Figure 3.1

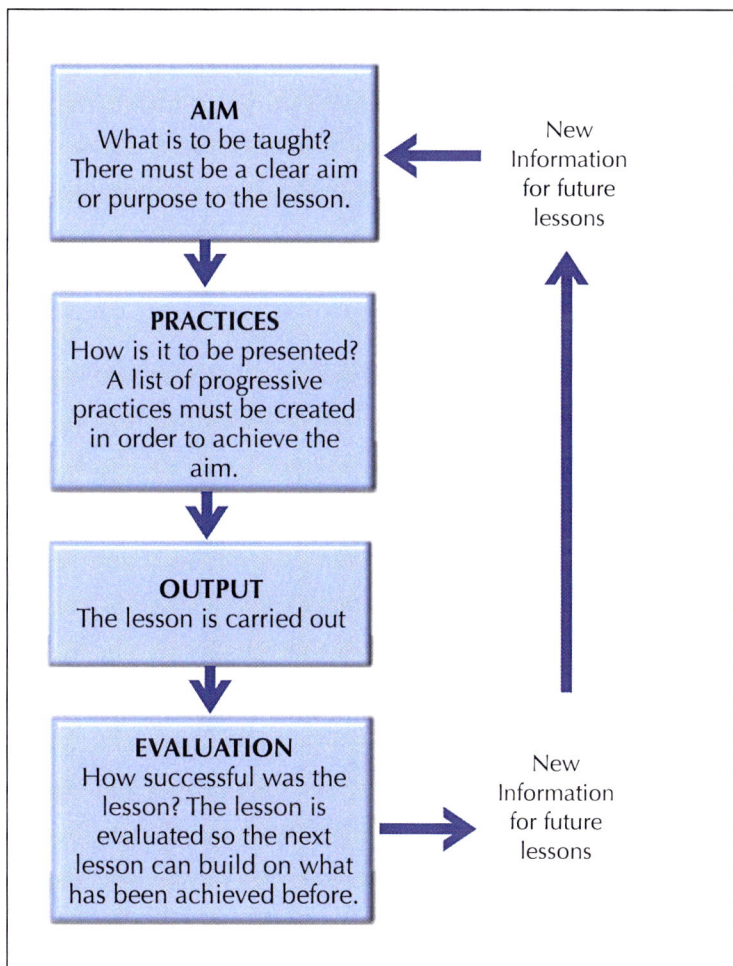

AIM
What is to be taught? There must be a clear aim or purpose to the lesson.

PRACTICES
How is it to be presented? A list of progressive practices must be created in order to achieve the aim.

OUTPUT
The lesson is carried out

EVALUATION
How successful was the lesson? The lesson is evaluated so the next lesson can build on what has been achieved before.

New Information for future lessons

New Information for future lessons

Figure 3.1
The key components in planning a lesson

A committed teacher will go through this process for every lesson they teach. There is no shortcut. All teaching requires:

- **Time spent before** the lesson preparing what will be taught and how it will be presented.

- **Time spent after** the lesson evaluating how successful it was?

Time spent before the lesson

Lesson preparation plays a very important part in a teacher's programme. They need to know exactly what it is that they want to teach and achieve.

Everything the teacher plans should be done for a reason and to be meaningful, the reason must be specific.

When asked what is their aim, a teacher often answers in very broad terms by saying *'to teach breaststroke'*. In a thirty-minute lesson they may then proceed to teach the whole stroke by working through a range of exercises covering all aspects of the stroke including kicking, pulling, breathing and co-ordination. At the end of the lesson, however, they have achieved nothing because they did not have anything specific in mind.

To set an aim 'to teach breaststroke' is not specific enough. Each lesson must have a specific aim. For example 'to introduce the breaststroke leg action' is a more specific aim. It gives the teacher and the lesson a focus, namely introducing the early leg practices in the building programme.

The clearer the teacher is about *what* is to be taught and *why*, the better the lesson is likely to flow.

Each lesson must not be viewed in isolation. There needs to be a progression with an overlap between one lesson and the next, so that a series of lessons guides the pupils through a number of stages, each one building on the previous lesson. Therefore the teacher needs to have an overall plan of what aspects they want to cover over a set period of time. This needs to continually be reviewed taking into account the rate of progress made by the pupils.

 Ideally, a pupil should not be made to move on, until they have mastered the required skills to do so. In a group situation, some pupils progress faster than others, and so the teacher must be prepared to work different ability groups within their lesson.

How is a lesson structured?

Once the aim of the lesson has been set, the lesson should then be broken down into a number of sections:

- An introductory activity.
- An explanation and/or demonstration.
- A main theme.
- A contrasting activity.
- A choice activity or challenge.

Each section includes a number of skills or sectional practices which must be progressive in nature. This means that each practice should build upon the one before to develop a skill further.

 For effective skill development, the teacher must take great care over the selection and order of their practices to ensure they are truly progressive. Practices which are not progressive become little more than activities just to occupy the pupils.

The aim of the lesson

The first point to consider is the aim. This is the objective of the lesson. The teacher should ask *'what is it I want the pupils to achieve?'*

Defining the aim

The words used to define the aim must be accurately reflected in the main part of the lesson. For example:

- **To introduce**: This means working through very basic exercises as the work is being done for the first time. So to introduce the backstroke leg action involves the very first leg practices in the building programme using plenty of support.

- **To improve**: This means to get better, so the work has already been introduced but the practices are harder and without support to improve the stroke.

- **To develop or strengthen**: This indicates that some stamina work is being done with the more advanced practices in the building programme.

Factors affecting the aim

There are also other factors that affect the aim of the lesson. They need to be considered at the start of each lesson. They are:

- **The number of pupils in the class:** With small classes, the aim can be specific to the whole group or to an individual as there is greater opportunity for the teacher to work on a one-to-one basis. Large classes can be split into ability groups and the teacher may have a different aim with each group.

- **The age of the pupils:** This is important because it colours the pace of the lesson and the approach of the teacher. For example, five-year-olds do not understand lengthy explanations.

- **The temperature of the water**: if the water is too cold, children are only interested in how soon they can get out. No one really enjoys swimming in cold water and children should not swim in water below 22 degrees centigrade. An ideal temperature is 26 to 28 degrees centigrade.

- **Time allotted**: It is essential to know how long the lesson is, allowing for necessary changing time if it is a school situation.

- **Equipment**: The number of floats available may dictate the type of exercise possible. There is little point in trying to use two floats, one under each arm for support, if there are not enough floats for all the pupils to have two floats each.

- **Staged reached**: As the teacher works through the building block programme, a certain level of competency needs to be achieved before the next building block is attempted. Progress can therefore be limited until such skills have been mastered.

Once the teacher has taken into account these limiting factors and has a clear idea of the aim, the lesson plan can be structured in the following way.

Introductory activity

The first part of the lesson is the introductory activity or the 'warm up'. The pupils want to get in, get wet and warm up. The entry is always a shock to the system so it needs to be done quickly, followed by some exercises to prepare the body and mind for work. Therefore this should quite literally be 'getting in time'.

 Teaching points are not be given at this stage, but the pupils need to be instructed about the activity you want them to do.

Explanation and demonstration

The next part of the lesson is explaining and demonstrating the aim.

Explain clearly but briefly what is required and how it is to be achieved.

Children always copy, so find a competent demonstrator who can show exactly the points that are being highlighted.

 If the teacher gives the demonstration, it has to be done accurately with consideration given to the pupils' view of it. Often teachers stand directly above the pupils demonstrating an arm action that is impossible for them to see or understand.

If it is a complicated demonstration and explanation, sometimes it is advisable to do it before the warm-up as the pupils, once wet, will soon get cold.

Main theme

Now we come to the main theme where the aim of the lesson is put into practice. Keep the aim firmly in mind when planning this section. The work must be both **progressive and interesting**.

If the pupils are swimmers, start with an attempt at the whole stroke. This gives the teacher a chance to assess the ability of the pupils and group them if required. It also gives the pupils a chance to try the stroke and understand what needs to be achieved.

Obviously, if the pupils are non-swimmers, an attempt at the whole stroke is not possible. For these pupils, the stroke needs to be broken down into isolated skills such as leg practices or arm practices with various aids.

Give relevant teaching points to re-enforce each exercise. It is not enough to just say:

'*hold the float and kick four widths*' .

There has to be a descriptive teaching point added to the practice such as:

'*point the toes' or 'turn the feet out*' .

For each practice given, the teacher must be aware of what it is designed to achieve.

Examples

When working through a series of practices on backstroke kicking, holding the float in different positions achieves different things:

	Position of the float	What is achieved?
1.	Two floats, one under each arm	Maximum support so the pupil can concentrate on the leg action.
2.	One float clasped to the chest	As the support is reduced, a float held at the chest gives a feeling of security.
3.	One float held over the thighs	Develops a good body position and prevents the knees from breaking the surface.
4.	One float held over head, arms extended	With the arms extended, this flattens out the body position, raises the chest and makes it easier to breathe.

These practices are in progressive order. The teacher must be careful to present the practices in the correct sequence, working from easier skills with plenty of support to harder practices with little or no support.

 Activities should never be given just to keep the pupils occupied. Time spent in the water is too valuable to be wasted in this manner.

Finally, finish this section with the whole stroke again to see if the aim was achieved. In this way, the structure of the main theme has followed what is often described as a '**whole – part – whole**' structure where:

- First the **whole stroke** is attempted.
- This is followed by a number of **part practices.**
- Finally the **whole stroke** is attempted again.

Contrasting activity

A contrasting activity changes the tone and tempo of the lesson. This part is just what the heading implies; a contrast from what has previously been done. It gives the lesson variation but it still has a purpose.

It can be an introduction of work to come (pre-planning) or focus on specific watermanship skills such as survival skills, preliminary diving or sculling practices. The list is endless. It is also a good time to gather the class into a group instead of working singularly. This is where a teacher's imagination can achieve a great deal. By adding a story or getting the pupils to use their own imagination (as described with the 'free fall parachuting' practice outlined in Chapter 1), interest is heightened and an ordinary exercise is transformed into something exciting and different.

Choice activity or specific challenge

There now only remains a few minutes left of the lesson. Usually this time is profitable to beginners because they may want to have another try at something they have learnt during the lesson. The teacher can observe while allowing the pupil to choose their activity.

All too often, however, teachers allow this time for free practice in the hope of ending the lesson with a fun element. This approach is extremely questionable, unprofessional and can even be dangerous. With water time at a premium, wasting five minutes of a twenty or thirty minute lesson is depriving the pupil of valuable learning time. This time is too precious to waste in this manner. Also, competent swimmers usually want to turn the time into a 'free for all' and it becomes difficult for the teacher to watch for everyone's safety.

🔑 Fun can be achieved profitably in an organised way.

A good idea is to use this time to have games, races or mini competitions that most pupils enjoy and at the same time can be productive.

Evaluation

It is essential for the teacher to evaluate the lesson as soon as possible after it has finished. Some attempt needs to be made to assess how successful was the lesson in achieving what was intended. Refer back to the aim, and then ask the following questions in each of the categories:

Category	Questions
Content of the lesson	Was the aim achieved? Could the lesson be improved? What is the next progression?
The pupils response	Did the pupils learn anything? How many pupils mastered the skill well? Were any pupils having difficulties? Were any pupils bored/inattentive?
Self-evaluation by the teacher	Did the lesson 'flow'? Were you comfortable with the lesson? Did you enjoy the lesson?

These evaluations should be used as an aid to planning the next lesson.

SAMPLE LESSON PLANS

We are presenting three sample lesson plans to help the novice teacher see how a plan can be put together. A blank pro-forma lesson plan and evaluation sheet is given at the end of this chapter.

SAMPLE LESSON PLAN 1

Limiting factors

Factor	Details
Number of pupils:	6+
Age range:	10+
Water time:	30 minutes
Equipment:	floats, arm bands
Stage reached:	Beginners who have completed confidence work and are ready to start on stroke work.

Aim of the lesson

To **introduce** the backstroke leg action.

Introductory activity (warm-up 2–3 minutes)

- Enter the water any way (jump, slither or slide)
- Jump up and down, shoulders under
- Total submersion
- Blow bubbles as they submerge; walk across the pool and 'bob' back.

Demonstration/explanation (1–2 minutes)

With a good demonstrator in the water, show the pupils the backstroke leg action. The teacher demonstrates walking on the side of the pool, emphasising:

- Working from the hip
- Slight knee bend
- Depth of the kick

Main theme (15 minutes)

	Practice	Teaching points
1	Push and glide and regain feet (with arm bands if necessary)	• Push gently and stretch
2	With two floats, one under each arm, push and glide from the side and start kicking. Several widths are attempted, depending on the distance.	• Pretend you are walking • Stretch your legs
3	With one float clasped to the chest, push and glide from the side and start kicking.	• Keep the legs close together • Work from the hip

If the above practices have been attempted with arm bands, repeat each exercise without. If not, carry on kicking varying the position of the float, first above the knees then beyond the head.

Contrasting activity (5 minutes)

Treading water practice

Practice 1	Teaching points
Sitting on the side, try an alternator kick	• Push the feet to the side and down alternately • The teacher shouts out 'one, two, one, two' and the pupils push down alternately in time with the teachers counting.

Practice 2	Teaching points
In the water, with two floats one under each arm, practise the alternator leg action.	Keep the knees outside the hips

Supervised choice activity (5 minutes)

Ask the pupils to choose which bit of the lesson they liked best and try this practice again.

Sample Evaluation Form

Evaluate your lesson

To evaluate the lesson the teacher must ask a number of key questions. The evaluation involves both a review of the lesson, how the pupils performed and a self-assessment on how the teacher (him or herself) has performed. Remember it is important to be honest if these evaluations are to be meaningful.

Content of the lesson

Key questions	Comments
Was the aim achieved?	
Could the lesson be improved?	
What is the next progression?	

The pupils' response

Key questions	Comments
Did the pupils learn anything?	
How many pupils mastered the skill well?	
Were any pupils having difficulties?	
Were any pupils bored/inattentive?	

Self-evaluation (teacher)

Key questions	Comments
Did the lesson 'flow'?	
Were you comfortable with the lesson?	
Did you enjoy the lesson?	

SAMPLE LESSON PLAN 2

Limiting factors

Factor	Details
Number of pupils:	6–8
Age range:	8-10 years
Water time:	30 minutes
Equipment:	floats, arm bands
Stage reached:	Beginners who have completed several lessons of breaststroke.

Aim of the lesson

To **improve** the breaststroke leg action.

Introductory activity (warm-up 2–3 minutes)

- Straddle jump into the pool and swim as many widths as possible in any stroke until told to stop.

Explanation 1–2 minutes)

Sitting on the side of the pool, trace with the heels, the breaststroke leg action emphasising the simultaneous movement of the legs, the turning out of the feet and bringing the legs back together again.

Main theme (15 minutes)

Working through a number of widths on the following practices:

	Practice		Teaching points
1	Attempt the whole stroke	•	Have a go
2	Breaststroke leg action on the back, one float under each arm	•	Watch legs working together
3	Breaststroke leg action on front, one float under each arm	•	Drive the feet back
4	Breaststroke leg action on the back, one float clasped to the chest	•	Trace circles with the heels
5	Breaststroke leg action on front, one float extended	•	Kick and glide
6	Push and glide, complete stroke to half way	•	Emphasise push and glide
7	Push and glide, full stroke across the width	•	Stretch and drive the feet back hard

Contrasting activity (5 minutes)

Preliminary work for surface diving

	Practice		Teaching points
1	Mushroom tucks	•	Tuck up knees close to chest
2	Working in pairs, ducking under arm and legs	•	Submerge completely
3	Handstands	•	Push head down

Supervised choice activity (5 minutes)

The pupils may choose any practice they may wish to do.

EVALUATION OF THE LESSON

Repeat the evaluation process outlined for Sample Lesson Plan 1 by asking the key questions under the categories:

- Content of the lesson
- The pupil's response
- A teacher's self-evaluation

Remember to be honest and critical of your own teaching performance. Review the teaching practices and teaching points you used and try to identify things you would do differently next time to improve the lesson.

   It is only by evaluating yourself in this way will you truly become a great swimming teacher.

THE PROGRAMMED LESSON

Once the pupils have mastered the strokes and have a degree of strength and skill, a programmed lesson may be introduced. This is a lesson where the pupils are given a set piece of work as a 'things to do' list, interspersed with set periods of rest. This allows the pupils to follow a written plan and work on their own.

There has to be some prior knowledge of the ability of the group, so that the work can be designed to develop and strengthen areas of weakness. It is not as difficult as it sounds.

- The teacher follows the pattern of a warm-up and explanation and then divides the class into groups.
- A work is prepared on cards or boards and is given to each of the different groups.
- Each programme concentrates on a different element of the selected stroke such as body position, legs, arms, breathing, and timing.
- The teacher may start the lesson with three different programmes, one for each group and can then move from group to group, giving help, teaching points and praise to each.

The main problem with this particular type of lesson is motivation. The pupils must be motivated to complete the work effectively.

   During the lesson, every child must have some positive words given to him or her by the teacher.

The programmed lesson is not a time for the teacher to sit back and 'let them get on with it'. It needs careful planning, as thoroughly as any other lesson. The teacher must get actively involved.

SAMPLE LESSON PLAN 3

Aim of the lesson

To **develop** the front crawl stroke

Introductory activity (warm-up 3 minutes)

Swim as many widths as possible in 3 minutes, with every other width being on front crawl.

Explanation/demonstration (4 minutes)

Watch a good demonstration, explaining salient points, such as:

- Flat body position.
- Entry of the arms.
- Propulsive phase of the arm action.
- Breathing.

Main theme (20 minutes)

Description of groups

Group A
These pupils are the weakest set and need to practice the leg action to support a good body position and a continuous arm action.

Group B
These pupils have problems with the breathing. They need to revise the leg action and then practice the co-ordination of the breathing with the arm action.

Group C
These pupils are the most proficient and need to strengthen their stroke with drill type practices.

Practice schedule for Group A

	Practice	Teaching points
1	6 widths full stroke	• Keep stroke long and smooth
2	6 widths leg kick with one float extended	• Work the legs from the hips
3	6 widths leg kick with one float extended, breathing to the front	• Head up for three kicks • Head down for three kicks
4	6 widths leg kick with no float; take a short rest between each width. Start with a push and glide.	• Stretch and kick hard • Keep arms extended and thumbs locked together
5	8 widths full stroke	• Keep legs close together • Keep leg action continuous

Practice schedule for Group B

	Practice	Teaching points
1	8 widths full stroke	• Keep stroke long and smooth
2	6 widths leg kick while holding float, one hand at the top edge and the other at the bottom edge. Turn the head to breathe.	• Roll the head down
3	4 widths holding float with one arm extended, on the non-breathing side; push and glide start the legs kicking, then pull with breathing side arm only; concentrate on entry.	• Touch the top of the float with first finger
4	4 widths as before, turning the head to breathe when the hand is under the chin.	• When you see the 'boomerang' position, turn your head to breathe
5	4 widths lifting the elbow high	• Brush thigh with thumb as you push back
6	8 widths full stroke	• Keep the legs working and concentrate on the breathing

Practice schedule for Group C

	Practice	Teaching points
1	10 widths full stroke	• Keep stroke long and smooth
2	10 widths arms only, using a pull buoy held between the legs	• Do the stroke slowly • Try to feel the pull
3	6 widths right arm only with left arm extended, 6 widths with the opposite arm working.	• Keep elbow high during the recovery
4	8 widths full stroke, bi-lateral breathing	• Kick hard
5	10 widths full stroke	• 5 widths explosive breathing, 5 widths trickle breathing

 The resting time between each practice and the number of widths performed, obviously depends on the size of the pool and the ability of the pupils.

Contrasting activity (5 minutes)

Sculling

	Practice	Teaching points
1	Sculling races across the pool on the back, feet first a) Individually b) In teams	• Keep the fingers together • Keep the fingers tilted down

EVALUATION OF THE LESSON

Use the model outlined previously in Lesson Plan 1 to ensure you are asking the right questions when you carry out your evaluation. In terms of a programmed lesson, you may also wish to comment on:

- How well the different groups worked when left on their own?
- Did this style of lesson cause any behavioural problems
- Did you have any organisational difficulties?
- Were you able to monitor the different groups both safely and effectively?

A programmed lesson is an opportunity for you to increase greatly the work load of the pupils to improve their ability to perform over longer distances.

The pupils should finish the lesson tired and have the feeling that they have been challenged.

Summary of lesson plans

Lesson plans are one of those areas which are vitally important for successful teaching, and yet few teachers do it well. Investing a little more time in preparation can produce more inspiring and effective teaching. The lesson must be approached with confidence and a good lesson plan will help this.

 Remember, however thorough your knowledge is about the sport, good teachers are those who successfully pass their knowledge on.

MAKING USE OF ASSISTANTS

Assistants can be of great use to a teacher but they do need to be told exactly what to do. Usually an assistant is needed if a pupil is more nervous or not able to progress as fast as the rest of the class. In such cases, the assistant may work with the pupil in the water on a one-to-one basis or with small groups. Assistants can also be a great help during a programmed lesson where they can work closely with one group while the swimming teacher gives more attention to the other groups.

To use an assistant effectively, the teacher needs to plan carefully:

- The tasks the assistant is to carry out.
- The instructions the assistant is to give to the pupils.

The teacher must remain in overall control of the lesson and provide the assistant with clear instructions about what is required.

The teacher must also be continually aware of how well the assistant is doing so they can evaluate their performance and give them feedback at the end of the lesson.

PLANNING A COURSE OF WORK

The teacher must know the route they are going to take over the coming weeks. Each individual lesson forms part of a course of work over a period of ten to twelve weeks (possibly a school term). To plan a course of work, a teacher needs to consider:

- The course length.
- The number of sessions.
- Time allocated per session.
- The number of pupils.
- The standard of the pupils.

When planning a course, a teacher also needs to consider:

- The overall aim of each course of lessons.
- At the end of each course, there should be a number of targets for each child to achieve; this is usually measured by tests or awards.
- Using these tests, the teacher can review the term's work and evaluate the results.

Assessments

The last week of each course is often reserved for testing the pupils. They may be asked to swim a certain distance or work through a number of skills to gain a recognised award. Alternatively, the teacher may set the test to specifically cover a list of what has been taught during the previous weeks.

The aim is to assess the pupil's progress. At the same time, this is also an assessment of how successful the teacher has been in achieving their aims over the past weeks.

At the end of each course, the teacher must review the term's work by asking:

- How successful was the course?
- How successful were the pupils?
- Which areas need more time spent on them during the next course?

In this way, the teacher is:

Planning the child's future swimming progress.

Examples of course plans for various ability groups

Non swimmers

Week	Area of focus
1	Confidence work – push and glide – regaining the feet – floating - making shapes – games (Ring-O-Roses, Simon Says)
2	Introducing backstroke leg action – games
3	Introducing breaststroke leg action – jumping in
4	Introducing front crawl leg action – playing with a ball
5	Developing backstroke leg action – sculling
6	Developing breaststroke leg action – treading water
7	Developing front crawl leg action – introducing the surface dive
8	Continue on with part practices – introducing new drills – games
9	Revision week covering a variety if skills learnt so far
10	Devise a small 'Can you do?' test

Learners

Week	Area of focus
1	Revision of main confidence work
2	Backstroke improvement – straddle jumps.
3	Breaststroke improvement – surface diving – underwater swimming
4	Front crawl improvement – playing with a ball
5	Introducing butterfly leg action
6	Introducing diving (shallow water practices)
7	Developing backstroke arm action
8	Developing breaststroke arm action – treading water practices
9	Developing front crawl arm action – various sculling practices
10	Assessment on a distance swim

Improvers

Week	Area of focus
1	Assessment of ability – discover weak areas
2	Backstroke programmed lesson – one skill from selected award
3	Breaststroke programmed lesson – one skill from selected award
4	Front crawl programmed lesson – one skill from selected award
5	Butterfly programmed lesson – one skill from selected award
6	Diving
7	Award practice
8	Award practice
9	Award practice
10	Assessment for awards

LESSON PLAN RECORDING SHEET

Class	Date	Start time	Venue	Water space

Limiting factors

Age range	Class size	Males	Females	Water time	Equipment needed

Stage reached

Aim	Key things to achieve

Introductory activity

Time:	Practices:	Teaching points:	Equipment/organisation:

Demonstration/explanation

Time:	Focus of the lesson:	Teaching points:	Equipment/organisation:

Main theme of the lesson

Time:	Practices:	Teaching points:	Equipment/organisation:

Contrasting activity

Time:	Practices:	Teaching points:	Equipment/organisation:

EVALUATION OF LESSON FORM

	Key questions	Comments
Content	Was the aim achieved?	
	Could the lesson be improved?	
	What is the next progression?	

	Key questions	Comments
The pupils' response	Did the pupils learn anything?	
	How many pupils mastered the skill well?	
	Were any pupils having difficulties?	
	Were any pupils bored/inattentive?	

	Key questions	Comments
Self-evaluation (teacher)	Did the lesson 'flow'?	
	Were you comfortable with the lesson?	
	Did you enjoy the lesson?	

Focus for next lesson	

LESSON PLANS

Lesson Plans some teachers dread,
They like to teach right out of their head.
Is it necessary to sit down and plan?
Before those little faces you scan.
Well yes! It's clear that you must have an aim
Oh dear, oh dear, we hear you exclaim!
Let's start at the top with a decision on stroke,
How to teach this, is the thought you provoke.
Shall we introduce, develop or strengthen the action?
Always remember, that there will be a reaction.
The warm up, is when the swimmer gets wet,
Perhaps a few little races you've set.
They are wet and warm and ready to learn,
Show them a good demo..must be your concern.
It's time get on and practice the task,
Kicking or pulling, whichever you ask.
Remember the theme: whole – part – whole
Give praise, aloud their virtues extol!
The contrast activity can be great 'Fun'
Because their lesson is almost done!

Pat Parkes

Why Things Happen In Water

Main Focus:

- What is buoyancy?

- Why is it we can float?

- What determines the floating position?

- Can you learn to swim more easily if you can float?

- What is resistance?

- How does resistance affect the swimmer?

- How does an understanding of resistance help the teacher?

- What are the main areas of resistance for each of the four strokes?

- What is propulsion?

- How do we use our arms and legs to generate propulsion?

- How important is it to trace a curved pathway with our arms through the water?

- How do our hands change their pitch as they pull through the water?

- A summary poem by Patricia Parkes

Be A Great Swimming Teacher

Chapter 4

Why Things Happen In Water

INTRODUCTION

Terms such as 'fundamental principles, scientific principles or the mechanics of swimming', often produce doubts, fears and concerns in the minds of teachers. Terminology can cause confusion. However, it is not enough for swimming teachers to simply know *how* and *what* to teach their pupils. It is also essential that they have a basic knowledge of *why* certain things happen in water when they ask their pupils to perform a range of skills and practices. Teachers need to understand what action to take when correcting any problems the pupils may have.

Our aim is to explain in a simple way 'why things happen in water'. This is really what swimming is all about. To do this we need to focus on three main areas:

- **Buoyancy**: What makes us stay up in water and what stops us from sinking?
- **Propulsion**: What makes us go forward in the water?
- **Resistance**: What stops us from going forward?

Throughout the sections on these topics we will be asking many questions to guide teachers' thinking and help their understanding.

BUOYANCY

What is buoyancy?

Buoyancy is the ability or tendency for an object to float in water (or other liquid).

The main fear of a non-swimmer, whether a child or adult, is 'going under'. They fear that they will sink to the bottom, be unable to breathe or come up again and drown. There are many questions surrounding the concept of buoyancy:

- Why do some objects float while others sink?

- Why can some people float better than others?
- What determines the floating position?
- Can you learn to swim more easily if you can float?

Why do some objects float while others sink?

Some objects, such as a polystyrene float, float very well and they are very difficult to even push under the water. Other objects can just about float with very little showing above the water such as an iceberg or indeed a human being. Still other objects sink straight to the bottom. Why is this?

The answer lies in the **density** of an object. The density of an object depends on two inter-related factors:

- Its **weight** (mass).
- How much **space** it takes up (volume).

Weight (Mass)

Put simply:

- If an object is heavy – it will sink.
- If an object is light – it will float.

Space (Volume)

If a rolled up ball of plasticine is placed in a bowl of water, it will sink. The ball is compact and takes up a small amount of space in the water. Yet if the same ball of plasticine is flattened out into a saucer shape, it will float. The plasticine now presents a much larger surface area to the water.

In both examples, the weight of the plasticine does not change, but the space it takes up or its volume does.

In the ball shape, the opportunity for the water to exert an **up-thrust** on the ball of plasticine is very limited because its volume is small. Therefore the weight of the plasticine (or the downward pull of gravity) is much greater than the up-thrust of the water and so the plasticine ball sinks.

In the flattened saucer shape, its volume is much larger and the water is able to exert an up-thrust, large enough to overcome the desire for the plasticine to sink. Therefore it floats in a saucer shape.

 Archimedes, the ancient Greek mathematician, discovered when his bath water overflowed that the amount of water an object displaces is equal to the volume of the object. He also discovered that the strength of the force pushing back by the water against an object depends on how much water it displaces. If an object displaces enough water to create a force or up-thrust large enough to support its weight, then the object will float.

⚡ Whether or not an object will float is determined by the object's density relative to that of water:

- If it is greater than water – it will sink.
- If it is less than water – it will float.
- If it is just less than water – it will only just float with most of its body still below the surface.
- If it is considerably less then water – it will float very high on the surface.

Specific gravity

Measuring and comparing an object's density with that of water, uses the concept of **specific gravity**. The specific gravity of water is 1.0. This is because the weight of a 1 centimetre cubic block of water is 1 gram.

Comparing an object's specific gravity to that of water, is a useful way of knowing whether an object will float.

⚡ If the specific gravity of an object is greater than 1.0 it will sink, while if it is less than 1.0 it will float.

If it is just less than 1.0, it will float with almost all the object immersed in the water. If it is some way below 1.0, it will float with most of the object above the water line.

Can people float?

Yes . . . just! To relate the concept of specific gravity to people, the human body is made up of many different components each with varying specific gravities. Bone is much heavier than water while muscle has a specific gravity slightly greater than water.

Despite this, people can still float because fatty tissue has a specific gravity less than water. Add to this the air in the lungs and the total make-up of the human body has a specific gravity just less than that of water. This results in the human body being able to float with most of its volume immersed in the water.

Why do some people float better than others?

Individuals differ in their ability to float because of their physical make-up. Clearly the greater the content of fatty tissue, the more easily a body floats, maintaining a horizontal position with ease. A muscular, large-boned individual is only just able to float and it is unlikely they will be able to maintain a horizontal position.

Generally, females float better than males because they have more fatty tissue covering their body and have a lighter bone structure. As a result, they find it easier to float in a horizontal position, resting relatively high in the water. Males usually have more muscle bulk and heavier bones (especially the legs). Often they are only able to float in a vertical position, with just their faces out of the water.

- The specific gravity of females is 0.97.
- The specific gravity of males is 0.98.

What determines the floating position?

In addition to its specific gravity, when a body is immersed in water, it has two forces acting upon it:

- Its weight acts downwards through the **centre of gravity**.

- At the same time, the up-thrust of the water acts upwards through the **centre of buoyancy**.

The floating position of a body is determined when the centre of gravity and the centre of buoyancy are vertically aligned. If these two points are not aligned, then the body is not stable. For the swimmer shown in Figure 4.1 the legs sink as the body rotates until these two forces are aligned and a stable floating position is reached as shown in Figure 4.2 (although in a near vertical position).

Notice in Figure 4.1 that the centre of buoyancy is higher than the centre of gravity. This is because the air in the lungs helps keep the torso up resulting in the centre of buoyancy being more towards the chest cavity. The weight of the legs causes the centre of gravity to act closer to the hip region.

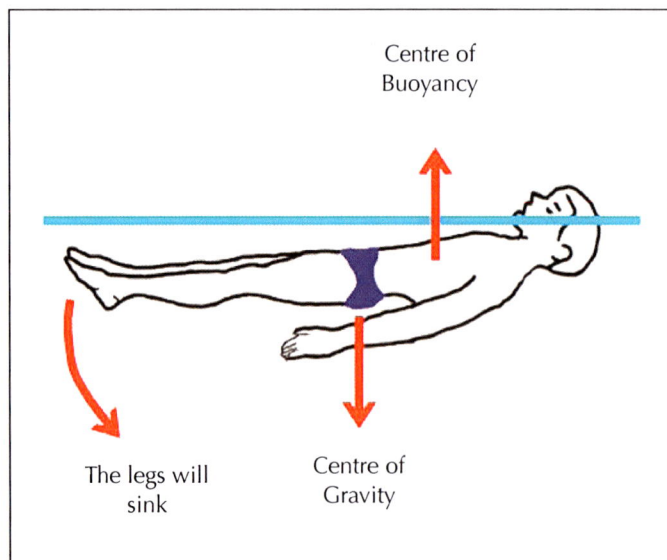

Figure 4.1
An unbalanced floating position

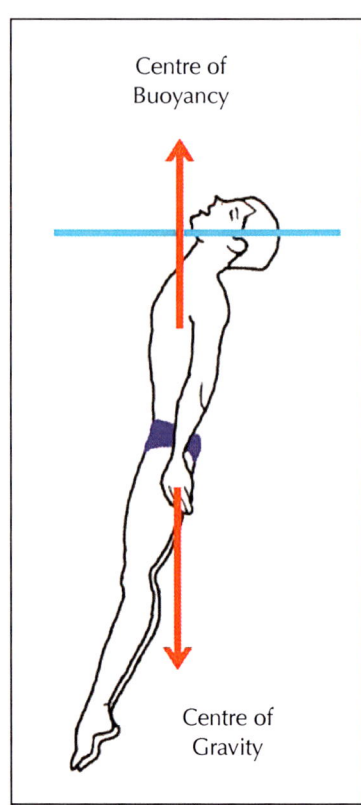

Figure 4.2
A balanced floating position

78

Mushroom float

An easy way to test a swimmers ability to float is to ask them to do a **mushroom tuck float**. If the swimmer can float well, their curved spine shows high out of the water. If the swimmer is a poor floater, they gradually sink to below the surface.

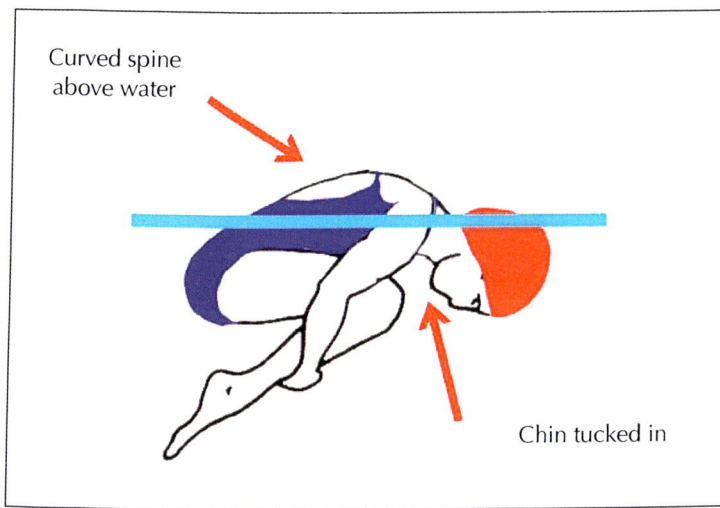

Curved spine
above water

Chin tucked in

Figure 4.3
A mushroom floating position

In Figure 4.3, you can easily see the curved spine above the water so this swimmer is a good 'floater'.

Why is it easier to float in the sea?

Seawater contains dissolved salt, so has a higher density than fresh water. The specific gravity is 1.03. This means that the human body is able to float more easily and often in a more horizontal position in seawater than it can in fresh water.

Can you learn to swim more easily if you can float?

It could be argued that a swimmer with a higher proportion of fatty tissue can learn to swim more easily. Swimming ability, however, involves a number of other factors in addition to being able to float motionless. The ability to remain on top of the water in a horizontal position has more to do with the generation of propulsion through muscular effort than on floating ability.

The ability to float does, however, give the beginner great confidence. **To know that the water will support you** if you take your feet off the bottom really boosts a beginner's confidence levels and it is a fundamental skill to develop and practise.

How can you improve the ability to float?

It is also interesting to note that the capacity to float can be increased by first filling the lungs with as much air as possible.

Buoyancy: a summary

- Buoyancy depends on the density of an object (its weight and volume).
- The object will float if the up-thrust acting on an object is greater than its weight acting downwards.
- The position a body floats in is dependent on the balance between the downward pull of gravity and the up-thrust created by the support of the water.

RESISTANCE

What is resistance?

Resistance is the slowing-down effect that water has on a swimmers attempt to propel themselves through the water.

When moving through water, you experience a slowing down or stopping effect. Most people are familiar with this – think how hard it is to wade through water waist deep.

How does resistance affect the swimmer?

With every swimming stroke, water is 'applying the brakes' as it tries to drag you to a halt. This is clearly visible from a push and glide off the wall when, after a strong push off the wall, the swimmer quickly slows down and eventually stops. If the swimmer adopts a good horizontal streamlined position off the wall where:

- the arms are extended behind the head
- the body is taut
- the legs are stretched out behind

they will glide further because in this position they experience the least resistance.

🗝 The greater the departure from a horizontal position, the greater is the resistance.

With a good horizontal body position the space taken up is small as shown in Figure 4.4.

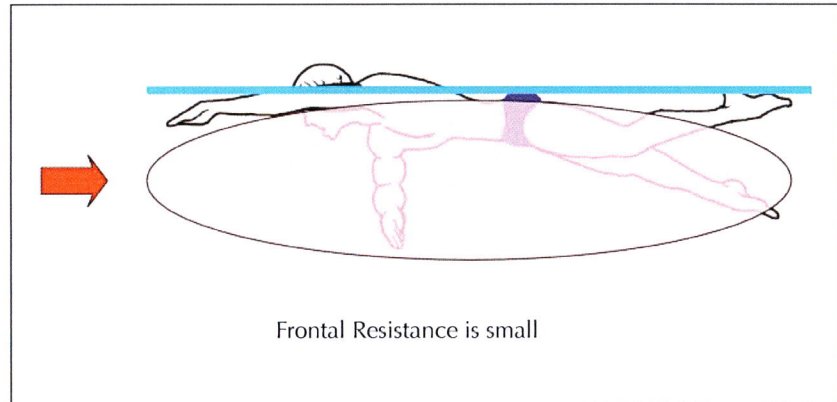

Figure 4.4
The total space occupied with a good body position when swimming front crawl.

Frontal Resistance is small

Figure 4.5 shows that with a poor body position, the space taken up is much greater so the frontal resistance of the swimmer is considerably higher.

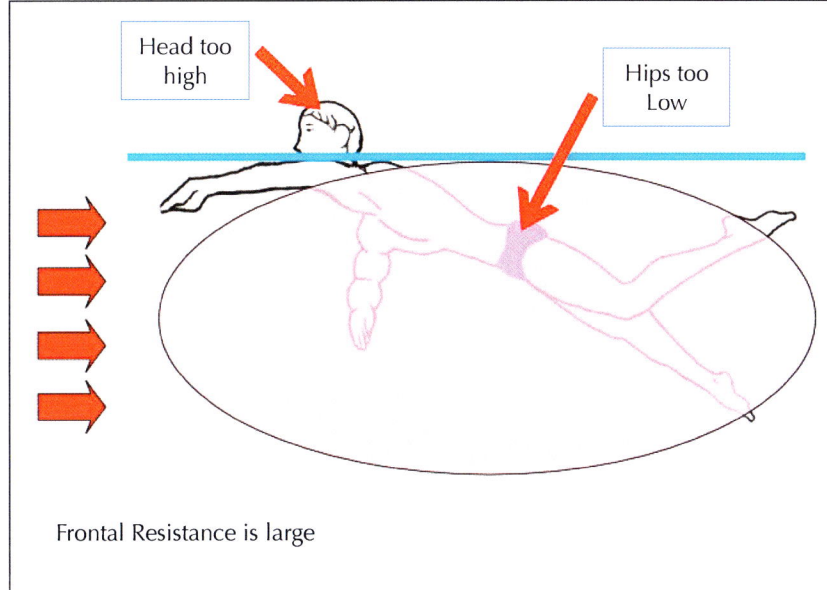

Head too high

Hips too Low

Figure 4.5
The total space occupied when the body position is poor

Frontal Resistance is large

What determines the total space a swimmer takes up?

The total space a swimmer occupies is determined by:

- The depth the swimmer occupies.
- The width (side to side) the swimmer occupies.

The resistance is increased when a swimmer takes up more space in the water. The teacher must continually look at the swimmer to see if streamlining can reduce the space they occupy. If a swimmer is inclined downwards from their head to their feet, they are occupying a much greater space in the water than if they were more horizontal and streamlined.

What determines the frontal resistance of a swimmer?

A swimmer's body also presents a cross sectional area to the oncoming water. This is described as **frontal resistance**.

If a swimmer presents a large frontal area, considerable resistance is created. This can easily be demonstrated to pupils by asking them to walk forwards holding a kick board vertically with its flat surface against the water. The water becomes a barrier that the swimmer has to push hard against to move forwards.

What does this mean for the teacher?

The swimmer is unable to prevent the water from resisting their forward motion but with guidance and feedback from the teacher, they can learn to reduce their resistance as much as possible.

The teacher must always be aware of:

- **How much total space** a swimmer is taking up in the water.
- **How big is the frontal area** a swimmer is presenting to the oncoming water?

What happens when a swimmer starts to swim?

A swimmer's shape presented to the oncoming water does not remain static. It is constantly changing as the swimmer performs the stroke.

When a swimmer starts to swim, they cannot avoid taking up more space, presenting greater frontal resistance to the water. There are for example, phases in both the breaststroke and the butterfly when the head has to be clear of the water to breathe causing an increase in frontal resistance. At other phases in the strokes, the body is more streamlined. One of the challenges for the teacher is to try to encourage their pupils to remain as horizontal as possible within the mechanics of the stroke.

Turbulence

Through their arm and leg movements, a swimmer also creates a certain amount of **turbulence** in the water. This turbulence creates **eddy currents** that act like a break dragging the swimmer back, particularly by the legs and the area behind the swimmer (sometimes called **tail suction**). The greater the turbulence created, the greater is the resistive force pulling the swimmer backwards.

Turbulence around both the arms and legs slows the swimmer down.

Turbulence "sucks" the swimmer backwards

Figure 4.6
The turbulence behind a swimmer

Figure 4.7
The turbulence around the swimmer's arms

Turbulence slows the swimmer down

 Where the turbulence is high, the teacher can see it as white water at the surface behind the swimmer and as air bubbles around the swimmer's limbs.

Wave drag

A swimmer also encounters further resistance if their stroke or speed of swimming generates excessive waves on the water surface. This form of resistance is called **wave drag**. As with the eddy currents, the waves act in a negative way, pulling the swimmer in a backwards direction. The teacher should observe the swimmer to avoid any excessive vertical or bouncing movements in the stroke and so reduce the effects of wave drag.

 It is interesting to note that a proficient swimmer can kick faster when completely submerged underwater than they can kick on the surface. This is because underwater, the swimmer's resistance is less since they are no longer affected by wave drag.

Skin friction

One other form of resistance is **skin friction**. This is the resistance caused by the water travelling over the surface of the swimmer's body. Unlike a competitive swimmer who may shave before a competition to reduce this form of resistance, a learner has little control over this other than ensuring their costume is not too loose. The teacher need not be concerned with this form of resistance when teaching beginners.

Resistance: a summary

A swimmer's forward progress is reduced by the resistance they encounter through being:

- **Pushed back** from the front due to the resistance of the water.
- **Pulled back** from behind due to the backward pulling effect of the eddy currents or the excessive creation of waves.

What is the combined effect of this *push and pull resistance* from the water?

Together, the frontal resistance from the water and the backward pulling effect of the eddy currents or excessive wave creation combine to form an overall negative **drag force**. This acts in the opposite direction to the one in which the swimmer's body is moving. The overall effect of this drag force is to slow the swimmer down. To move forwards, enough propulsion has to be generated by the swimmer to overcome this drag force.

What are the golden rules for the teacher?

The following are some stroke guidelines for the teacher:

- Focus on working to achieve a good horizontal and lateral alignment for all strokes.
- Always think about trying to minimise the amount of space a swimmer takes up in the water.
- Always try to present the smallest surface area to the oncoming water.
- Look to keep the arm and leg actions inside the body line as much as possible.
- Within the demands of the stroke, encourage the pupils to keep their head down where possible.
- Ensure the leg kick is not too deep.

What are the main areas of resistance for each of the four strokes?

The main area of resistance varies with the different strokes.

Strokes	Main area of resistance
Backstroke	• The propulsive arm movement because it occurs to the side, outside the body line.
Front crawl	• Kicking too deep in an attempt to generate greater propulsion. • Pulling too far outside the body line or too far across the centre line. • The front crawl creates the least resistance of the four strokes because the arm pull is directly under the body. Also, the breathing is performed to the side.
Breaststroke	• Frontal resistance due to the head being lifted to the front to breathe, resulting in an angled body position. • Eddy resistance, caused by the swirls of water around the limbs (arms and legs) as they move outside the body line.

Strokes	Main area of resistance
Butterfly	• As with the breaststroke, the main area is frontal resistance due to the head being lifted to the front to breathe, resulting in an angled body position. • Excessive turbulence around the arms as they enter the water.

 To achieve minimal resistance, all strokes must aim to be performed smoothly and efficiently with the least disturbance to the water as possible.

PROPULSION

What is propulsion?

Propulsion is the net effect of using the arms and legs to propel the body in either a forward or backward direction.

This net effect is dependent on first overcoming any resistance offered by the water.

How do we use the arms and legs?

By using the arms and legs to push backwards against the water, a propulsive reaction is created in a forward direction. In this way, the swimmer is able to achieve the fundamental principle of all movement based on the physicist Sir Isaac Newton's Third Law of Motion which states:

For every action in one direction, there is an equal reaction in the opposite direction.

A backward push on the water by the swimmer's hand and forearm causes a reaction in the opposite direction that moves the swimmer's body forwards. This is shown in Figure 4.8.

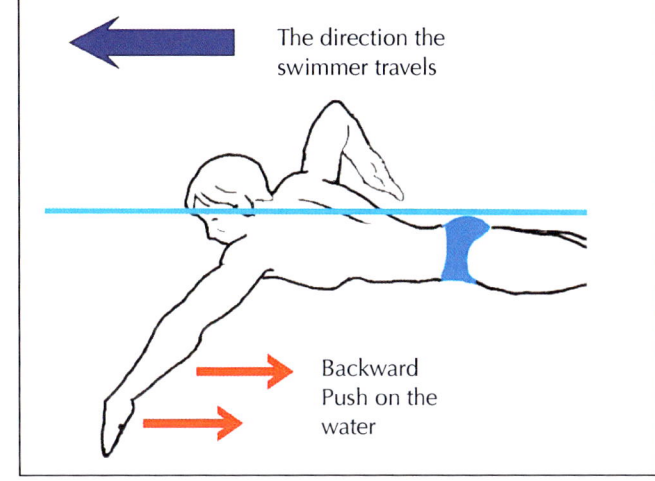

The direction the swimmer travels

Backward Push on the water

Figure 4.8
The principal of action/reaction in swimming.

A swimmer has the impression that the hand travels backwards from the point of entry to when they exit the water. In practice, however, because of the nature of the water, once the hands and forearms gain a purchase, they 'fix' themselves allowing the swimmers body to first be pulled towards them, before being pushed away.

 The shoulder acts as a pivot as the swimmer's body is pulled past the anchored hand.

The concept of the hand anchoring itself in the water and the swimmer pulling their body towards, over and past the hand is a useful one. This action normally takes place once the **catch point** is reached. This is the point after entry when the swimmer begins to apply real purchase on the water. It is essential that this position is achieved as early in the stroke as possible. Once in this position the hand is ready to fix its position in the water to pull the body past the hand and propel the swimmer forwards.

The total force generated to propel the swimmer in a forward direction is called a **propulsive force**. Most of the literature refers to this, as a **drag force**. This is confusing to the trainee teacher because the same term is also used to describe the total resistance acting on a swimmer. We have chosen to use the term 'propulsive force' as we feel it is more descriptive and it aids clarity.

Should the swimmer focus on pushing back in a straight line?

No! When a swimmer presses their hand against the water, the water behind the palm starts to move backwards, away from the palm of the hand. The propulsive force a swimmer can generate is much less if the hand continues to try to press against water that is already moving away from it.

For a swimmer to pull effectively, they must try to push continually against water that is relatively still so the hand can gain the most purchase on the water. To achieve this, a swimmer should be encouraged to think of their hands as tracing a **curved pull** through the water. By following a curved pathway, the hands continually press against still water throughout the pull. Figure 4.9 shows an example of the curved pathway used in the front crawl.

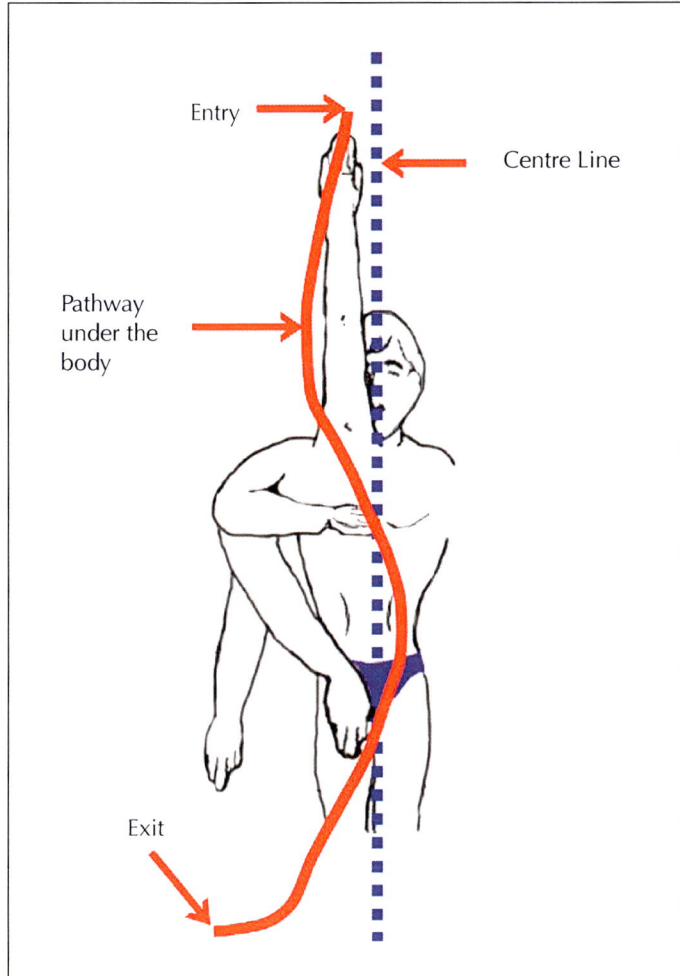

Entry

Centre Line

Pathway under the body

Exit

Figure 4.9
The 'S' shape pulling pattern for the right arm in front crawl.

The pull is often known by the pattern the hand follows. You can see from Figure 4.9 that the front crawl pattern is an 'S' shape. The pulling pattern for the front crawl is therefore known as an **'S' shaped pull**. All four strokes however, use this principle. These are described in greater detail in each of the stroke chapters (Chapters 5, 6, 7 and 8).

When swimming, the pupils can easily visualise these pulling patterns and copy them. The teacher must therefore describe these pulling patterns in relation to the swimmer's body.

Do the hands remain still during the 'S' pull?

No, the hands must change their pitch several times as they follow their 'S' shaped pull. This is shown in Figure 4.10.

By continually changing the hand pitch, the hands use a sculling action throughout the propulsive phase of the pull. The first part of the pull is performed with the thumb down. This changes to a thumbs up during the middle part of the pull and changes again to a thumbs down as the swimmer pushes back to complete the underwater phase.

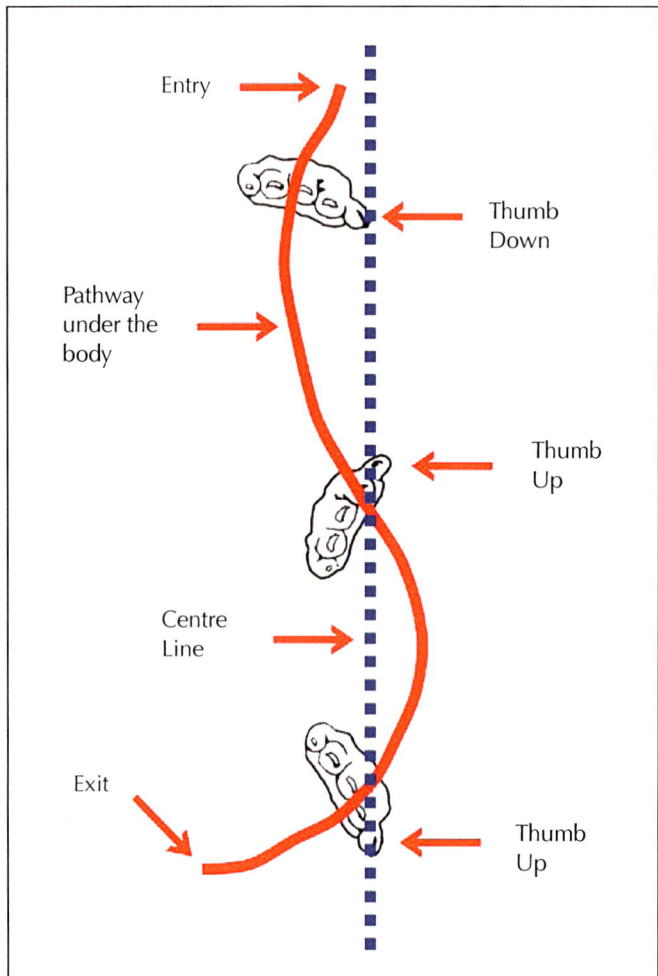

Entry

Thumb
Down

Pathway
under the
body

Thumb
Up

Centre
Line

Exit

Thumb
Up

Figure 4.10
The changes in hand pitch for the
right arm during the 'S' shape pull in
front crawl.

🔑 The swimmer must displace water backwards to go forwards.

This is achieved by changing the hand pitch as they pull through the water. This sculling action helps the swimmer to continually direct water in a backwards direction creating a propulsive force in a forwards direction.

Hand tracks

We have said that from a swimmer's point of view, the hand follows an 'S' shaped pull through the water. This is not however, the complete picture. Let us look at the pulling pattern from a different perspective.

The track that the hand actually takes through the water is one pathway with three components:

1. Forwards and backwards.
2. Up and down.
3. Side to side.

A clear example is the **hand track** for front crawl. Figures 4.11a to 4.11c shows the three components of the hand track through the water. These three components combine together to form one three-dimensional pathway through the water.

By looking at the swimmer from three views, you can see how a complete picture of the actual track that the hand takes through the water is best understood. To describe these pathways, the track that the hand follows is broken down into a number of **sweeping movements** as follows:

Sweeps	Where are they used?
Out-sweep:	Initial underwater sweep in breaststroke and butterfly
In-sweep	Second sweep used in all strokes
Down-sweep	Initial underwater sweep in backstroke and front crawl
Up-sweep	Final sweep in front crawl and butterfly

 You would not describe this to pupils who are learning to swim. They are only asked to view the pulling pathway in relation to their body using the terms 'pull' and 'push'. A teacher, however, can use their own knowledge of the three-dimensional pathway when analysing a swimmer's strokes to think about any corrections they might make.

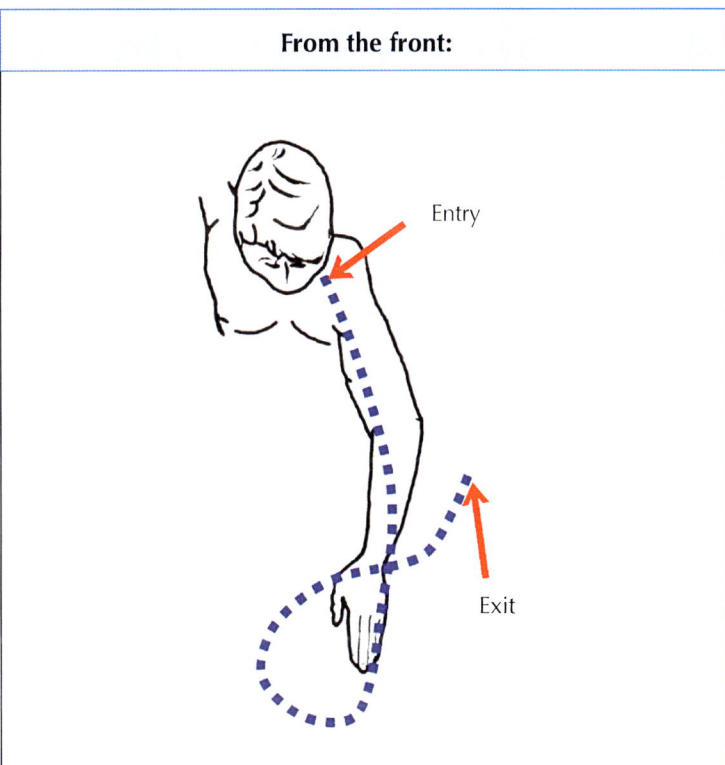

Figure 4.11a
The front crawl hand track through the water as viewed from the front.

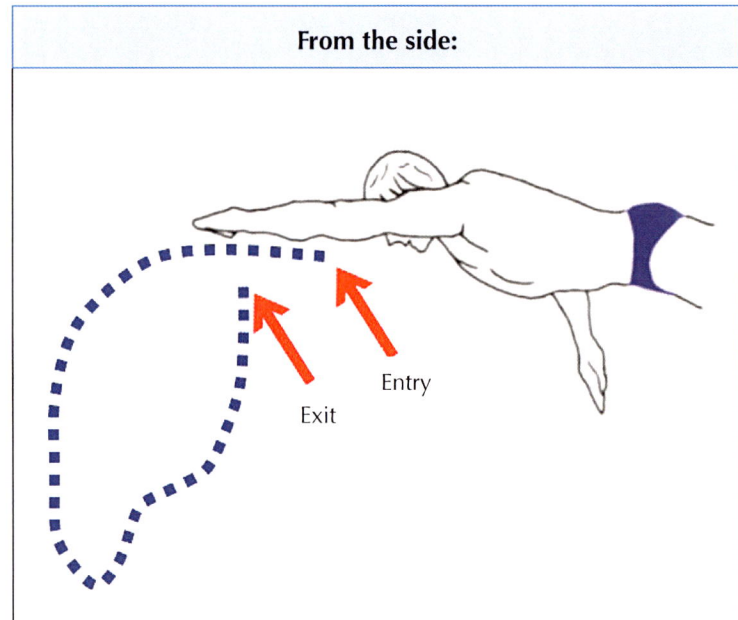

From the side:

Figure 4.11b
The front crawl hand track through the water as viewed from the side.

Entry

Exit

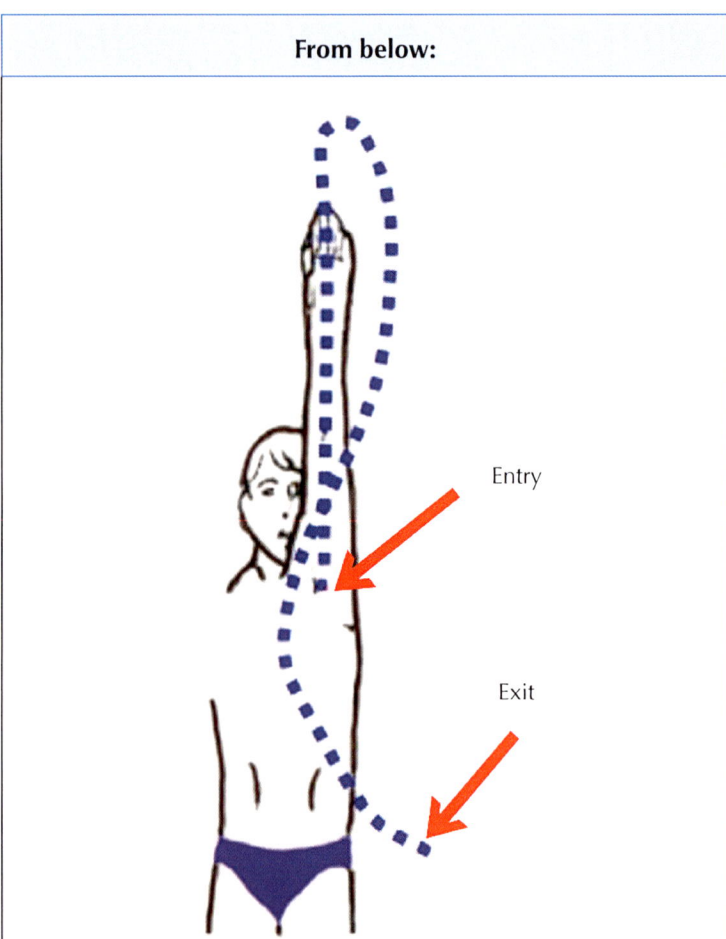

From below:

Figure 4.11c
The front crawl hand track through the water as viewed from the beneath.

Entry

Exit

Figure 4.11
The three-dimensional hand track through the water for front crawl.

How does propulsion apply to the leg kick?

While the main source of propulsion for front crawl, backstroke and butterfly is the arm action, the feet can also contribute to propulsion. In front crawl for example, a swimmer with good ankle flexibility is able to direct more water back with the top of the foot adding to propulsion in a forward direction. This is shown in Figure 4.12.

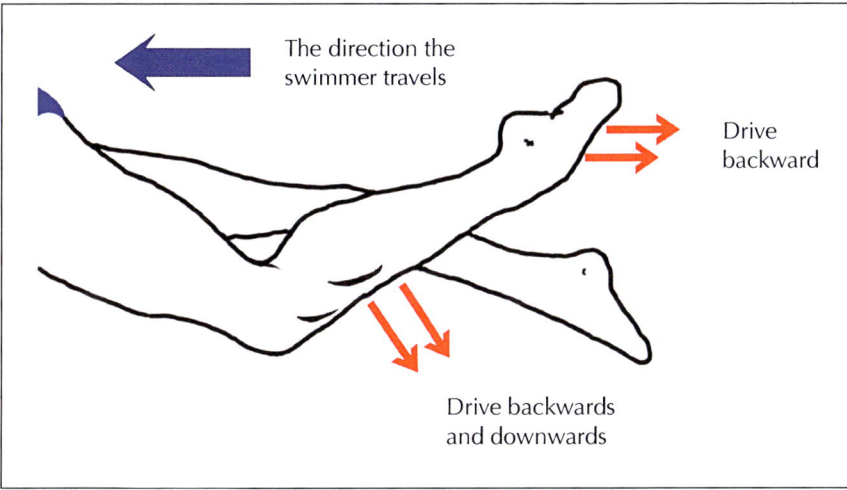

Figure 4.12 Directing the water backwards with the kick down in front crawl.

The legs also trace a curved pathway allowing the feet to continually kick down in water that is fairly still. During each down beat, the upper part of the foot is able to kick against relatively still water, gaining a strong purchase and driving the water backwards with each kick. The kicking pattern produced for front crawl is shown in Figure 4.13.

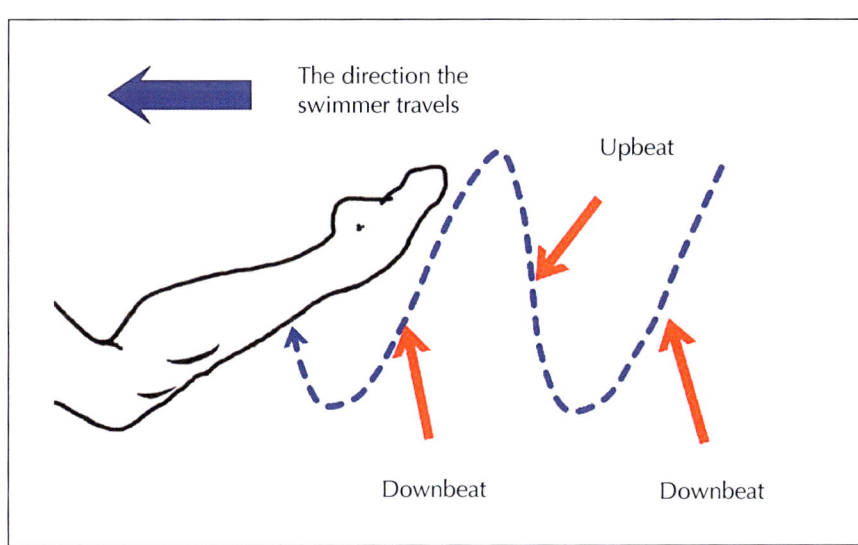

Figure 4.13 The curved pathway followed by the front crawl leg kick.

Remember the effectiveness of the leg kick in contributing to the overall propulsion of the swimmer may be small. The main function of the leg kick in three of the strokes namely, front crawl, backstroke and butterfly, is to keep the body in a horizontal position to reduce resistance and balance the arm movements.

Butterfly follows a similar pattern to front crawl while in backstroke the water is directed backwards on the drive up. In breaststroke, the kick is more likely to contribute a greater proportion to the overall propulsion of the swimmer. The feet and lower leg follow a circular pathway on the drive back. Combining this with the rotation of the ankles allows the swimmer to again displace water in a backwards direction, adding to the propulsive force of the swimmer. This is looked at in more detail in Chapter 8.

WHAT IS SWIMMING ALL ABOUT?

What is swimming all about?
Buoyancy and floatation without a doubt.
The density of water is one point nought,
Sea water is more, because of the salt.
Ladies are blessed with fatty tissue
A point about which, they might make an issue.
But with it 'hey, we can float'
They say with a superior gloat!
Men sink down to just their face
Some submerge without a trace.
Swimming is about being streamlined
Keeping the strokes, smooth and refined.
Propulsion is gained by pushing limbs back
Enter the hand, seek the angle of attack.
Swimming is about the resistance we find
As legs are drawn up, their swirls behind.
Resistance called profile, eddy or viscosity
Words to provoke deep curiosity.
Newton's Third Law talks of the action
How each stroke must have an equal reaction
That is what swimming is all about!

Pat Parkes

Chapter 5

Backstroke

Main Focus:

- Why is backstroke a good stroke to teach first?

- What to look for in a good stroke?

- Why is the horizontal position so important?

- What is the depth of the kick?

- What is the nature of the recovery?

- What are the two types of arm pull?

- Why is the push back so crucial for an effective stroke?

- How does the - **S** - shaped pulling pattern apply to backstroke?

- How does the body roll affect the stroke?

- A 7 stage building programme

- The identification of 7 main problems

- An improvement circle built on three core skills

- A summary of what to look for

- Usable stroke assessment sheets

- A summary poem by Patricia Parkes

Be A Great Swimming Teacher

Chapter 5

Backstroke

INTRODUCTION

Backstroke is performed lying in the water on the back (supine position). For this reason, it is one of the easiest strokes to teach. Beginners like to swim backstroke simply because their faces are kept clear of the water and they do not experience too many difficulties with the breathing. The stroke also remains popular as the swimmer becomes more proficient.

 It is interesting to see how often pupils choose to swim backstroke when a distance test is held. They find it less tiring than the other strokes.

Backstroke: the first stroke to learn?

There are sound reasons why the backstroke should be the first stroke taught in a learners' programme. These are:

- The leg action is straightforward (a simple up and down movement) and can be learnt quickly.

- The leg action can easily be co-ordinated with a sculling motion performed by the hands. Since the teaching of sculling is essential for the development of all strokes, teaching backstroke first allows this skill to be introduced early into the learners' programme.

- On the back, the pupil can see the teacher. This visual contact gives confidence and is enhanced when helpers in the water are used to support and encourage the pupils.

There are, however, two aspects to teaching the backstroke that may cause the pupil some concern:

- **Firstly, the beginner has an initial fear of lying backwards in the water.** This is overcome if the pupil learns to regain their feet easily.

- **Secondly, the idea of swimming backwards without being able to see where they are going causes some apprehension.** It is all too easy for pupils in crowded classes to collide 'head to head'. The teacher must organise the class to avoid this and encourage the pupils to always look over their shoulder before they start to swim.

Using supports for backstroke

Initial support is best achieved in the following way:

- A woggle is placed around the back of the swimmer.

- The pupil rests his or her forearms onto the woggle and holds on to it as they lean back.

Figure 5.1
A support position for the backstroke using a woggle.

Using a woggle, float or arm bands allows the beginner to experience movement through the water. When the support is removed, they can kick with the legs and scull with the hands and they are 'swimming'.

🔑 This achievement early in a learner's career is important, since there is nothing like success for breeding success.

If children are having difficulty lying back in the water, direct support by an assistant in the water can be used as shown in Figure 5.2

Hands support shoulders

- The assistant stands behind the swimmer.

- Using their hands and forearms they support the tops of the shoulders, keeping the hands visible at all times.

- They have their face at water level, close to the pupil's head.

Figure 5.2
The correct support by an assistant in the water for the backstroke

 Physical contact with learners

Many authorities advocate no physical contact by the assistant in the water as part of their policy to ensure the teaching environment is one where the safeguarding of children is paramount. We wholeheartedly endorse this and recommend that teachers attempt to resolve any problems without using physical support.

There are however, some children who after everything else has been attempted, still lack confidence and therefore experience difficulties, particularly with the backstroke. In the end, the only way to overcome it is by using some physical support by assistants in the water. If this is the case, it is important that teachers have knowledge of the correct support position to be used (and those to be avoided) and that any support is done openly and ideally with both pupil and parental consent.

Two support positions to be avoided are:

a) Standing behind a swimmer with the arms extended because this creates a wash that splashes over the pupil's face.

b) Standing at the side of a swimmer, as this impedes the arm movements and there is a tendency to 'roll' the swimmer onto their side away from the helper.

WHAT TO LOOK FOR IN A GOOD STROKE

Body position

The teacher must view the stroke from two different angles:

- **The side** – the horizontal position.

- **The front** – the swimmer moving away.

Each view tells the teacher something about the swimmer's body position.

From the side

It is most helpful to use the classic 'back glide' as a frame of reference when thinking about the horizontal body position in backstroke. The focus should be to look at the position of the head, hips, legs and feet relative to the surface of the water.

Look for:
• The head resting on the water. • The water just covering the ears and level with the crown of the head. • The hips just below the surface. • The legs fully stretched, held together with toes pointed.

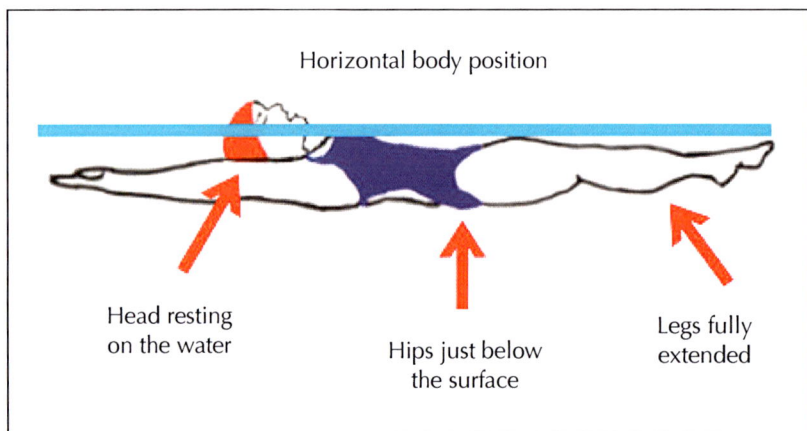

Figure 5.3
The back glide position

The 'head' controls the body position.

Tilting the head forward or pushing the head back alters the body position in the following way:

- If the head is tilted too far forward, the hips drop, creating a 'sitting' position in the water. This is often brought about by teachers asking the pupils to 'look at their toes breaking the water surface'.

- If the head is pushed too far back, the face submerges, the hips rise close to the surface and the knees come out of the water. Fear and tension often then cause the pupils to breath hold.

From the front

As the swimmer moves away from the teacher:

<table>
<tr><td>

Look for:

- Any sideways (lateral) movement of the hips and feet.
- The head should remain perfectly still.
- The hips should remain relatively still.
- The movement of the legs should be kept inside the width of the shoulders.

</td></tr>
</table>

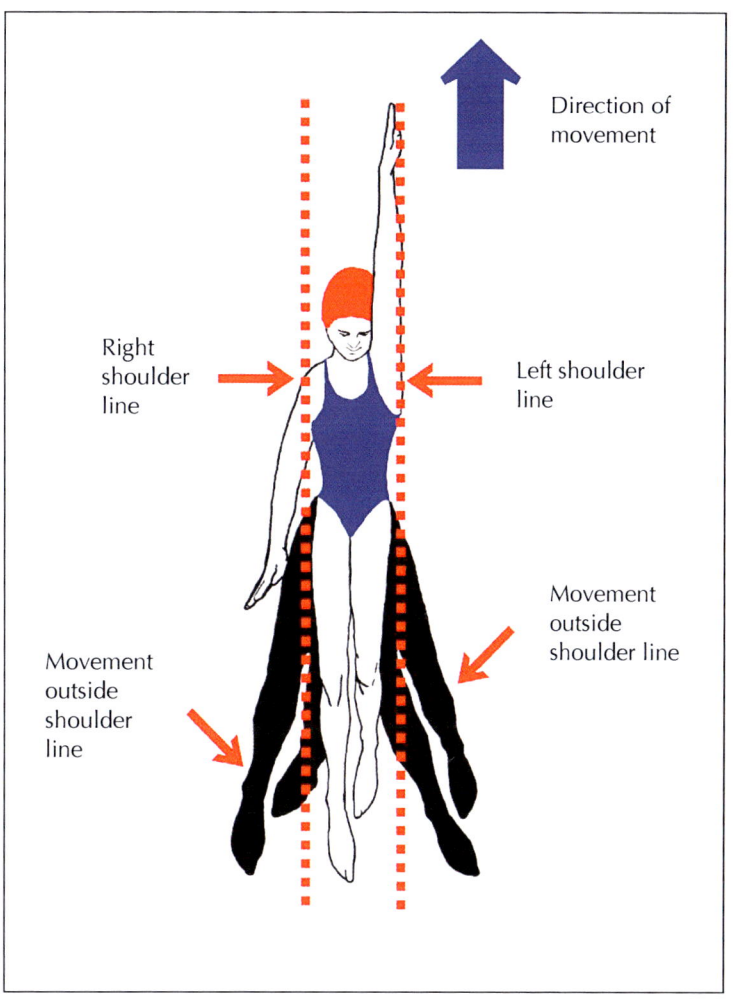

Figure 5.4
The backstroke body as the swimmer moves away from the teacher

 The lateral movement of the body only becomes evident when the arm pull is co-ordinated with the leg kick. Clearly any unnecessary sideways movement slows the swimmer down. As the swimmer moves away from the side, the check should be that the head, hips and feet are kept in a straight line . . . 'straight like a sentry'.

Discussion on the body position

The teacher must allow a level of tolerance as the size, shape and buoyancy of an individual will make it more difficult for some to attain an ideal horizontal position.

- A very buoyant swimmer needs to position their head with the chin tucked slightly in towards the chest to keep the hips from rising too high in the water.

- Conversely, the non-buoyant swimmer has to tilt their head back to keep their hips and legs from sinking too low.

The irony is, teachers usually ask pupils to lie as flat as possible on the water, emphasising a stretched position with the tummy up. There is nothing wrong with this. It is a way of achieving one thing by asking for another. The problem arises if

101

the instruction is taken literally. When performing the full stroke, the legs should be low enough to allow the kicking action to be performed under the water, with the toes just breaking the surface. We are therefore really looking for a shallow curved shape, with the emphasis being on the word **shallow**.

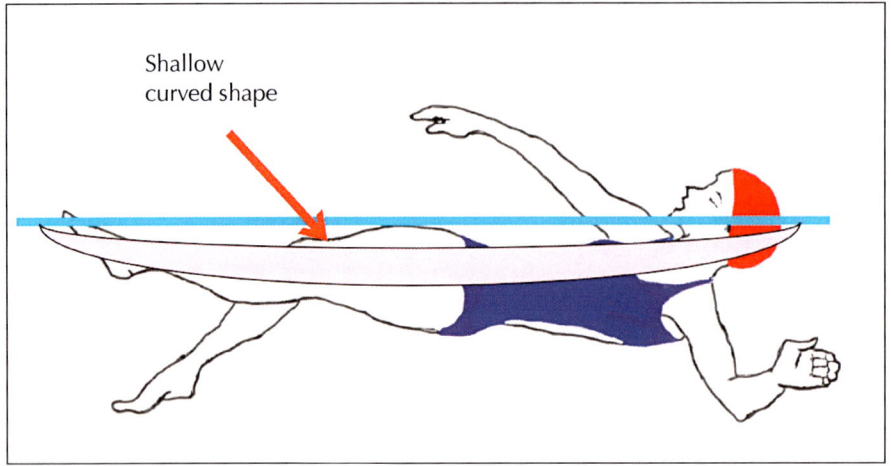

Figure 5.5
The shallow curved shape body position when swimming backstroke

 A critical factor: In the early stages of learning, it is critical to develop a correct horizontal body position because it is so closely related to the leg action. One could argue that the body position and leg kick are more inter-related in the backstroke than in any other stroke. A poor body position invariably makes a correct leg movement difficult. If the pupil is having a problem with the leg kick, first check the horizontal body position.

Leg action

The basic movement of the kick, is an alternating up and down motion in a vertical plane, with the legs passing as close as possible to one another.

The upbeat

Look for:
• The leg driving up towards the surface in a 'whip-like' movement with the ankle and toes extended.   • The knee being fully extended and the toes just breaking the surface as the leg finishes its upbeat.

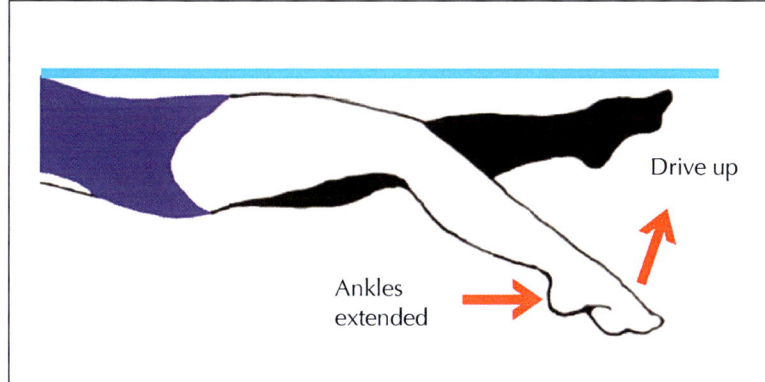

Figure 5.6a
The 'whip-like' dive up to the surface of the lower leg

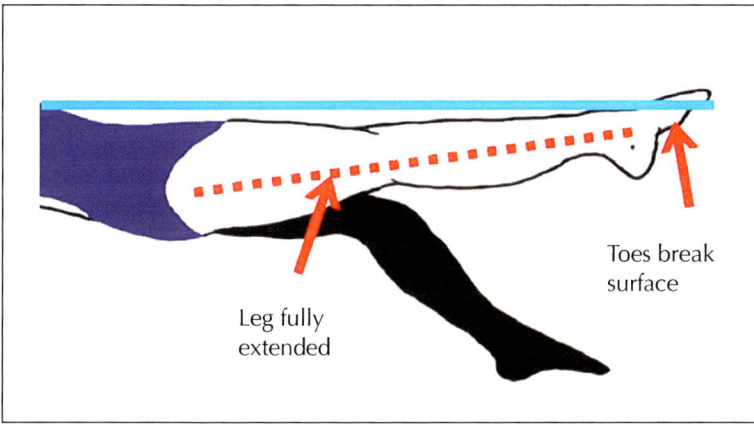

Figure 5.6b
The leg extension at the end of the upbeat

The downbeat

Look for:
• The action starting at the hips. This initial movement is carried out with a straight leg.
• The knee bending slightly as the leg drops down further.

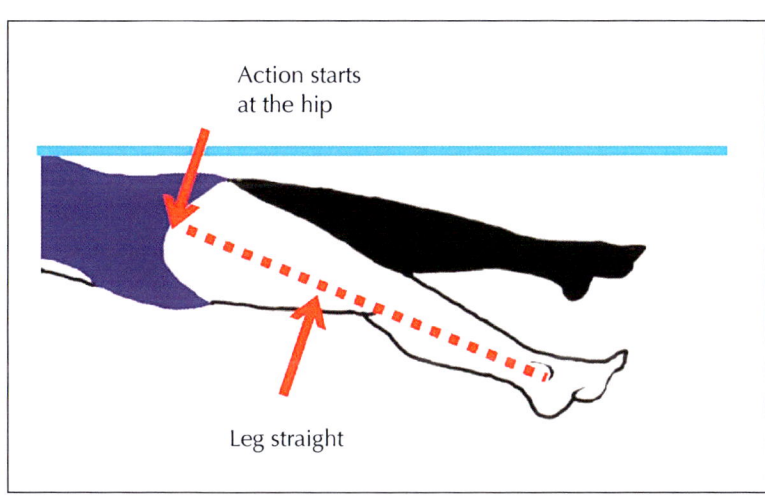

Figure 5.7a
The first part of the downbeat

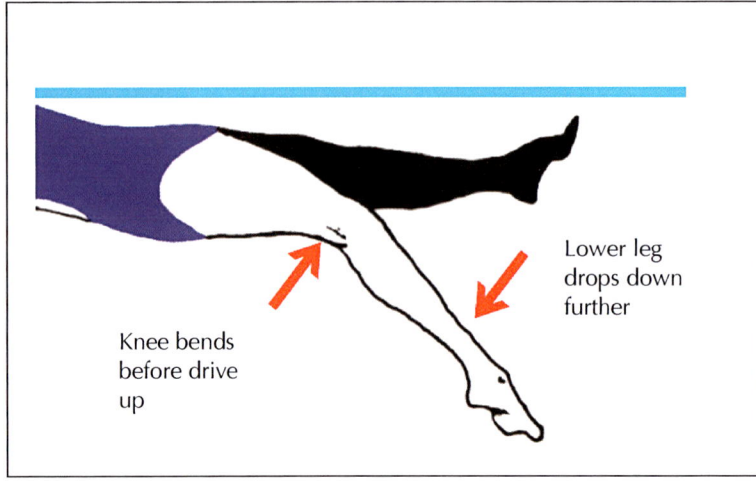

Figure 5.7b
The end of the downbeat

Lower leg
drops down
further

Knee bends
before drive
up

Discussion on the leg kick

There are two features of the kick that are important:

- The first is the depth of the kick.
- The second feature concerns the actual function of the leg kick.

The depth of the kick

🔑 The depth of the kick is relative to the length of the leg.

In a very small child, the kick is only about fifteen to thirty centimetres deep, but with an older pupil, it is deeper. The true depth of the kick is not always appreciated; it is deeper than many believe. All too often teachers are seen using their hands to demonstrate the action to a class, a demonstration which shows a flutter type of movement only a few centimetres deep. The pupils then copy this and the result is a very shallow kick, working from the knees.

In an attempt to describe the correct movement, we have likened the action in the building block programme to **walking**. The alternating movement gives a good picture of the action and rhythm of the kick. A deeper, slower leg action must be developed to give the pupils **time** to think about what they are doing and perform the action correctly. This is vital when the arms are later co-ordinated with the legs.

Functions of the leg kick

The main functions of the leg kick are:

- **To balance and stabilise the stroke.**
- **To maintain the body in a streamlined horizontal position.**

Teachers often believe the main function of the kick is propulsion. One can appreciate how this belief is fostered when a beginner is seen propelling him or herself across the width using only a leg action. The propulsion derived from the leg action comes from the upbeat. If the foot is extended (toes pointed) as the lower leg is whipped up towards the surface, the top of the foot can drive against the water.

The main source of propulsion, however, comes from the arm pull. The legs work hard to maintain a horizontal streamlined body position.

When the arms are added to the leg action, the kick is no longer performed entirely in the vertical plane. Some of the leg action becomes a diagonal up and down motion because the whole body, including the legs, rolls slightly onto the side in time with the arm action. The effects of this body roll on the leg action can best be seen as the swimmer moves away from the teacher as shown in Figures 5.8a to 5.8c.

Look for:
• A diagonal action when the body rolls onto either side. • A vertical action when the swimmer is mid-way through the roll from one side to the other.

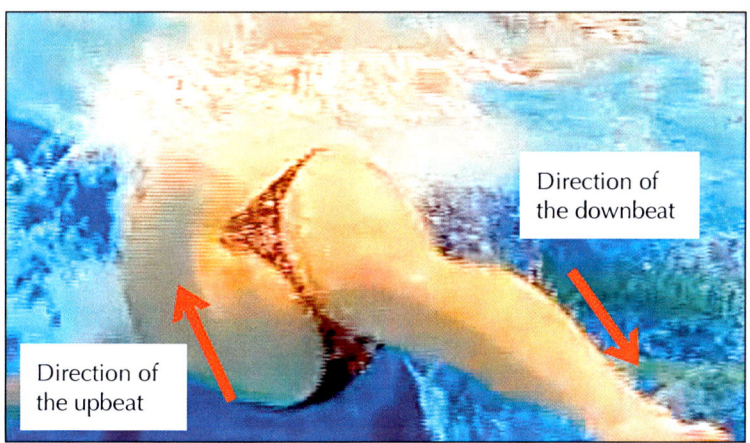

Figure 5.8a
The diagonal action when the body rolls onto the right side.

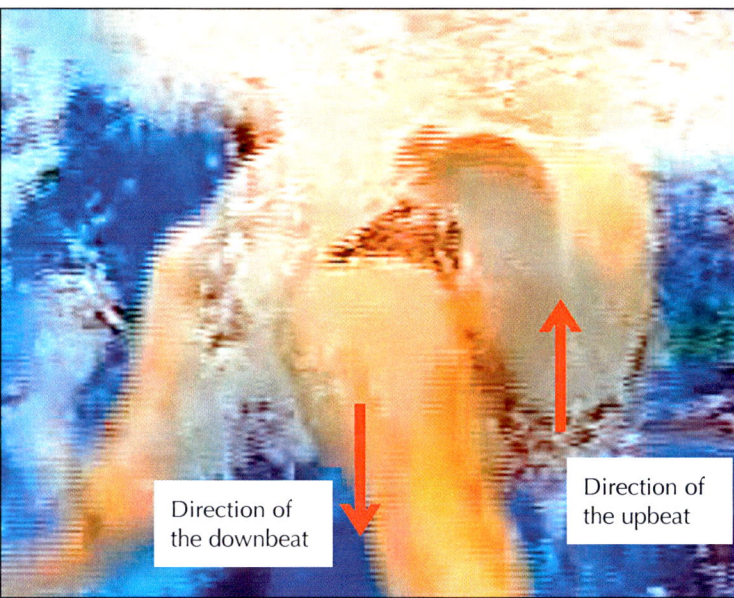

Figure 5.8b
The vertical action when the swimmer is mid-way through the roll from one side to the other.

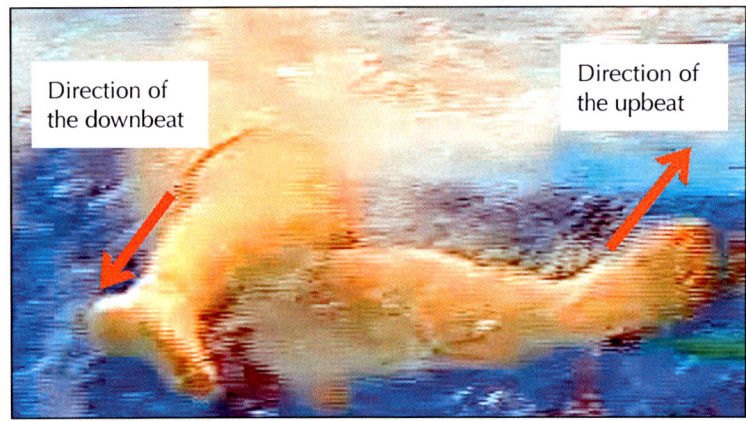

Direction of
the downbeat

Direction of
the upbeat

Figure 5.8c
The diagonal action when the
body rolls onto the left side.

Arm action

The arm action is basically a continuous 'windmill-like' movement. The alternating action allows one arm to recover over the water, while the other pulls through the water. A distinction is made between two types of arm pull:

- The **straight** arm pull.
- The **bent** arm pull.

The recovery and the entry is the same for both.

Recovery

The recovery starts as the hand and arm are lifted out of the water by the thigh. The hand is taken smoothly backwards over and beyond the head to a position in line with the shoulder. This action is carried out with a completely straight arm.

Look for:
• The hand exiting the water, little finger first.   • The hand tracing a semi-circular path, reaching as high as possible as it passes over the head.   • The hand reaching behind the head, arm extended.

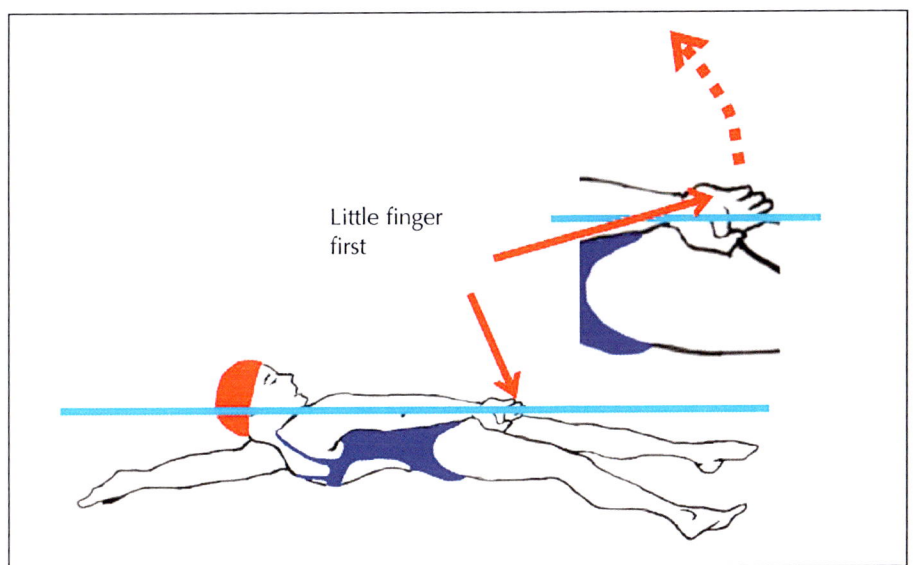

Figure 5.9
The start of the recovery

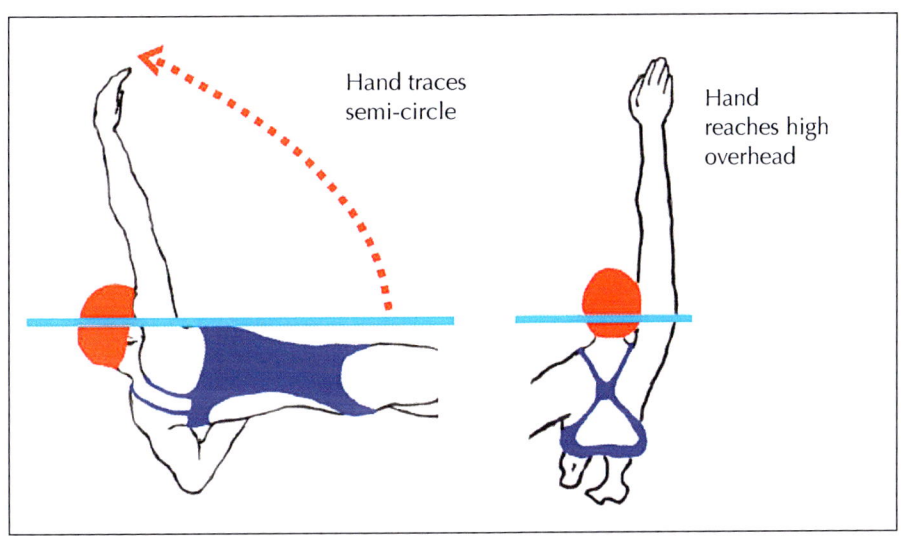

Figure 5.10
Mid-way through the recovery

107

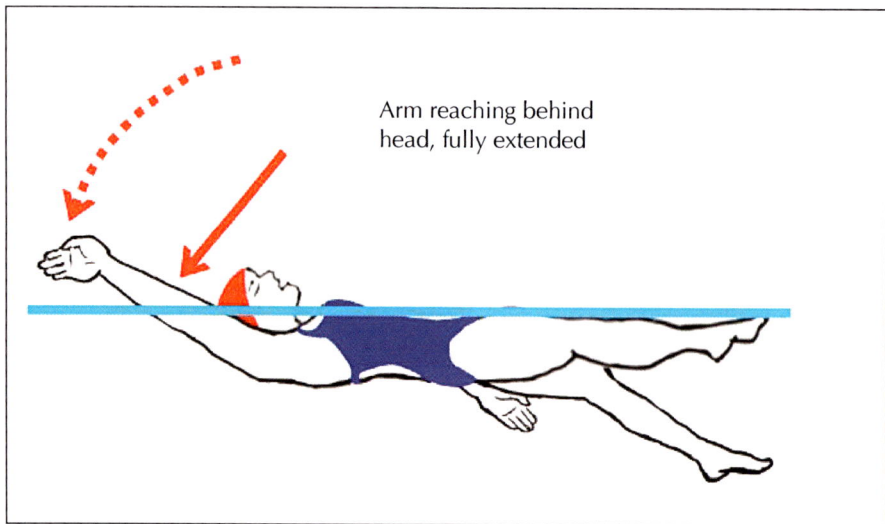

Arm reaching behind
head, fully extended

Figure 5.11
The end of the recovery

Throughout the recovery, it is essential the little finger leads the movement to open up the shoulder girdle.

 If the hand leaves the water thumb first, somewhere during the recovery it has to be consciously turned palm out to prepare for a little finger first entry. The novice swimmer already has a lot to think about so it is easier to teach them to turn the hand just before it leaves the water.

Entry

Look for:
• The hand entering the water, little finger first. • An entry point beyond the head and in line with the shoulder. • The hand pressing down and out to approximately 15 to 30 cm below the surface.

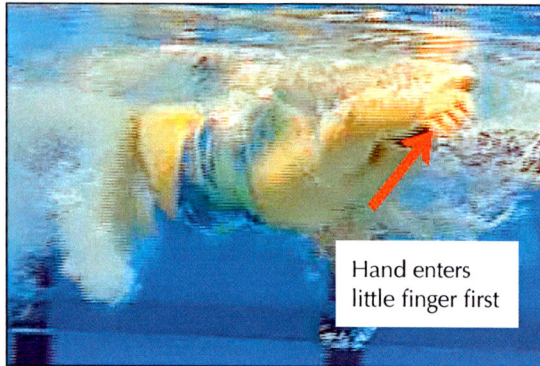

Hand enters
little finger first

Figure 5.12
The entry position as viewed from behind

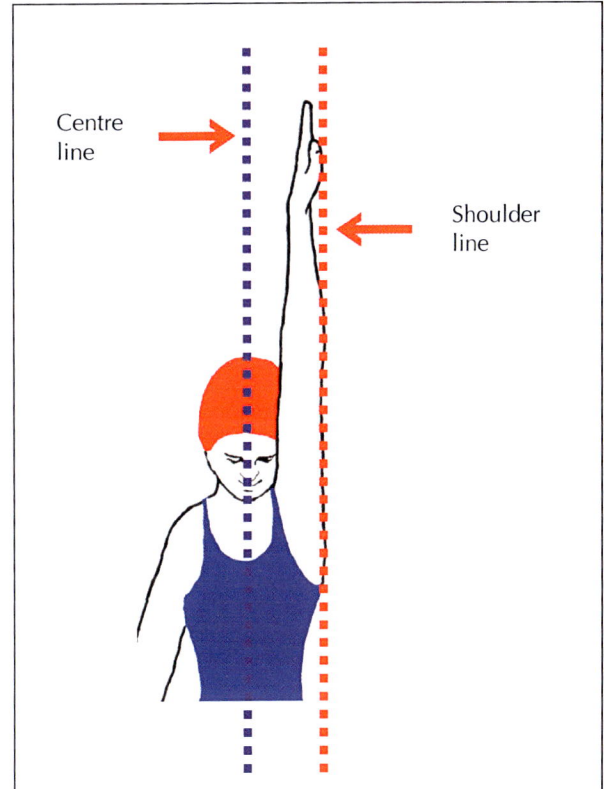

Figure 5.13
The entry position viewed from above

The straight arm pull

The straight arm pull is initially taught to beginners because:

- It is easy to describe and demonstrate.

- It enables the development of a correct arm recovery.

- Once a straight arm pull is mastered, a bent arm pull is easier to develop; it becomes a matter of refinement.

When the hand enters the water:

Look for:
• The hand pressing down and out to the side in a wide semi-circular path, until it reaches a point outside and in line with the shoulders. • The hand movement changing mid-way through the pull to a sweep in towards the thigh, before starting its recovery.

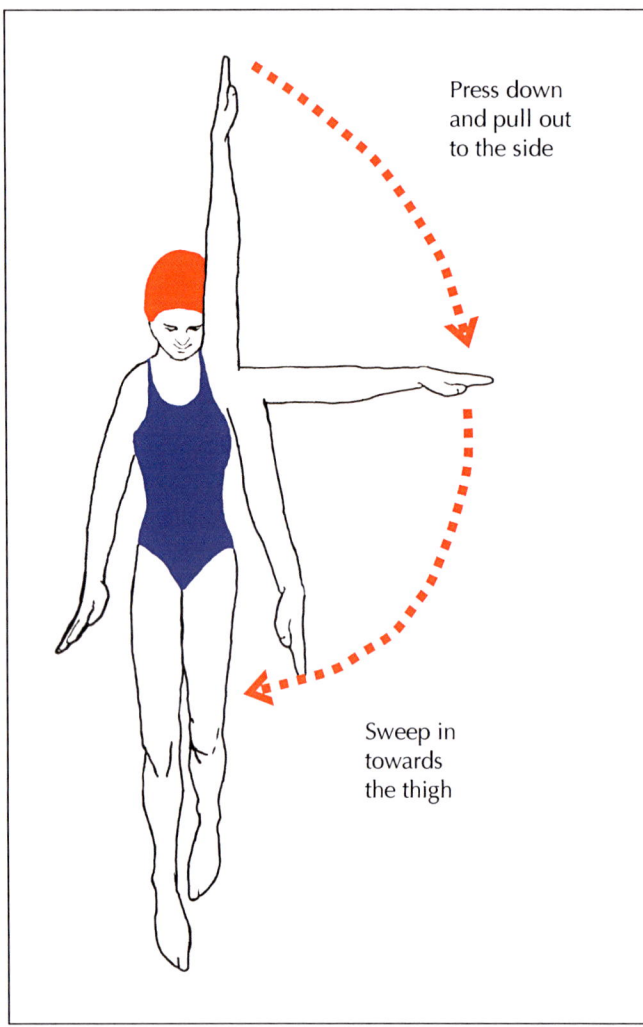

Press down
and pull out
to the side

Sweep in
towards
the thigh

Figure 5.14
The straight arm pull pathway in
backstroke

Although called a straight arm pull, the trained eye will notice, that in practice the arm bends slightly at the elbow. This is because the beginner is not strong enough to pull with a completely straight arm as the pressure offered by the water is too great. This is shown in Figure 5.15.

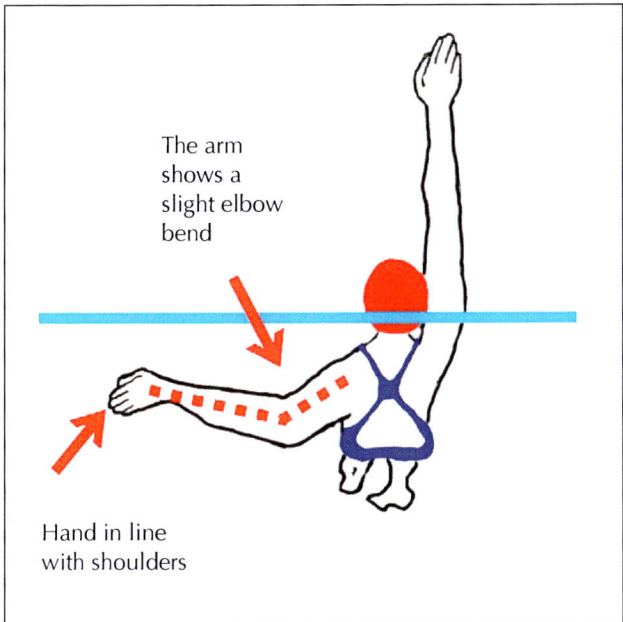

The arm shows a slight elbow bend

Hand in line with shoulders

Figure 5.15
The view from behind the swimmer mid-way through the straight arm pull

It is important, however, that the movement is first demonstrated as a straight arm pull. Problems arise by trying to teach a bent arm action before the pupil has reached a certain level of skill. The main problem is that the learner follows through with a bent arm during the recovery, destroying the entry.

Some children may adopt a bent arm action naturally from the start and this should not be discouraged, unless the elbow is bent excessively (more than 90 degrees when in line with the shoulder).

Two points to note are:

- **The teacher needs to demonstrate the arm action in an over-simplified form.** To do this they stand sideways and trace a 'backward circling movement'. When this is copied by the pupils, the path that they trace is more out to the side due to:

  - The pressure of the water.

  - The restriction of their shoulder girdle.

  This is also another good example of the teacher asking for one thing with the intention of achieving another.

- **It is possible that some novices appear to achieve the impossible and copy literally the movement (a deep backward circling of the arms) demonstrated by the teacher.** This becomes just a slow tracing movement, without providing any propulsion. In this instance, the propulsion is coming almost entirely from the legs. This is most common among young girls with weak arms but strong legs.

111

The bent arm pull

The bent arm pull is introduced as a development from the straight arm pull. It requires more strength and skill to be performed well but when mastered, it is a more effective pull. This is because it allows the hand to follow an **'S' shaped path** rather than the semi-circular path of the straight arm pull. Bending the elbow during the first part of the pull causes the 'S' pathway. This brings the hand in closer to the body and enables a much greater push back towards the feet during the last part of the stroke. It is this which helps to propel the swimmer forward.

The pull to the catch point

After entry, the hand continues to press down and out. The wrist flexes so the fingers point out to the side, thumb up. As the hand sweeps down and out, the elbow starts to bend. This flexing of the elbow allows the hand to gain a strong purchase on the water. The point at which the swimmer begins to feel their hand gaining a purchase on the water is called the **catch point**.

Look for:
• The hand sweeping out to the side to a point in line with the shoulders.   • The elbow bending approximately 90 degrees as the hand reaches 30 to 45 cm below the surface of the water.

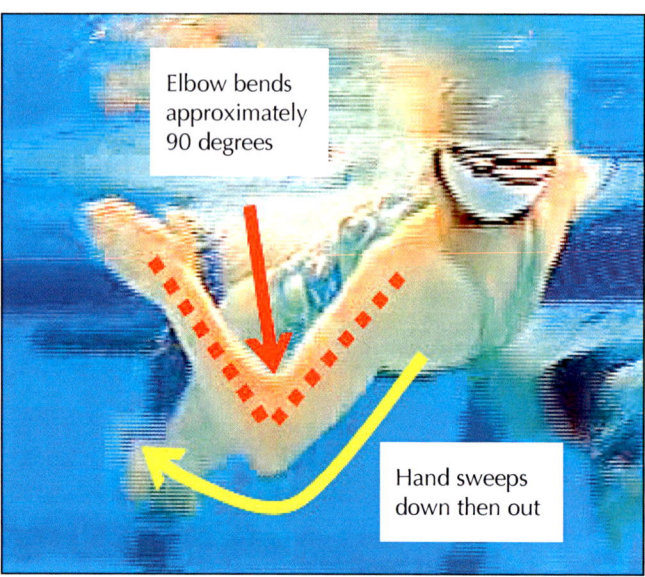

Elbow bends approximately 90 degrees

Hand sweeps down then out

Figure 5.16
The pull to the catch point in backstroke

In backstroke, the catch point is made late in the stroke. The pull phase ends close to the point of catch. This is due to the restriction of the shoulder girdle taking the hand and forearm out to the side. As a result the catch point and pull phase is best described as one movement.

By comparison, this is different for front crawl. In front crawl the catch point is made much earlier in the stroke, therefore the catch point and pull phase is best described as two separate movements.

As the swimmer's proficiency in backstroke improves, the catch point is made earlier in the stroke, before the hand reaches a point in line with the shoulder.

At the end of the pull phase:

Look for:
• The hand being ready to start a strong push back towards the feet.

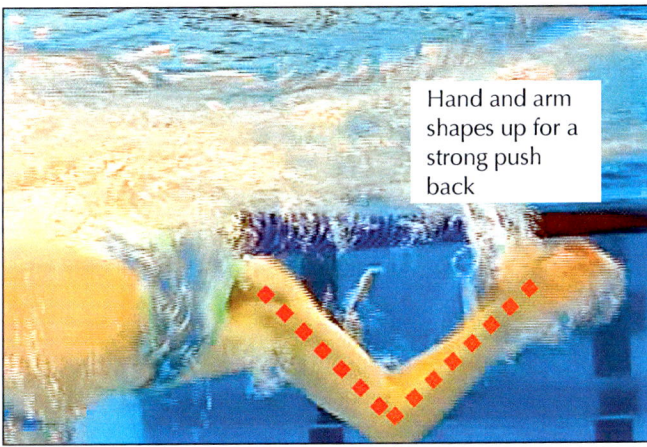

Hand and arm shapes up for a strong push back

Figure 5.17
The end of the pull phase in the backstroke.

Push phase

Look for:
• The upper arm remaining relatively still at the end of the pull phase as the hand and forearm sweeps in and down towards the thigh.

The feeling is one 'pushing back' until the elbow is straight.

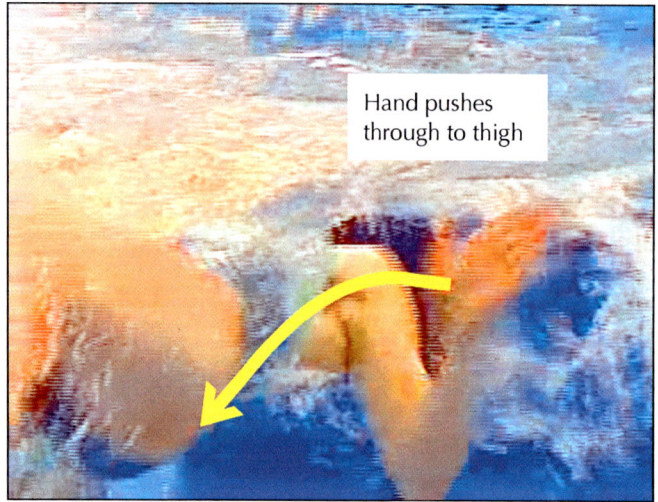

Figure 5.18
The push phase in backstroke

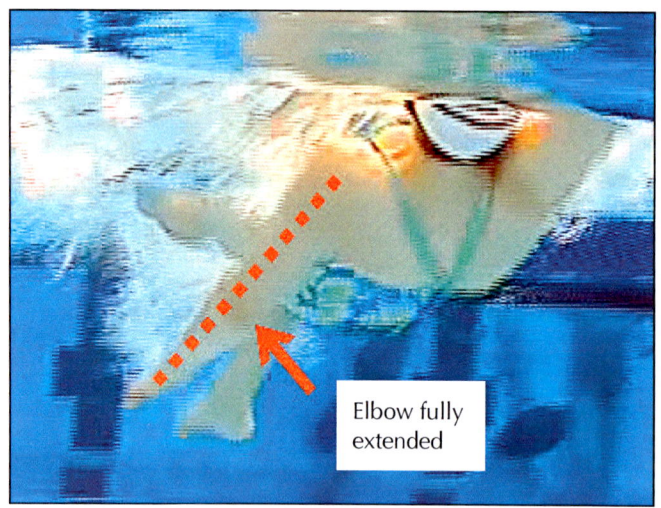

Figure 5.19
The push through the full extension in backstroke

During the bent arm pull:

Look for:
• The hand tracing an 'S' shaped pulling pattern as shown in Figure 5.20.

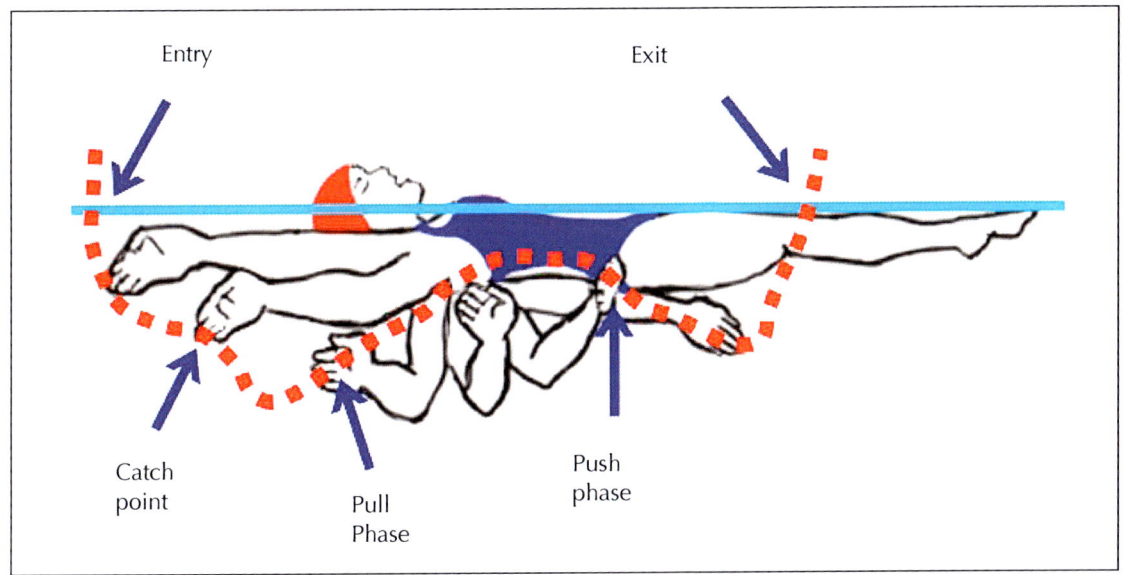

Figure 5.20
The underwater 'S' pull in backstroke

 The 'S' shape to the pull can only be seen from the side view so the teacher must be careful when demonstrating the bent arm action.

Discussion on the backstroke arm action

The arm action is the 'power house' of the backstroke as it provides the main source of propulsion. Two factors have a key influence on the effectiveness of the pull:

- The effect of the body roll.
- The track the hand takes through the water.

The importance of the body roll

With a straight arm pull, a body roll is not important. The shallow, semi-circular arm action does not allow for a body roll to be created. With a bent arm pull, however, a body roll becomes necessary. During the first part of the pull the arms are in a fairly weak position due to the restriction placed upon them by the anatomical weakness of the shoulder girdle. Consequently the main power from the arms occurs later in this stroke than any other.

The key therefore, is the ability to get the hand and forearm ready as early as possible in the stroke for a strong push back. This is assisted by a body roll and the bending of the elbow to approximately a 90 degree angle.

A question often asked by teachers is how much should the swimmer roll? To talk about this in degrees is somewhat meaningless. At this level it is something you do not have to consciously teach. Providing the swimmer is encouraged to lift the shoulder on the recovery, this will cause a sufficient roll of the body.

As the swimmer moves **towards** the teacher:

Look for:
• One shoulder lifting to aid recovery, while the opposite shoulder rolls down on the pulling side. This is what is meant by 'body roll'.

As the right arm pulls, the left shoulder is lifted to aid recovery.

Figure 5.21
The roll onto the right side in backstroke

As the left arm pulls, the right shoulder is lifted to aid recovery.

Figure 5.22
The roll onto the left side in backstroke

116

It is not essential that a rolling of the shoulders be seen immediately the arm action is co-ordinated with the legs. Some swimmers may develop a roll quite naturally and this should not be discouraged. Others keep their shoulders flat on the water surface. This is quite acceptable when first learning the arm action, but to develop the arm pull further, the rolling of the shoulders has to be encouraged.

Also, remember the legs in turn, are affected by the body roll as previously described. These diagonal kicks help maintain the lateral alignment of the body and balance the effects of the arm pull.

Also look for:

Look for:
• The whole body rolling, shoulders, hips and legs, while the head remains perfectly still.

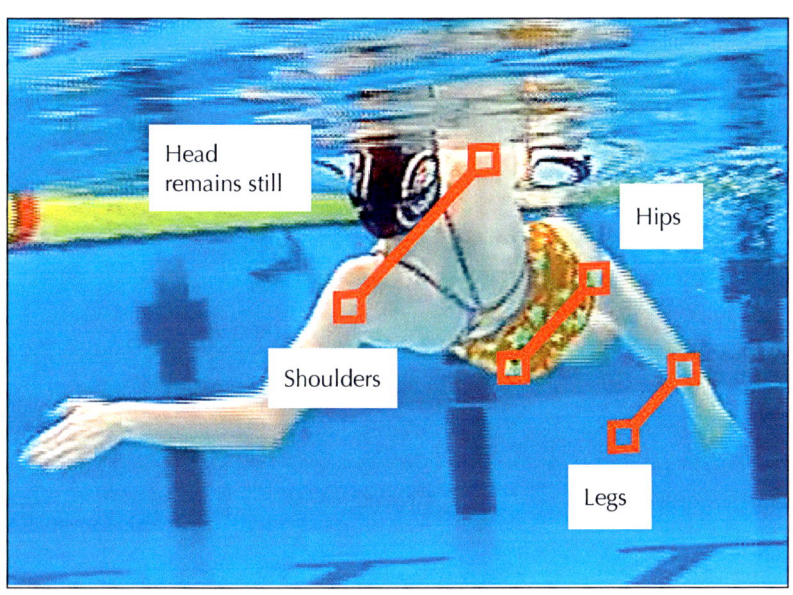

Figure 5.23
The whole body roll in backstroke

The hand track 'through the water'

In Chapter 4 we discussed the concept of the actual 'track' the hand takes through the water. The three components of this track for backstroke are shown in Figures 5.24a to 5.24c. These three components combine to form one three-dimensional pathway.

While this pathway is not described to the pupil, it nevertheless is important for the teacher to have an appreciation of this hand track to fully understand the arm action. They need to try to visualise the track from each view shown.

There are individual variations to this pathway depending on size, strength, flexibility and skill of the pupils. The teacher must decide if any variation is having a negative effect on the arm action and where necessary make appropriated stroke corrections.

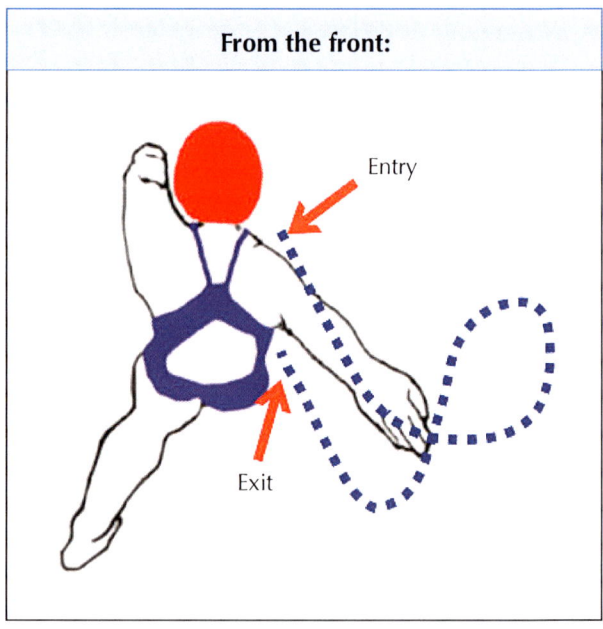

Figure 5.24a
The backstroke hand track through the water as viewed from the front

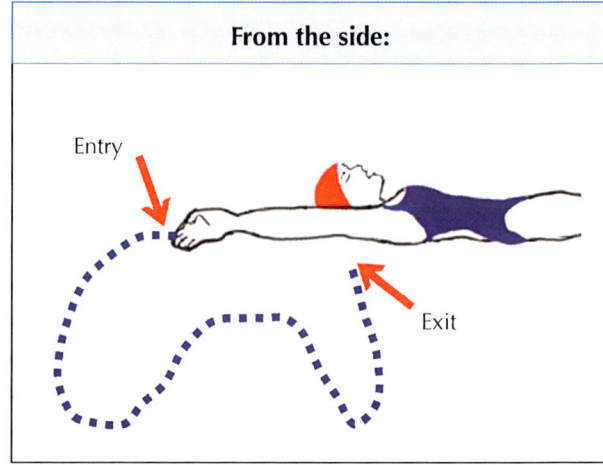

Figure 5.24b
The backstroke hand track through the water as viewed from the side

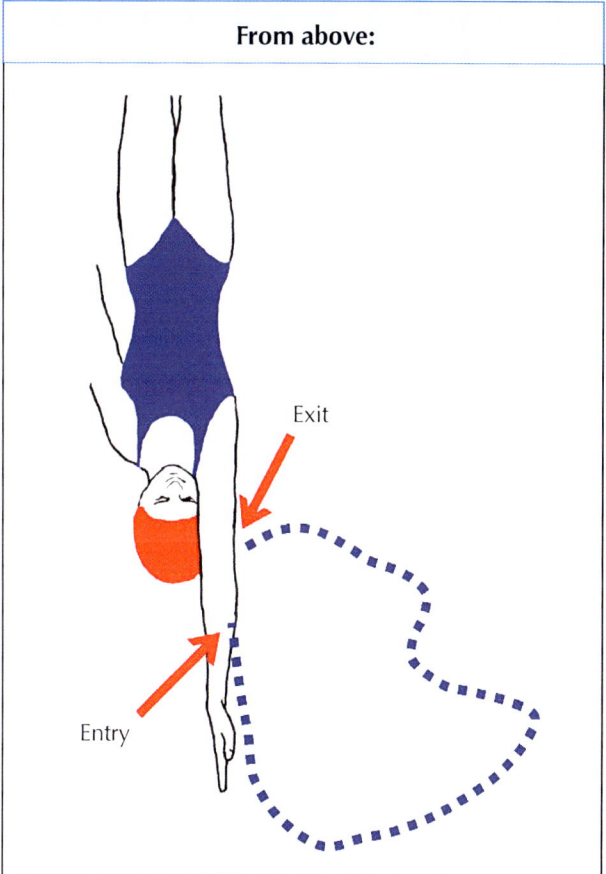

Figure 5.24c
The backstroke hand track through the water as viewed from above

Figure 5.24
The three-dimensional hand track in backstroke

Breathing

With the face clear of the water, the pupil is free to choose when to breathe. The teacher, however, must not assume that the pupil will breathe automatically.

🔑 Pupils need to be told to breathe out during the early stages of learning.

Beginners always inhale but they tend to hold their breath. We have all seen children struggling across the pool, eyes tightly closed, faces screwed up and gradually turning purple with effort. This limits practices severely to only a few strokes before they have to stop to regain their breath.

The swimmer should be taught to breathe regularly, in on one arm pull and out on the other so that they build up a regular rhythm to their breathing. These breathing skills are not difficult but require constant attention and regular practise early in the beginners' programme.

Timing and rhythm

The end result should be a **flowing rhythm** where the action is continuous and each arm cycle leads smoothly into the next one. The timing involves two key aspects:

- With a continuous leg action, six leg kicks fit into one stroke cycle. This timing fits together quite naturally and does not normally have to be specifically taught.
- As one hand starts its pull, the other hand is ready to start its recovery. The overall rhythm to the stroke is not unlike the rhythm set up when walking and one stride, together with the accompanying arm swing, leads smoothly into the next one.

Both walking and swimming backstroke share the following characteristics:

- They both have short cycles, one to three seconds.
- Both actions are highly repetitive, with little variations.
- Both involve an alternating leg and arm action that must be co-ordinated.
- The head is kept still throughout.

Let's examine this relationship a little more closely. When walking, the back is kept straight, the head is still and the movement of the leg is initiated from the hips. Throughout, a slight bending of the knees occurs. All of this also applies to backstroke. The only difference is that when walking, a 'heel to toe' motion is used but in the backstroke this action is reversed, leading with the toe on the kick up and the heel on the kick down. In other respects, the body position and the leg action in the backstroke is very similar to that of walking.

While the leg actions and body positions are similar, so is the **rhythm**. This is because the length of your stride when walking is the same as the depth of your kick when swimming backstroke. Both are relative to the length of the leg. In walking, the length of your stride determines the rhythm to the movement, while in backstroke the depth of the kick is the key to setting up the rhythm for the whole stroke.

If the following instruction is given to a beginner:

'*Push and glide on your back and kick the legs as if you are walking*' ,

the result is good. There are a number of advantages to this simile:

- The pupils can easily relate the movement to something they are very familiar with.
- There is a tendency for the pupils to adopt the correct body position.
- The teacher can easily demonstrate the action of walking on the pool side, emphasising the movement from the hips and the depth of the kick by drawing

attention to the length of their stride. This is more effective in reinforcing the correct action than the teacher trying to demonstrate the action using their hands and arms.

- Finally, if the knees are brought up out of the water during the early practices, an exaggerated demonstration by the teacher 'marching' and lifting their knees, highlights this error effectively and usually produces smiles into the bargain!

Above all, the likening of the backstroke kick to the rhythm of walking:

- **Slows** the leg action down.
- Buys the novice swimmer **time** . . . time to kick deep enough and feel the pressure of the water on the feet and time to co-ordinate the action of the arms with the legs.

This 'buying of time' is crucial during the early stages of learning the stroke.

Slowing things down may also be achieved by reducing the kick to four beats per stroke cycle in the first instance. This encourages a slower stroke with a more propulsive component to the leg action and helps to give the novice swimmer the time they need to co-ordinate the leg action, arm action and breathing into an effective stroke. As the leg kick becomes more proficient, the novice swimmer often slips quite naturally into a more regular six beats to one arm cycle pattern.

THE BUILDING UP OF TEACHING PROGRESSIONS

The purpose of practices and drills:

- Teachers must always be clear about why they are going to do a particular practice.
- The practice has to create a situation where something of value is going to be achieved.
- The practice has to make the pupil do something in a certain way or force them to feel a particular rhythm.
- Practices are not merely used for variety. Teachers who use practices in their lessons to add variety are usually boring teachers.

In a teaching situation the purpose of any practice should be to:

- Break down the complete stroke into smaller parts so the pupil only has to concentrate on the skill being taught.
- To school the limbs into the right track.

- To increase the pupils awareness of what is required.

 No drill or practice is performed exactly as it would be in free swimming; it simply creates an environment where certain things can happen.

For these reasons, our building programme for the backstroke and for the other three strokes places great emphasis on not just identifying the practices to use but also on the reasons for performing the practice and on the teaching points to emphasise.

BUILDING BLOCK 1

Preparation to learning the kick
At the onset, two skills have to be mastered:

- Lying back in the water.
- The ability to regain the feet.

Lying back in the water
With the pupils wearing arm bands, this can best be achieved in two ways:

- If there are helpers in the water, the pupils lie on their backs supported by the helpers as shown in Figure 5.2.
- Using two floats, one under each arm, the pupils lie back in the water.

Some pupils may be reluctant to stretch out as they lie back. If there is a bar available, this can be used to encourage a full stretch position. The pupils can put their back to the bar or wall, hold their arms along it and raise their legs. The pupils can also be eased into the correct position by tucking their toes under the bar and lying back while the helpers still give support.

Alternatively, a shallow water practice may also be helpful. The pupils sit on the steps, place their hands on the pool floor and then straighten their bodies out. This practice creates a more stable feeling and gives the pupils security as they are still in contact with the side or floor of the pool.

The ability to regain the feet
Often, beginners get onto their back and panic if they cannot confidently get back on their feet. Therefore this skill must be mastered initially with, but later without, arm bands.

The practices are:

Practice 1	Teaching points
From a stationary position, the pupils are asked to draw their knees up to their chest, push their head forward and push their hands forward underwater, palms up.	• Draw your knees up to your chest. • Put your chin down on your chest. • Push hands forwards, palms up.

Reason To eradicate fear and to demonstrate how to stand up from the supine position.

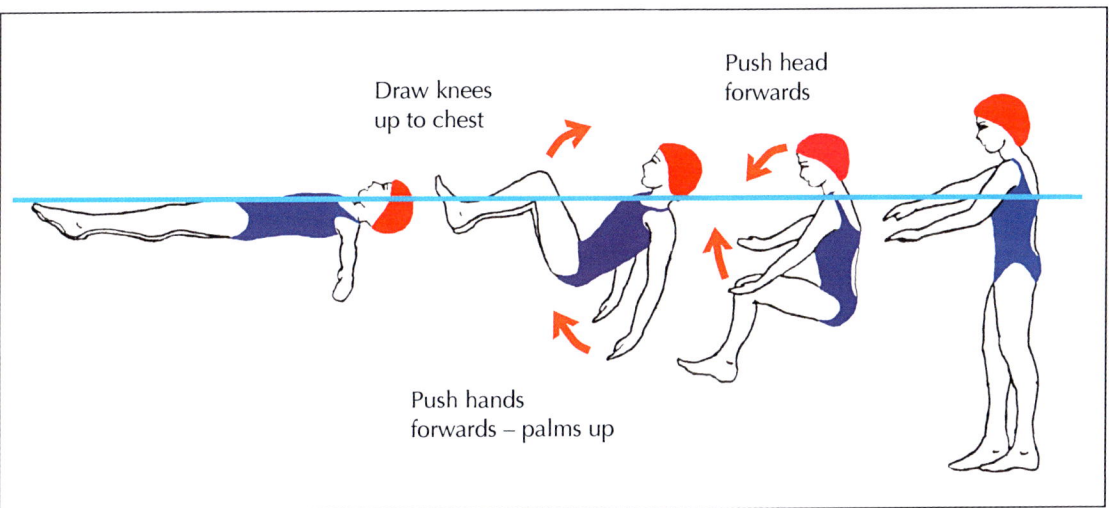

Figure 5.25
The sequence to regain the feet from lying on the back

Practice 2	Teaching points
Push and glide and regain feet.	• Re-emphasise the teaching points outlined for Practice 1.

Reason This is the first step towards getting the pupils to stretch the body out and regain their feet while moving.

Some pupils stop using arm bands from day one, while others continue to wear them throughout many of the later building blocks. This depends on their confidence. The teacher must be flexible. It is important not to force a child before they are ready to take the arm bands off.

At the same time, their wearing arm bands should not prevent them from continuing on with the building programme. If, however, they work through the programme with the arm bands on, they will have to go back and work through the programme again without them at a later stage.

Once the pupils are able to regain their feet from a push and glide with arm bands on, it is necessary to get them moving using a simple leg action.

Practice 3	Teaching points
Wearing arm bands and with two floats, one under each arm, push off the wall and kick.	• Kick the legs up and down. • Lie back on the water.

Reason   To get them moving and give them confidence.

Practice 4	Teaching points
Repeat Practice 3 without the arm bands holding two floats, one under each arm.	• Emphasise again the lying back in the water. • Look at the ceiling.

Reason   To progress from Practice 3.

BUILDING BLOCK 2

Developing the leg kick

Once the pupils are moving, the next stage is to develop the kick.

Practice 5	Teaching points
Teacher demonstrates the 'walking' action, emphasising the length of stride.	• Emphasise the length of the stride.

Reason   The pupils watch the demonstration to make them aware of the movement and depth of kick.

Teacher
emphasise
walking
action by
pointing

Width of
stride

Figure 5.26
Teacher demonstrating the walking action

Using their arms, the teacher then demonstrates the action both from a side view and one facing the class.

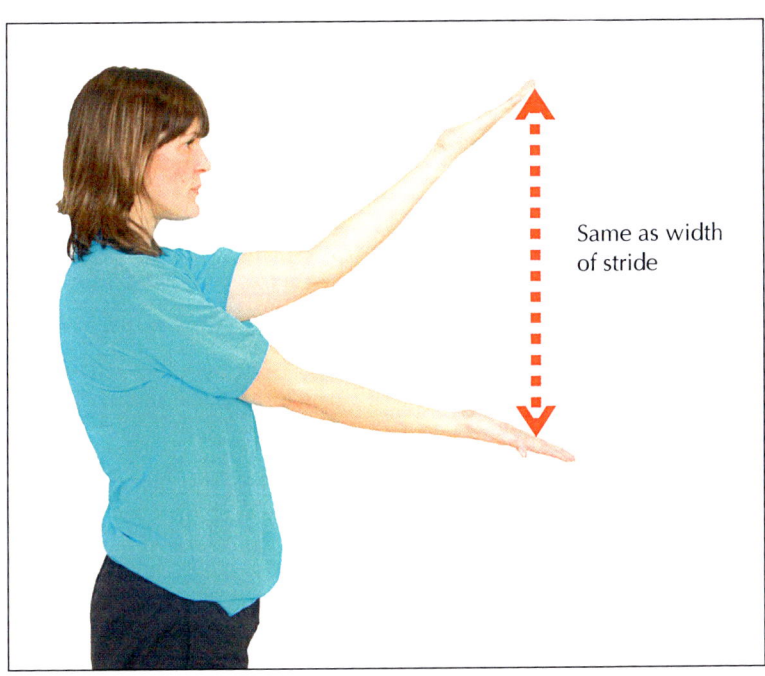

Same as width
of stride

Figure 5.27
Side view of the teacher
demonstrating the kicking
action

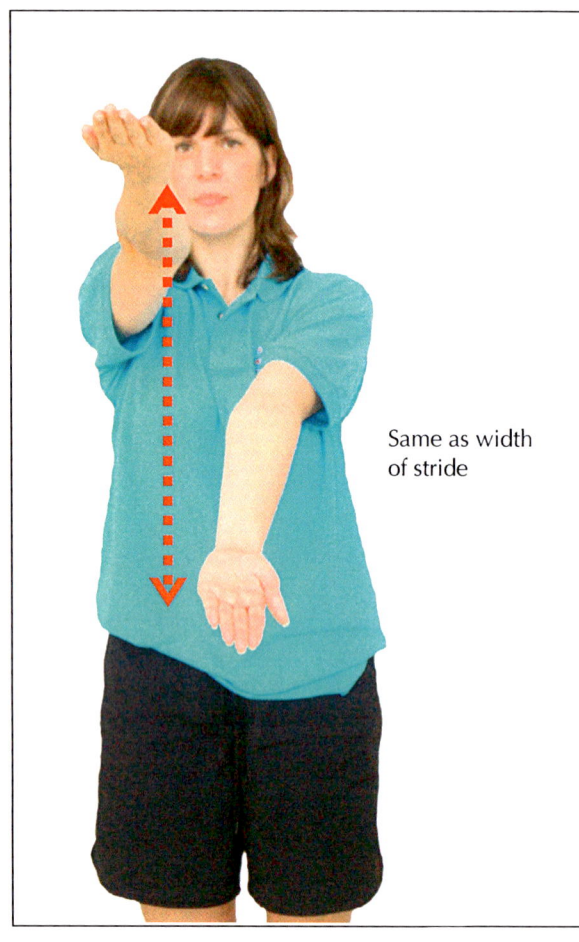

Same as width
of stride

Figure 5.28
Front view of the teacher demonstrating the kicking action

Practice 6	Teaching points
With two floats, one under each arm, push and glide on the back and introduce the walking leg action.	• Kick from the hips as if you are walking. • Kick the length of a stride.

Reason   Support from the floats is needed so the pupil can concentrate on the leg action.

The following practice using one float clasped to the chest causes a slight change in the body position. The shoulders become rounded and the spine curved, resulting in the hips dropping a little. Although this is not normally desirable, at this stage in learning its benefit is to force the swimmer to work the legs hard from the hip. Novice swimmers also tend to hold their ankles stiff and so it is necessary to emphasise the movement of the ankles.

Practice 7	Teaching points
With one float clasped to the chest, perform the walking leg action.	• Work the legs hard from the hips.

Reason   To reduce the amount of support but to continue the development.

 A teaching point frequently used is *'point the toes'*. We have avoided this because we are looking for ankle movement. Asking the pupils to point their toes, causes them to hold the ankles in a very stiff position. The ankle needs to be loose similar to when kicking a football. Then the foot is under the ball and follows through, lifting the ankle. This is the same kind of action to encourage in the upbeat on the backstroke. During the kick down, however, the ankle must relax. Look for a fairly loose ankle movement.

As the kick is developing, support is still needed. The temptation is to develop the kick simply by giving the pupils a number of practices in which they hold the float in different positions. The teacher must be aware, however, that every time the area of support changes, the body position also changes.

It is important that early practices develop the kick while still maintaining the correct body position. The two go hand in hand. Two practices frequently used are kicking with the float held behind the head and kicking with the float held over the thighs. These practices are not necessary at this stage in the building programme, but they are more useful as corrective practices later on.

BUILDING BLOCK 3

Introducing sculling

It is a logical step that once the support from a float has been reduced to a minimum, an attempt is made at kicking with no support. For the learner this is a big step and to give them confidence, the leg kick is best co-ordinated with a **sculling** movement from the arms as this helps maintain a horizontal body position.

The ability to scull is a fundamental skill for learners to acquire. It lays the foundations for learning how to pitch the hands correctly when swimming. Skilful swimming is a combination of many things but one of the most vital is the ability to vary the way the hand is pitched throughout the pull.

So often, however, sculling is taught badly because teachers have not fully grasped what it is they are actually trying to achieve and where its place is in swimming. All too often the teaching point given is *'slap your bottoms'* or *'wave your hands'*. It is difficult to see how these teaching points produce the desired movement. It is very, very important that this skill is taught accurately at this early stage.

What exactly do we mean by **hand pitch**? Hand pitch is simply the way the hands are held as they are move through the water. With learners, we only need to introduce the following three hand positions:

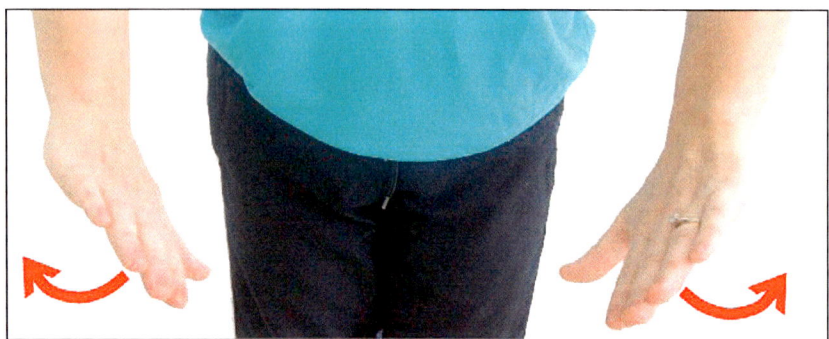

Figure 5.29a
Hands pitched with the thumbs down

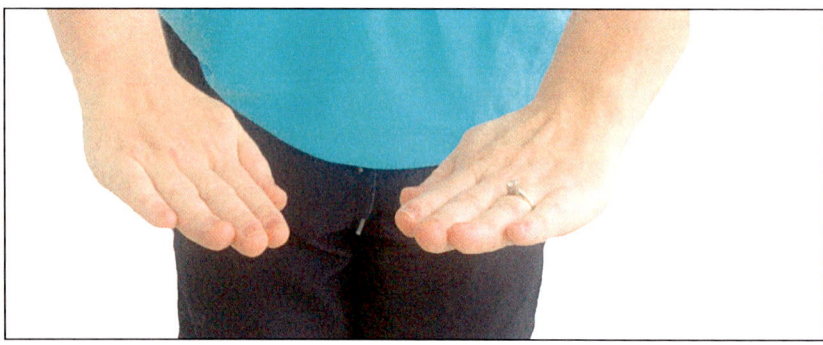

Figure 5.29b
Hands pitched with the thumbs in a flat position

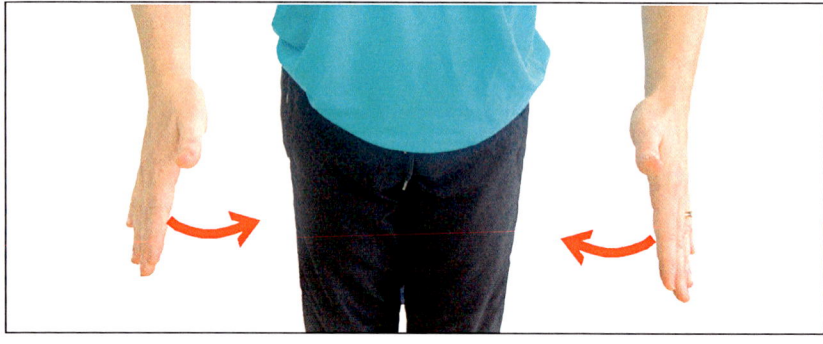

Figure 5.29c
Hands pitched with the thumbs up

Figure 5.29
Teacher demonstration of the three hand positions in sculling

With these three positions in mind, we can look more closely at the actual skill of sculling.

- Sculling is a smooth movement of the hand, wrist and forearm, tracing a **figure of 8 pattern** in the water. This figure of 8 stroke pattern occurs in a narrow, well defined area.

- As the hand moves through the stroke, it involves an alternating thumbs up/ thumbs down movement. In this way the pitch of the hand is continually changing.

- Figure 5.30 shows that the hand is held with the thumbs down as the hand presses out away from the centre line of the body. This changes to a thumbs up position as the hand sweeps back in towards the centre line.

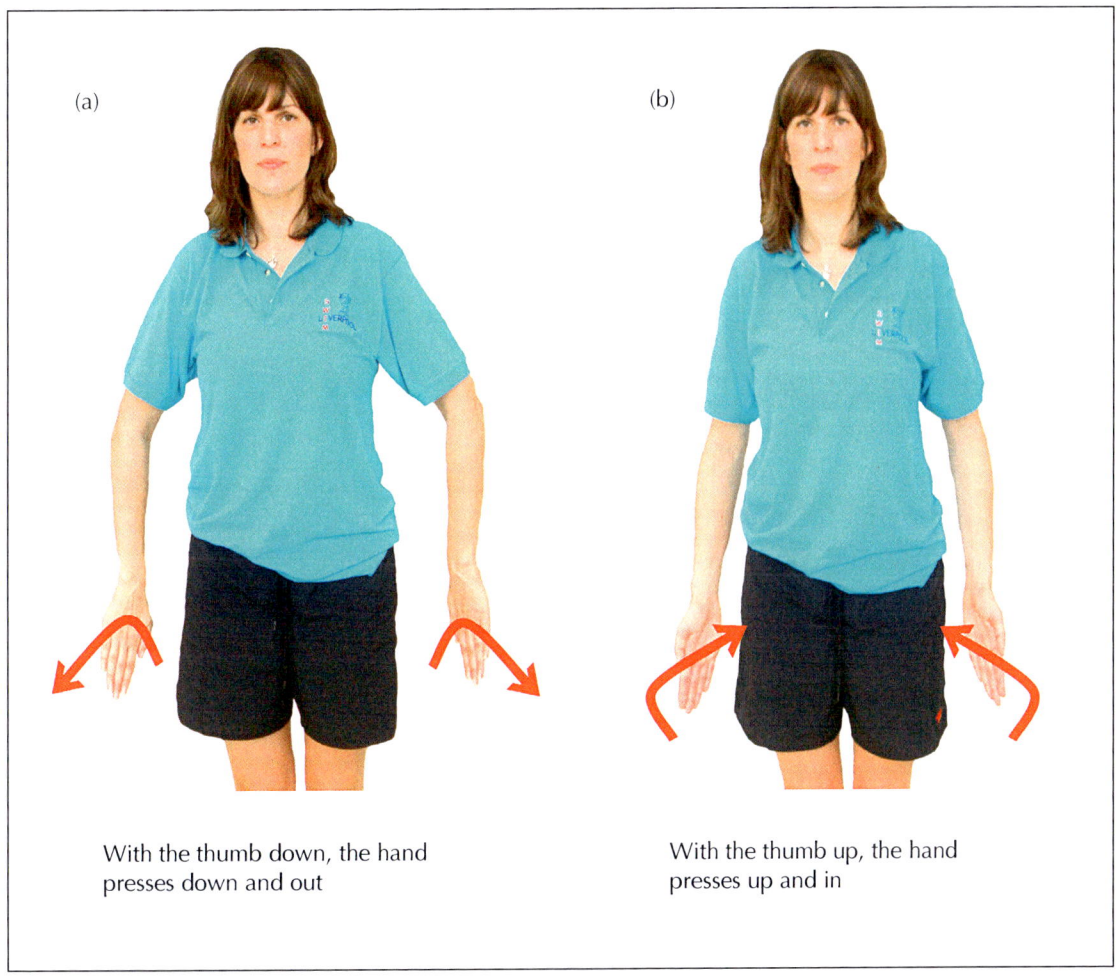

(a)

(b)

With the thumb down, the hand presses down and out

With the thumb up, the hand presses up and in

Figure 5.30
Teacher demonstration of the figure of 8 scull

By following a figure of 8 path, the palms are able to press against the water throughout the movement.

Note that the movement is **medial rotation**. The medial bones of the lower arm rotate while the upper arm remains relatively still. As such, the size of the figure of 8 pattern depends on the size of the swimmer's forearm. A variety of sculling positions is outlined in Chapter 9.

Young children move their hands, wrist and forearm through a very small figure of 8 stroke pattern, while adults produce a much bigger movement. The important points to emphasise are:

- The pitch of the hand alternates between a thumbs down/thumbs up position.

- The lower part of the arm performs all the movement while the upper arm remains relatively still.

- The scull is performed in a small, well-defined area.

Practice 8	Teaching points
Standing in shallow water, elbows tucked into sides, arms in front, palms down. Pupils follow the demonstration of the teacher, thumbs down on the press out, thumbs up on the press in.	• Keep fingers together. • Keep elbows in. • Thumbs down as you press out, thumbs up as you press in.

Reason 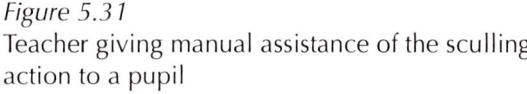 To give a clear understanding of the movement required.

If a child is experiencing difficulty grasping the correct movement it is often a great help to do a manual demonstration. The teacher stands behind the pupil, places their hands over the child's hands and together they trace the correct sculling movement.

Figure 5.31
Teacher giving manual assistance of the sculling action to a pupil

130

Physical contact with the pupil
Care must be taken when carrying out any practice which involves contact with the pupil. Ideally get permission from the parents. It must be carried out openly and quickly, preferably with another adult present to safeguard the teacher from any false allegations. This practice may be seen by some authorities as unacceptable but physical assistance in this way can assist greatly the learning process of a child who has difficulty understanding the correct movement.

Practice 9	Teaching points
Push and glide, kick the legs hard and use your hands to scull down by your hips.	• Concentrate on the leg action. • Kick as if you are walking. • Keep the sculling going.

Reason   To take away the support completely and develop the leg action in preparation for the arms.

BUILDING BLOCK 4

Introducing the arm action

If the pupils have mastered these first practices, they are now ready for the arm action to be introduced. The teacher must give a precise demonstration of the movement required. At first, this is best carried out with the teacher standing **sideways** to the class and with the children standing in the water. Care must be taken that the demonstration is a **sideways view** for two reasons:

- The children will mirror exactly a frontal demonstration, and their arms end up revolving the wrong way round, that is, forwards instead of backwards. How many times have teachers stood facing a class demonstrating the backstroke arm action and then have to correct the children by saying backwards not forwards?

- A sideways view emphasises the palm facing out with the little finger leading and the actual depth of the pull is seen more easily.

Once the pupils have tried the arm action, further demonstrations may be carried out by the teacher facing the class.

The development of the straight arm pull

The teacher demonstrates the complete movement while the pupils copy as outlined in Practice 10.

Practice 10

Standing in the water, copy the arm movement required, as demonstrated by the teacher.

Reason   To develop an awareness and understanding of the total arm action.

Figure 5.32
Entry position

Little finger
first entry

Figure 5.33
Mid-way through the pull

Pull out to the
side, in-line with
the shoulders

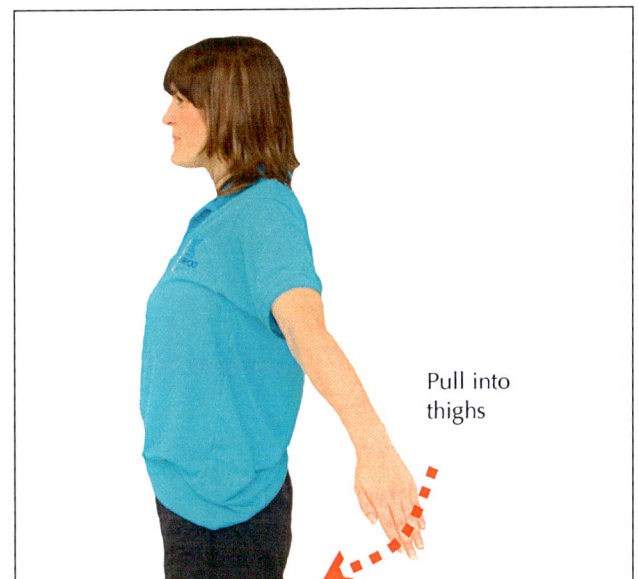

Figure 5.34
End of pull

Pull into
thighs

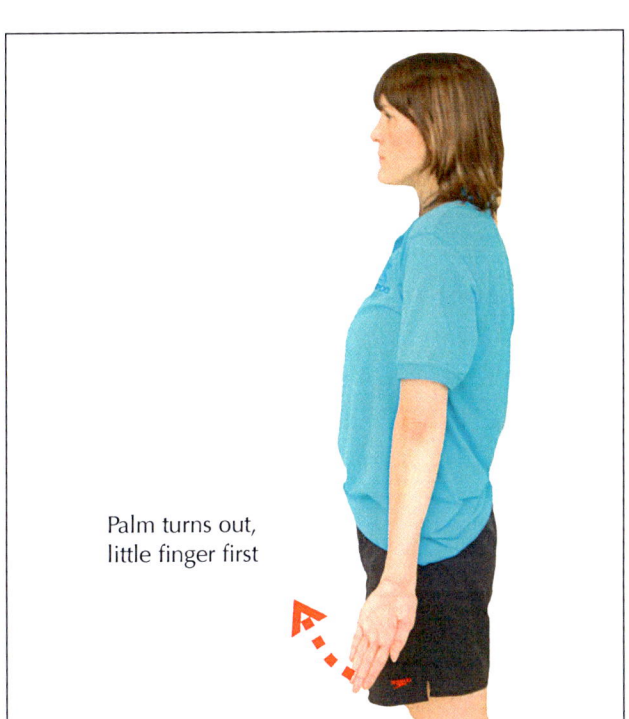

Figure 5.35
Exit

Palm turns out,
little finger first

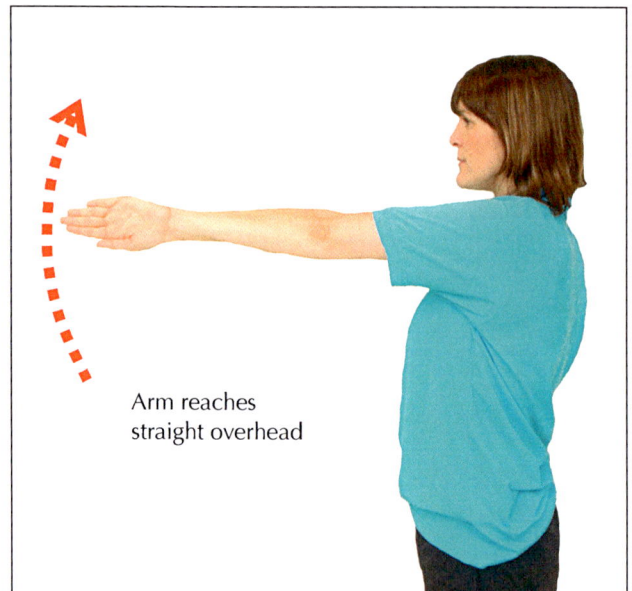

Arm reaches
straight overhead

Figure 5.36
Recovery

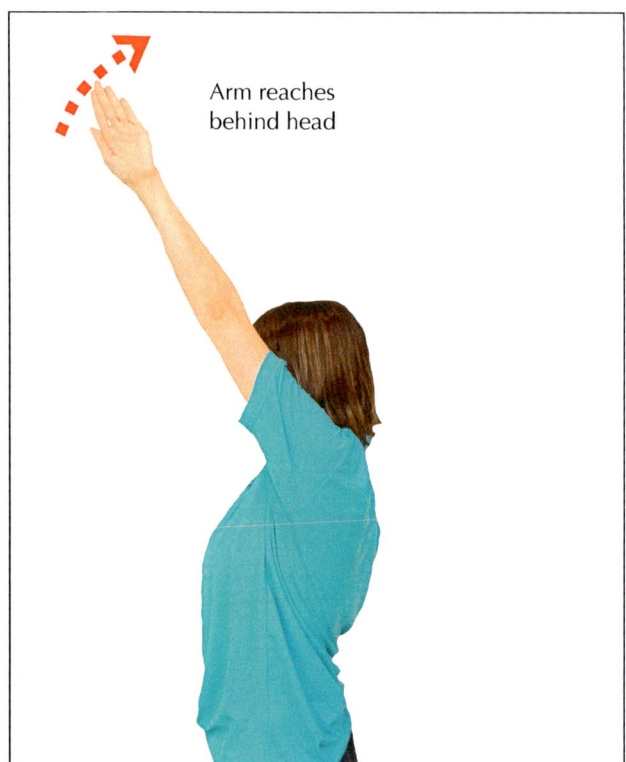

Arm reaches
behind head

Figure 5.37
Preparation for entry

Practice 11	Teaching points
With one float under one arm, push and glide, kick the legs and perform the movement with the other arm. Change the arms in alternate widths.	• Keep the legs kicking. • Lift the hand out of the water little finger first. • Keep the arm straight.

Reason   To practice the arm movement with some support so the pupils can concentrate on the correct limb track.

BUILDING BLOCK 5

The co-ordination of the leg and arm actions

Having established the leg action and introduced the arm movement, it is now time to co-ordinate the two together.

Practice 12	Teaching points
Push and glide, pick up with the leg action and scull with the hands by the side to halfway across the pool. Then attempt one complete stroke cycle. As competence improves increase this to two stroke cycles.	• Push and glide, arms by your side. • Kick hard.

Reason   The first part is to get the pupils moving with the correct body position. Only one or two arm pulls are then attempted because at this stage they tire very quickly and the stroke can break down.

Practice 13	Teaching points
Extended Practice 12 by gradually increasing the number of strokes performed until a whole width can be completed.	• Stretch the arms straight, chin up and breathe.

Reason   To build up the distance covered . . . slowly.

BUILDING BLOCK 6

Breathing

In the backstroke building programme, the breathing is left until much later than in the front crawl programme, simply because it does not present the learner with the same sort of problems. It does, however, need to be taught, otherwise children tend to breathe in but not out causing an early breakdown in the stroke.

A rhythm needs to be established based around breathing in as one arm leaves the water and breathing out as the other arm leaves the water.

Practice 14	Teaching points
Push and glide, attempt a complete width.	<ul><li>Breathing in as your right arm leaves the water.</li><li>Breathe out as your left arm leaves the water.</li></ul>

Reason   To develop the correct co-ordination and timing of the breathing.

 In these early stages of learning the backstroke, the stroke must be slowed down sufficiently to allow the pupils time to perform the correct arm movement. If not, the pupils tend to do a 'thrashing' movement of the arms with a lot of water being thrown over the face (alarming to the novice swimmer) and much of the arm action degenerates into short, circular movements out to the side.

Although the arm pull sought at this level is essentially a straight arm pull, it is vital that the pull is made through a **full range of movement**, entering in line with the shoulder and finishing down close to the thigh.

BUILDING BLOCK 7

Further development of the arm action

Now is the time to break the arm action down into specific phases and focus on one element at a time.

Practice 15
Following a demonstration by the teacher emphasising the specific teaching points to focus on, the pupils start with a push and glide and attempt the complete arm action concentrating on the teaching points given.

Reason   To develop awareness of where and how each of the phases should be performed in the backstroke arm action.

 With less confident pupils, it may be necessary to first carry out Practice 15 using a single arm, with the other supported by a float. The support gives the pupil time to concentrate on what is required of them. Again, make sure the swimmer is given the chance to practice equally with both arms. As soon as possible however, change to building the arm action up using full stroke as this gives greater balance and rhythm to the stroke.

The key phases of the arm action are broken down by the teacher. Each phase is individually demonstrated and the specific teaching points given before the pupils attempt the complete action focusing on what they have been told.

Previously, the teacher has demonstrated the arm action from the side view. It is now important that the teacher demonstrates while facing the class. It is easier for the teacher to highlight the specific phase and to give the teaching points to the class while facing them.

Entry

Teaching points

- Enter the water, little finger first.
- Keep the arm straight.
- Keep the head still.

Figure 5.38
Teacher demonstration of the entry position

137

First part of the straight arm pull

Teaching points

- Reach well back behind the head.
- Keep the wrist firm.

Figure 5.39
Teacher demonstration of the first part of the straight arm pull

Mid-way through the pull

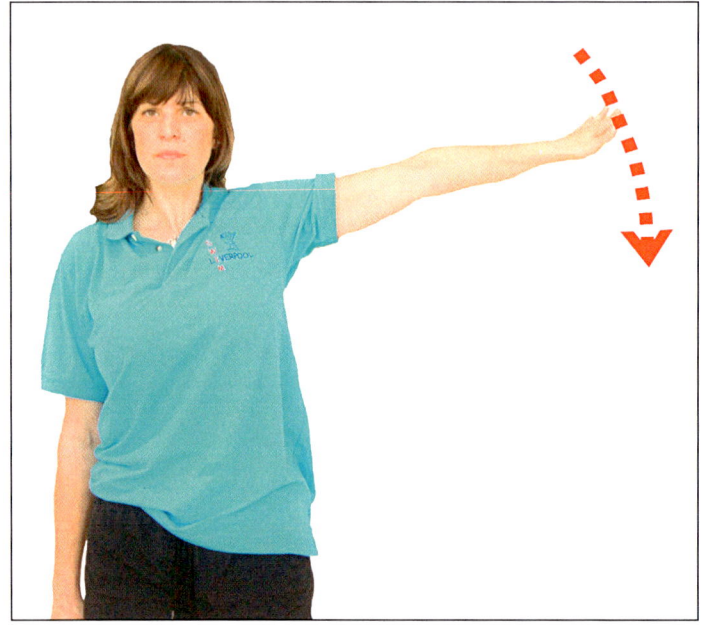

Teaching points

- Press down and out until the hand is level with the shoulder.

Figure 5.40
Teacher demonstration of the hand in line with the shoulder in the straight arm pull

Pull in towards the thigh

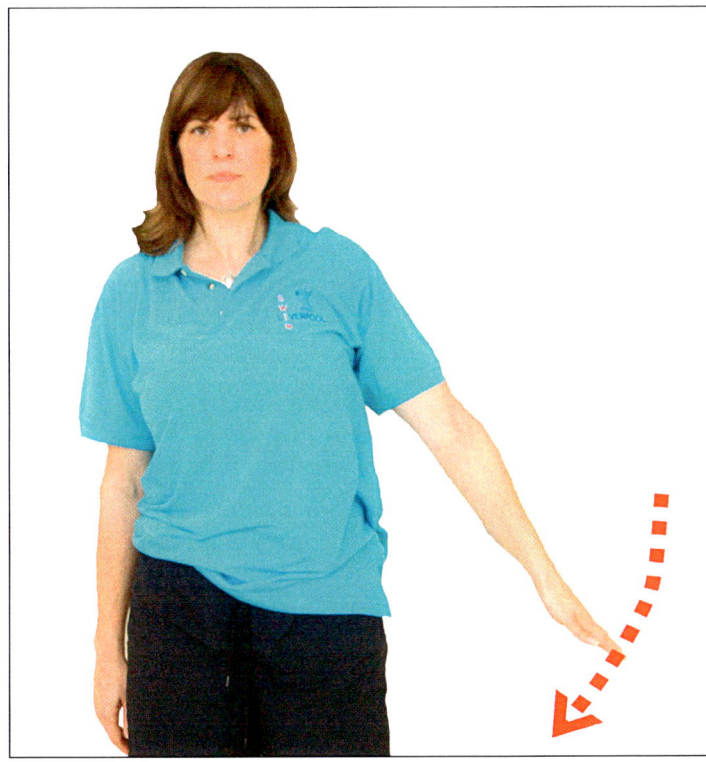

Teaching points

- Press the hand down and into the body.

Figure 5.41
Teacher demonstration of the pull into the thighs

The exit

Teaching points

- Turn the palm out.

Figure 5.42
Teacher demonstration of the end of the straight arm pull

The recovery

Teaching points

• Lift the arm, little finger first out of the water.
• Reach for the ceiling.

Figure 5.43
Teacher demonstration of the recovery

PROBLEMS AND SOLUTIONS

We have discussed the good points of technique, but life has a habit of dealing a poor 'deck of cards' to some teachers, so let's look at some of the difficulties that can arise.

Leg action

Problem 1: Knees breaking the water surface

This is the most common error by far. It is often described as a 'cycling' action, but in truth is more of a 'pumping' movement with the legs. There are two distinct reasons for this occurring:

Cause/effect

The head is pushed back raising the chest is too high and bringing the hips close to the surface. This poor body position causes the knees to come out of the water.

Solution

To attain the correct body position, the leg kick should be practised with a float held over the knees, preventing them from breaking the surface.

Cause/effect	Solution
The head, chest and hips are in the correct position but the hips are flexed (bent) too much, again causing the knees to come out of the water.	The teacher has to revert back to earlier practices, using two floats, one under each arm, emphasising working from the hips (similar to walking). A practice which may prove helpful is kicking across the width holding a float behind the head. This forces the pupil to adopt a flatter body position by reducing the amount of flexion at the hips.

 In both cases, the body position has to be studied carefully to see which of the causes is responsible for the error. This is critical, as the correction is different for each problem.

Problem 2: Kicking with a shallow flutter-type action

Cause/effect	Solution
This is the result of the pupil being unaware of the true depth of the kick.	Revert to earlier practices, emphasising the walking movement.

Problem 3: Kicking with the feet in a dorsiflex position (square feet).

Cause/effect	Solution
The pupil holds the feet and ankles rigid. This is more noticeable when the pupils have been taught breaststroke first.	To overcome this difficulty, revert back to earlier practices with two floats, one under each arm, and emphasise the pointing of the toes, using a simile such as 'kicking a football'.
	This exercise is to extend the feet and make the pupils use the ankle joints.

 Earlier we stated that likening the leg action to kicking a football was a poor simile. As a description of the whole movement, this is true. It can, however, be used effectively here to correct the above problem. As the pupil kicks up to the surface, they visualise kicking a football with the top of the foot.

Arm action

Problems associated with the arm action can be divided into two kinds:

- Problems that have a direct effect on the swimmer's body position.
- Problems that occur specifically with the arm movement itself.

Problems affecting the body position

As with the leg kick, a swimmer's body position is also very closely linked to their arm action. The alternating recovery over the water, followed by an arm pull which takes place largely out to the side, continually acts to pull the body first to one side, then to the other.

Problem 4: Excessive movement of the hips and legs from side to side giving the impression of a snaking motion as the swimmer moves away from the teacher.

There are three main causes of this **snaking motion**:

Cause/effect	Solution
An incorrect entry position, too wide or one crossing over the centre line.	Using a clock face as a simile, the teaching point to emphasise is entry at eleven o'clock and one o'clock.

Cause/effect	Solution
A pull that is too shallow, sweeping the hand out wide to the side.	Encourage the pupils to 'brush their ear' with the inside of their arm before entry.

Cause/effect	Solution
A recovery that sweeps across the centre line.	Focus on the arm coming out of the water, little finger first.

In short, anything that takes the arm pull outside the correct arm track increases the likelihood of snaking.

Problem 5: A bouncing rhythm to the stroke

Whereas **snaking** is action/reaction from side to side, **bouncing** is action/reaction up and down. A bouncing rhythm to the stroke is caused by either:

Cause/effect	Solution
A weak irregular leg kick, often only two or four beats, working primarily from the knee and not from the hips.	Build up a continuous six beat leg action by reverting back to the earlier building practices.

A two or four beat leg kick may occur if the early leg practices are rushed and progress onto the arm pull is made before the pupil is ready. A two or four beat leg kick will not balance the arm action as well as a six beat kick and can cause the swimmer to bounce or bob along the surface of the water.

 Remember, a good stroke is developed from a strong leg kick.

Cause/effect	Solution
The arms pulling too deeply under the body, often due to a straight arm pull, forcing the hips to rise.	Much greater focus should be placed on developing an 'S' shaped pull to re-educate the limb track.

 We have not used the excuse 'the pupil misunderstands the movement' as a reason for a problem. This phase can be all too conveniently used to cover a multitude of sins, so many as to be meaningless. If a demonstration has been given and the movement copied by the pupils, then the pupils understand the movement. If a fault then occurs when swimming, misunderstanding of the movement cannot be the answer.

Problems associated specifically with the arm movement itself

Problem 6: An incorrect entry position

As the swimmer cannot see where their hands enter the water, they have to rely on their 'feel' for this. Avoid an entry position too wide of the shoulder line or across the centre line.

Cause/effect	Solution
Some children may have difficulty visualising where the ideal position is.	To overcome this, reference to a clock face can prove useful, describing the correct positions as being at eleven o'clock and one o'clock. In this way, over-reaching towards the centre line can be described as the twelve o'clock position, while an entry wide of the shoulder line is at ten or two o'clock.

Problem 7: A dropped elbow

The main difficulty children experience is mastering the bent arm pull movement. They tend to bend their elbow too much and omit the first part of the pull. The elbow 'drops' and travels in advance of the hand, so the thumb almost scrapes down the side of the body. This error is commonly referred to as a **dropped elbow** or the 'lavatory chain pull' (for those who still remember what a lavatory chain is!).

Cause/effect

This is most common with pupils who lay very flat on the water, relying on their legs rather than their arms for propulsion. This gives them a false sense of efficiency. On entry, the arm is allowed to 'slip' through the water, elbow first, before lifting it out for the recovery.

Solution

Emphasis must be placed on lifting the shoulder during the recovery to encourage the body to roll and place the pulling arm in a better position to gain a strong purchase on the water. There are two practices to emphasise this:

- A single arm drill while holding a float across the chest and using a leg action to balance the stroke.
- A progression from this is holding a pull buoy between the thighs, practice the arm action using both arms, still emphasising the lift of the shoulders and the roll of the body.

Teaching points

- Roll the body towards the pulling arm.
- Bend the elbow during the pull phase.

The secret throughout is the lift of the arms on the recovery. This produces a much better body position for the pulling arm to follow an effective limb track through the water.

THE IMPROVEMENT CIRCLE

The key elements to a successful backstroke are:

- Maintaining a **good** body position at all times.
- An **effective** and **continuous** leg action.
- An arm action **deep** enough to gain effective purchase on the water.
- An overall **smooth** and **free flowing** rhythm.

A key factor to achieving these is the development of an effective body roll. A rotation of the hips and upper torso assists the pulling arm to be deep enough and aid the recovery of the opposite arm as it is lifted clear of the water. The improvement circle for backstroke is built around three core skills.

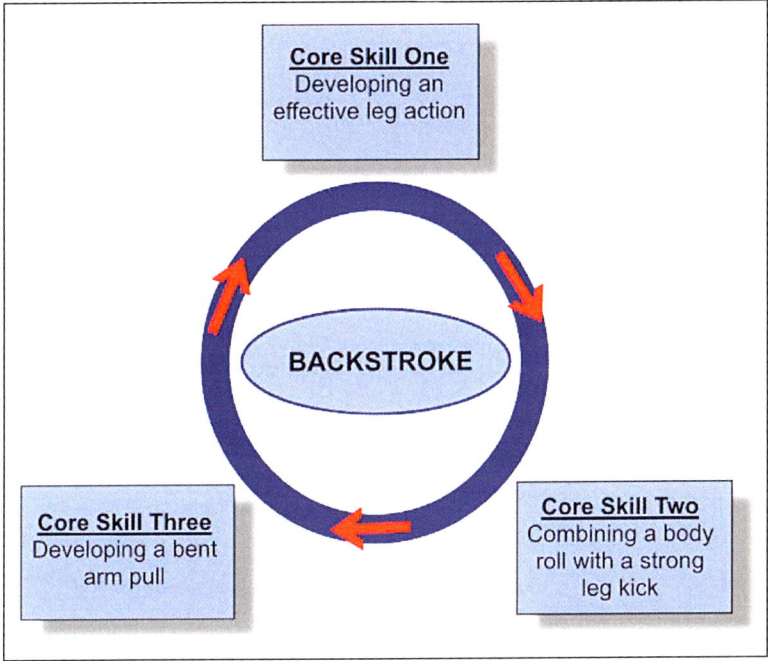

Figure 5.44
The improvement circle for backstroke

Core skill 1: Developing an effective leg action

Remember, a competent leg action:

- Balances and stabilises the stroke.
- Helps maintain the body in a streamlined position.
- Adds to forward propulsion.

It is therefore essential to strengthen and condition the movement early on. In addition to the practices outlined in the building block programme, the following can be used;

Backstroke kicking practices with support

1. Kick holding a float to the chest with both arms.
2. Kick holding a float over the top of the thighs.
3. Kick holding a float with both arms stretched out behind the head.

Backstroke kicking practices without support

1. Kicking with both hands sculling down by the side.
2. Kicking with both hands on top of the thighs.
3. Kicking underwater for short distances either with both arms down by the side or stretched out behind the head.

Regular exposure to kicking without support is a vital skill as it not only develops the leg action but also forces the pupil to work harder at maintaining a good horizontal body position. It is important that the teacher continually reinforces the need to maintain a good streamline position.

Core skill 2: Combining a body roll with a strong leg kick

A body roll is best developed while kicking with both arms held down by the thighs. Kicking in this position allows the hips and upper torso to rotate freely.

Backstroke kicking practices with arms held down by the thighs

1. Keeping the head still, kick and roll the left hip upwards and the left shoulder around towards the chin. Perform one width on one side then perform the same on the other side.
2. As for Practice 1 performing 12 kicks on one side before rolling onto the other side and completing 12 more kicks.
3. As for Practice 2 gradually reducing the number of kicks on each side; for example from 12 down to 4 each side.
4. Repeat Practices 1 to 3, kicking with one arm extended behind the head and one arm held down by the thigh, making sure the pupil rolls towards the extended arm.

It is essential that when developing the body roll, the head is kept perfectly still, eyes focused on the ceiling, while the hips and the upper torso are encouraged to rotate around the long axis of the body.

Core skill 3: The development of a bent arm pull

The teacher must first demonstrate the action to the pupils. The teacher lying on a ledge or bench as shown in figures 5.45a to 5.45j best achieves this.

Pull phase of the bent arm pull

Teaching points
• Press the hand down. • Keep the wrist firm. • Bend the elbow.

When the teacher presents a side view, they can talk through the main teaching points and the 'S' shaped pulling pattern is more easily seen.

Figure 5.45
A teacher demonstration of the bent arm pull from a lying position.

Figure 5.45a

• Enter little finger first.

Figure 5.45b

• Press hand down.

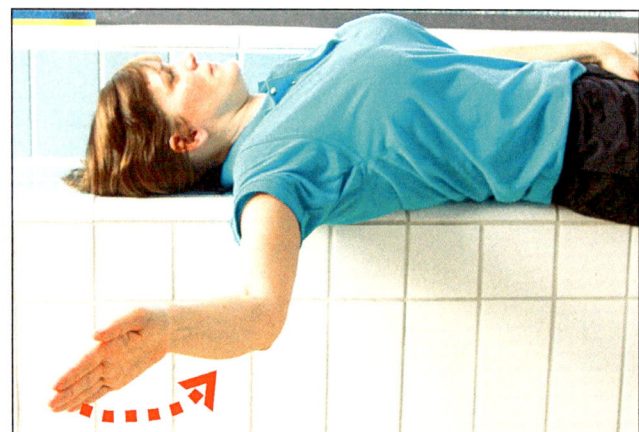

Figure 5.45c

- Start to bend the elbow.

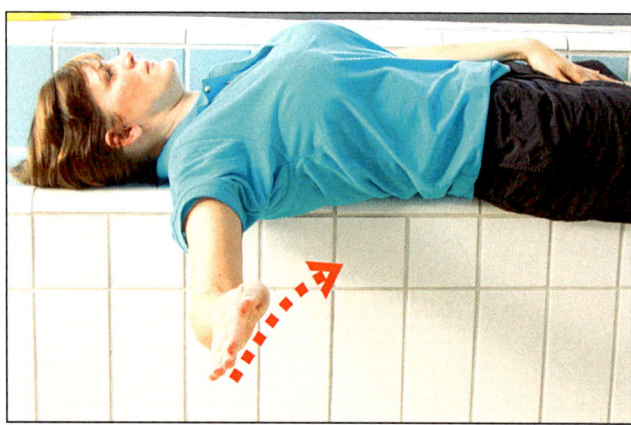

Figure 5.45d

- Bend the elbow.
- Start to sweep the hand up.
- Keep the wrist firm.

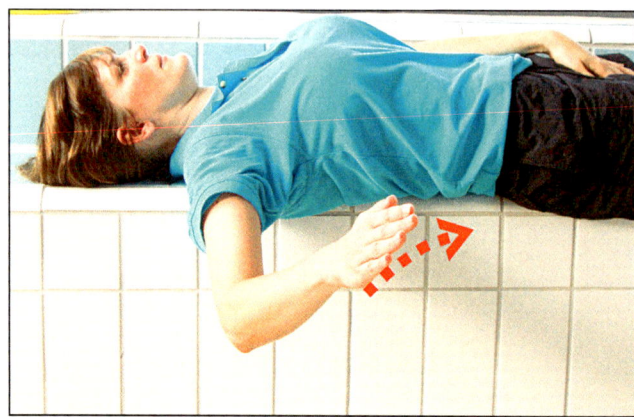

Figure 5.45e

- Push back.

Figure 5.45f

- Push the hand into the side.

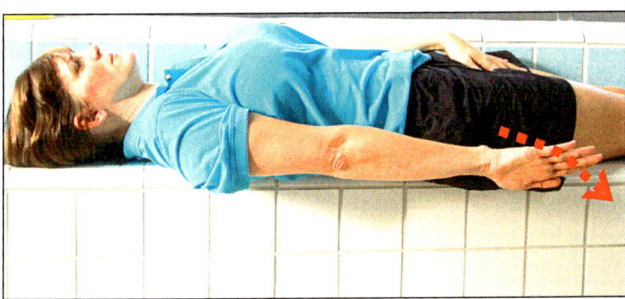

Figure 5.45g

- Stretch the arm and push the hand down to the thighs.

Figure 5.45h

- Exit little finger first.

Figure 5.45i

• Reach for the ceiling.

•

Figure 5.45j

• Stretch for entry behind the head.

Following the demonstration by the teacher, the pupils copy the arm movement while in shallow water. This practice is to develop an awareness and understanding of the action required. Throughout the teacher focuses on the following teaching points:

Teaching points
• Lift the arm high out of the water.
• Little finger first.
• Press the hand down.
• Keep wrist firm.
• Push down and into your side.

Backstroke

The pupils are then encouraged to 'have a go' by placing one float under one arm, push and glide, kick the legs and perform the movement with the other arm, changing arms on alternate widths.

Through a variety of single arm practices both with and without support, the bent arm action is developed. Throughout the practices the teacher also has the opportunity to focus on combining the leg action and the body roll with the arm action.

 Two body positions are normally used for a single arm practice. These are:
- With the supporting arm down by the pupils side.
- With the supporting arm stretched out behind the swimmers head.

When developing the backstroke, the first of these two body positions enable the pupil to more easily combine the arm action with the body roll.

Backstroke practices to develop a bent arm pull

Single arm practices with the supporting arm holding a small float.

1. Perform a single arm practice holding one small float under the other arm.
2. Perform a single arm practice with the supporting arm holding a small float down by the side.
3. Perform a single arm practice with the supporting arm stretched out behind the head holding a small float
4. Include full stroke into the practice by first performing one width right arm only, followed by one width left arm only, then two widths full stroke.

Single arm practices without support

The same Practices 1 to 4 listed above can be performed without a float. It is now easier to also include a range of combinations for example:

1. Performing five strokes right arm only, followed by five strokes left arm only.
2. Performing five strokes right arm only, followed by five strokes left arm only, then five complete stroke cycles before starting the same sequence over again.
3. Performing any of the practices listed pulling with a pull buoy or with the fingers closed and held in a fist position.

 Using a pull buoy between the legs can cause problems by the pull buoy 'popping' out. Pupils end up spending all their time recovering the aid rather than attempting the exercise.

151

A 'catch-up' backstroke practice

Catch-up backstroke can be performed in two ways:

Catch-up with both arms by the side: Starting with both arms down by the side, the right arm works through a complete stroke cycle, while the left arm remains still. When the right arm returns back to the right side, it is held still while the left arm works through a complete cycle.

Catch-up with both arms above the head: Starting with both hands stretched out behind the head, the right arm works again through one stroke cycle, while the left arm remains still. When the right arm returns back to its starting point, it is held still while the left arm works through a complete single arm stroke.

Remember:

- Ensure that equal practice is given to both the left and right arms so the stroke is developed in a balanced way.

- During the single arm practices, both with and without support, the pupils should be encouraged to roll around the long axis of the body while keeping the head perfectly still.

 Notice that the skill of kicking backstroke on the side is not specifically highlighted. When swimming full stroke, diagonal kicks do occur as a result of the alternating arm action and the effects of the body roll. The rotation in backstroke, however, is not so pronounced as in the front crawl. This is because in backstroke the rotation is restricted by the shoulder girdle. In front crawl, the body is able to rotate more freely in the prone position. As a consequence, we have identified kicking on the side as a core skill for front crawl but have not done so for backstroke.

SUMMARY OF THINGS TO LOOK FOR IN A GOOD BACKSTROKE

Body position
• A shallow curved shape with the hips just below the surface. • Head – hips – legs remain in line throughout the stroke. • Hips lead the body roll so legs and shoulders roll with the hips. • Body rolls in time with the arm action. • Head remains as still as possible throughout the stroke.

Leg kick

- Legs kick up and down close together.
- Leg action smooth and continuous.
- The depth of the kick is similar to the length of the stride.
- Kicking action initiated from the hips.
- Slight knee bend at end of downbeat.
- Leg drives up in a strong 'whip-like' action.
- Feet extended on upbeat – relaxed ankles on downbeat.
- Toes should just break the surface.
- Lateral movement of the legs should be kept inside the shoulder lines.

Arm pull

- Arms enter in line with shoulders.
- Entry made with palms facing out – little finger first.
- Hands drive down and out into catch position.
- Elbow fixes and bends as hand starts to pull.
- The elbow bend reaches approximately 90 degrees when in line with the shoulder.
- At the end of the pull phase, the fingers remain below the surface.
- Hands push through and finish close to the thighs.
- Hand traces a sideways 'S' pattern.
- The arm pull is smooth and continuous.
- The arm action is symmetrical.

Arm recovery

- Hands leave the water little finger first – palm out.
- Recovery is made with a straight arm, high overhead.
- Lift shoulders on recovery.
- Palm remains turned out throughout the recovery.
- Arm remains straight ('like a sentry').
- Towards the end of the recovery, the hands prepare to enter palm out, little finger first.
- Recovery is symmetrical.
- Recovery is smooth and continuous.

Breathing

- Breathe in on one arm recovery; breathe out on the other arm recovery.
- Breathe every stroke cycle.
- The breathing does not have any effect on the head position.

153

Timing, co-ordination and rhythm

- Smooth, balanced and flowing rhythm.
- Six kicks to one arm cycle.
- Arms balanced and symmetrical.
- Propulsion applied in a continuous manner.

BACKSTROKE ASSESSMENT SHEET

Name of swimmer:		Age:	
Stroke/activity:		Date:	
Analysis carried out by:			

BODY POSITION

Key questions to ask	Teachers observations and comments
• How streamlined is the body? • What is the position of the head, hips and feet throughout the stroke? • Do the head, hips and feet form a shallow curved shape? • How still is the head during the stroke? • How close to the surface are the hips? • How close to the surface is the leg kick? • What is the extent of the body roll? • Is there any lateral (side to side) movement of the body? • Do the legs and shoulders roll with the hips? • Is the body roll even on both sides? • Do the shoulders, hips and legs roll together as one? • Is the swimmer very buoyant?	

LEG ACTION

Key questions to ask	Teachers observations and comments
• How strong is the leg kick? • How close are the legs during the kick? • What is the depth of the kick? • Is the leg kick continuous? • To what extent do the feet break the surface? • How strong is the 'whip' up of the lower legs? • Are the ankles extended on the upbeat? • How does the body roll effect the leg kick? • How many kicks are there per stroke cycle? • What is the rhythm/tempo of the kick?	

155

ARM ACTION

Key questions to ask	Teachers observations and comments
• Is the entry made in line with the shoulder line? • How do the hands enter the water? • Is the pull a straight arm or bent arm pull? • Where is the initial catch made? • What is the degree of elbow bend? • Do the hands push back towards the thigh? • Do the hands trace an 'S' shaped pulling pattern to the side of the body? • How do the hands exit the water? • Do the hands exit the water close to the hips? • Is the arm action continuous? • Is the arm pull effective in generating propulsion?	

ARM RECOVERY

Key questions to ask	Teachers observations and comments
• What is the action of the recovery? • How straight is the arm recovery? • How high do the hands pass overhead? • Is the recovery symmetrical? • What is the speed of the recovery? • How do the arms approach the entry point? • Which way are the palms facing as they approach the entry point? • Is the recovery a smooth continuous action?	

BREATHING

Key questions to ask	Teachers observations and comments
• When is the breath taken? • When does the swimmer breathe out? • How often does the swimmer breathe? • What is the effect on the overall stroke? • Does the breathing have any effect on the head position?	

TIMING AND CO-ORDINATION

Key questions to ask	Teachers observations and comments
• How many kicks are there in one stroke cycle? • What is the timing between the leg and arm actions? • What is the timing between the breathing and the arm action? • Are there any pauses in the stroke? • What is the overall rhythm of the stroke? • Is the arm pull symmetrical? • How smooth and continuous is the overall stroke? • Is propulsion applied in a continuous manner?	

FINAL IMPRESSIONS AND COMMENTS

Key questions to ask	Teachers observations and comments
• What contribution do you think the legs make to propulsion? • What contribution do you think the arms make to propulsion? • How flexible do you think the swimmer is? • How strong do you think the swimmer is? • What is good about the stroke? • What would you like to improve?	

ALTERNATIVE BACKSTROKE ASSESSMENT SHEET

Name of swimmer:		Age:	
Date of assessment:		Date:	

Body position (focus on head, shoulders, hips and feet)	
Horizontal	
Lateral	
Rotational	
Streamlining throughout stroke cycle	

Leg action (Focus on hips, knee bend, lower leg, feet and ankles)	
Action of recovery	
Action of kick down	
Rhythm/tempo	
Effectiveness	

Arm action (Focus on hands, elbow and shoulders)		
	Left arm	Right arm
Entry and stretch		
Initial pull into catch (sweep down)		
In-sweep		
Push back		
Release and exit		
Recovery		
	Left arm	Right arm
Hand track through the water		
Left and right symmetry		
Overall action		

Breathing (Focus on head, shoulders, hip rotation)		
Rotation of head		
When is breath taken?		
Smoothness of movement		
Breathing pattern		
Effect on stroke		

Timing/co-ordination/rhythm		
Timing of leg and arm action		
Co-ordination of breathing		
Co-ordination of body roll		
Continuity of stroke		
Rhythm/tempo		

General impressions

Main focus for future improvement

BACKSTROKE

Backstroke is swum in the supine position,
From being upright, it's an easy transition
Start from the side,
With a strong push and glide
Head back, chin up, the easier to breathe
True you can't see the path that you weave.
You can see the teacher patiently talking
Kick from the hips, as if you are walking.
The arms lift up, over and round
They're supposed to be straight, not like a mound.
Eleven o'clock is the point of entry,
Body straight, just like a sentry.
Pull and push down with the wrist and the hand
You want to start moving away from the land.
The shape in the water is a letter 'S'
This is backstroke at its very best!

Pat Parkes

Chapter 6

Front Crawl

Main Focus:

- Why is front crawl the fastest of all the strokes?
- What to look for in a good stroke
- The value of a body roll
- A simple leg kick; but why is it so important?
- Why is the arm action the power house of the stroke
- The key boomerang shape during the in-sweep
- The nature of the recovery
- The crucial breathing action
- A 10 stage building block programme
- The key elements of breathing and rhythm
- The identification of 12 main problems
- The improvement circle built on three core skills
- A summary of what to look for
- Usable assessment sheets
- A summary poem by Patricia Parkes

Be A Great Swimming Teacher

Chapter 6

Front Crawl

INTRODUCTION

Front crawl is probably the most natural of all the strokes for children to learn. Small children instinctively move their legs up and down when supported in water. It is also the stroke that most teachers like to teach, because success can usually be achieved quickly. Early practices are relatively easy and it is not long before a dog paddle stroke can be attempted without any support and yes, the child is 'swimming'.

Front crawl is the fastest of all the strokes

Why is this?

- **It is the most streamlined.** A flat horizontal body position is maintained throughout the stroke cycle. Although the swimmer is face down in the water (prone position), there is less disturbance to their horizontal body position as the head is turned to the side to breathe. This enables the swimmer to maintain the streamlined position from one stroke to the next.

- **Propulsion can be applied in a more continuous manner.** The alternating arm action allows each arm in turn to generate propulsion. As soon as one arm has finished its pull, the other one is ready to begin.

- **The arms pull under the body, where they can create more propulsive force than any other stroke.** The strong muscles of the upper body, namely the chest and shoulder girdle, can be used effectively by the swimmer to pull close to the centre line, applying a strong propulsive force throughout the full range of movement.

What is the main problem to overcome when teaching the front crawl?

The main problem is:

Fitting the breathing smoothly into the arm pattern.

Beginners have an initial fear of putting their faces down into the water. This has to be overcome early in the learners' programme. If the teacher is content with 'swimming at any cost', this aspect of the stroke is all too often hurried, or even worse, ignored. Teachers can easily become very busy teaching the arm and leg movements and yet spend very little time teaching the breathing. As a result, pupils either struggle to swim with their heads up, or their efforts are limited to a few complete strokes with their heads down, before they have to stop to regain their breath.

 We cannot emphasise enough, that the breathing in front crawl has to be taught early in the learners' programme. This means spending **time** to teach the skill correctly and time to co-ordinate it into the full stroke. To highlight this, we use the analogy of learning to be an opera singer. The first thing opera singers learn, is how to breathe correctly – singing comes later.

WHAT TO LOOK FOR IN A GOOD STROKE

Body position

It is most helpful to use the classic 'front glide' as a frame of reference when thinking about the horizontal body position for the novice swimmer.

Look for:
• A body as flat and streamlined as possible. • Arms extended, with one hand placed on top of the other. • Head held comfortably with the water cutting between the hairline and the crown. • The legs stretched, held together with toes pointed.

Horizontal body position

Figure 6.1
The front glide position from underwater

Figure 6.2
The teachers view
of the front glide
position

 This streamlined body position needs to be achieved before the front crawl leg kick is introduced. For this reason, push and glide practices cannot be emphasised enough during the early stages.

A discussion on body position

As with all strokes, this rather static body position changes into a dynamic one once the arms, legs and breathing are co-ordinated into the complete stroke.

Look for:
• A slightly more angled body position when swimming front crawl to allow the alternating leg action to be performed entirely in the water.

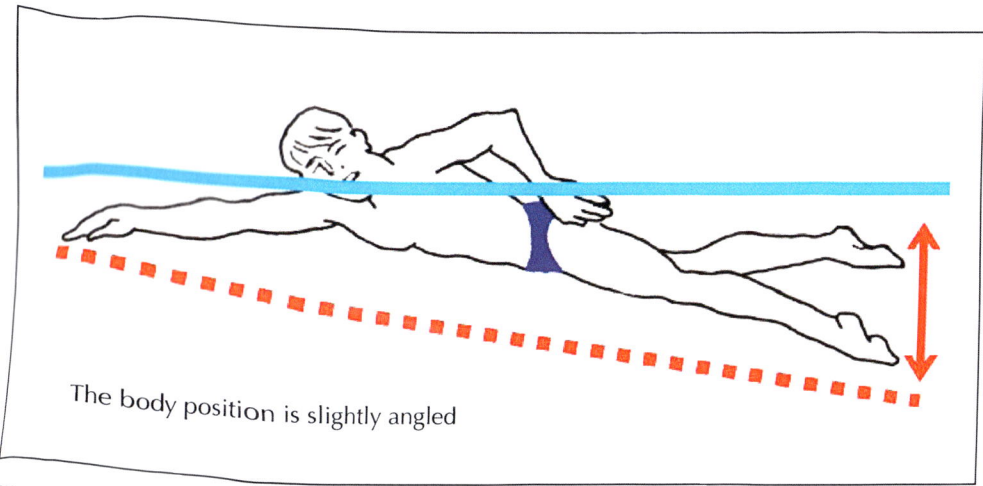

The body position is slightly angled

Figure 6.3
The horizontal body position when swimming full stroke

The position of the head is the most critical factor:

- If the head is lifted too high, the hips and legs sink low in the water, increasing the swimmer's resistance.
- If the head is pushed down too low, the hips rise and much of the leg kick is performed out of the water making it less effective.

In the front glide position, the shoulders remain flat on the water but when the full stroke is performed, this is no longer the case. The whole body (shoulders, hips and legs), **rolls around the long axis** due to the alternating arm action and the turning of the head to the side to breathe.

An axis of rotation is an imaginary line or point about which the body rotates. In swimming, the **long axis** goes right through the body from the head to the feet.

Look for:

- The rolling of the shoulders around the long axis of the body as the swimmer swims towards you.

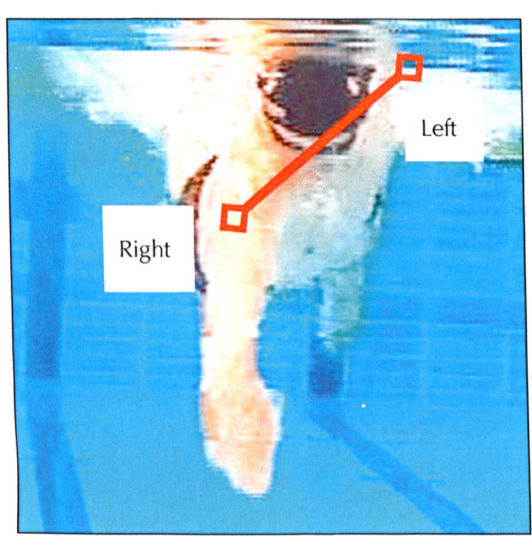

Figure 6.4a
The roll onto the right side.
As the swimmer rolls onto their right side, the right shoulder is lower than the left.

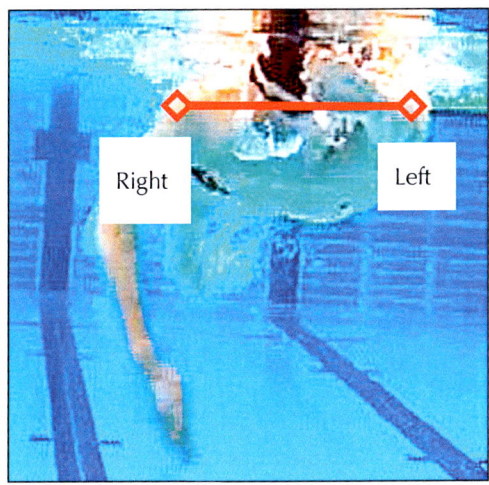

Right　Left

Figure 6.4b
The mid-way point as the body rolls from the right side to the left.

As the swimmer rolls from the right to the left side, the shoulders are flat at the mid-way point.

Figure 6.4c
The roll onto the left side.

As the swimmer rolls onto their left side, the left shoulder is lower than the right.

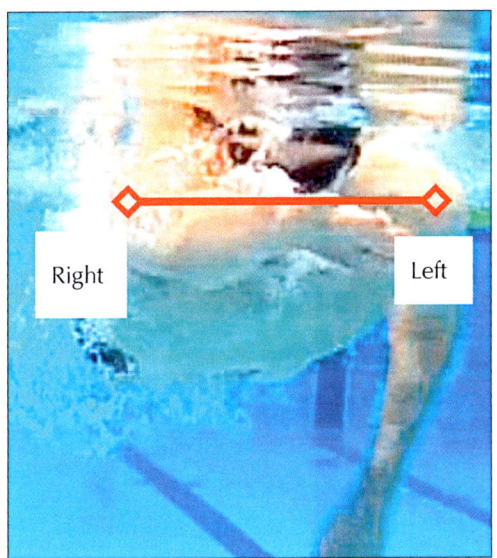

Right　Left

Figure 6.4d
The mid-way point as the body rolls from the left side to the right.

As the body rolls back again from the left to the right side, the shoulders are flat at the mid-way point.

169

Look for:
• The 'whole body' rolling around the long axis, (shoulders, hips and legs).

Figure 6.5
Rotation around the long axis in front crawl

 The amount of roll seen at the shoulders should be around 45 degrees, though a swimmer may not roll as much on the non-breathing side.

Leg action

The basic movement is a continuous, alternating up and down movement with the legs passing as close as possible to one another. The action is broken down into two phases, an upbeat and a downbeat.

The upbeat

The upbeat is the recovery phase of the front crawl leg kick.

Look for:
• A straight leg during the first part of the upbeat as the movement is initiated from the hip.
• A slight knee bend as the leg lifts up further. At the top of the recovery, the heels come close to or just break the surface.

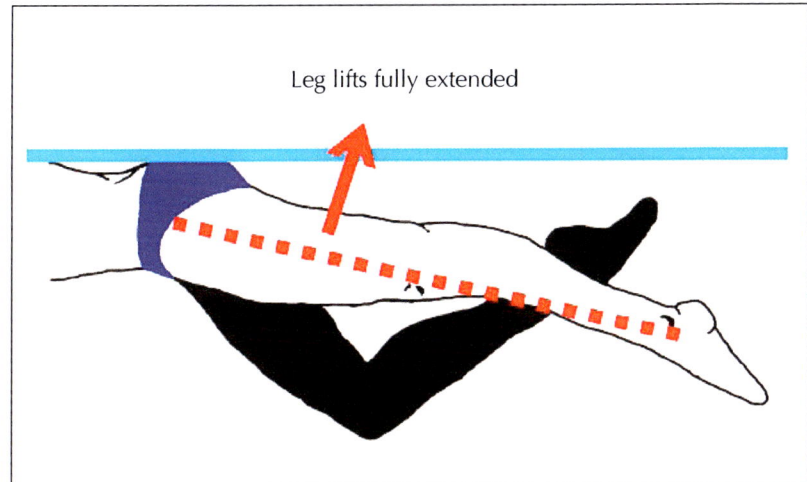

Leg lifts fully extended

Figure 6.6a
The first part of the upbeat

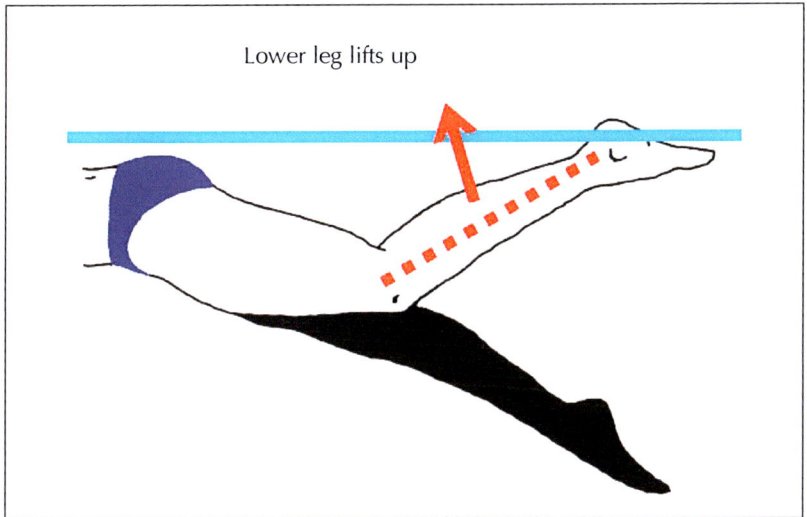

Lower leg lifts up

Figure 6.6b
The second part of the upbeat

Figure 6.6
The upbeat phase of the front crawl leg kick

The downbeat

The downbeat is the main propulsive phase of the front crawl leg kick.

Look for:

- A greater knee bend as the thigh initiates the drive down.
- The lower leg 'whipping' down with the toes and ankles extended.
- The action finishing with the leg fully extended.

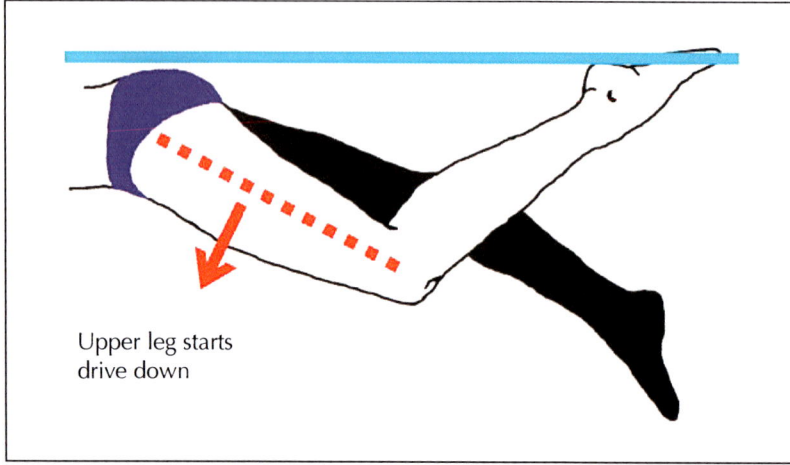

Figure 6.7a
The initial drive down of the hip

Upper leg starts drive down

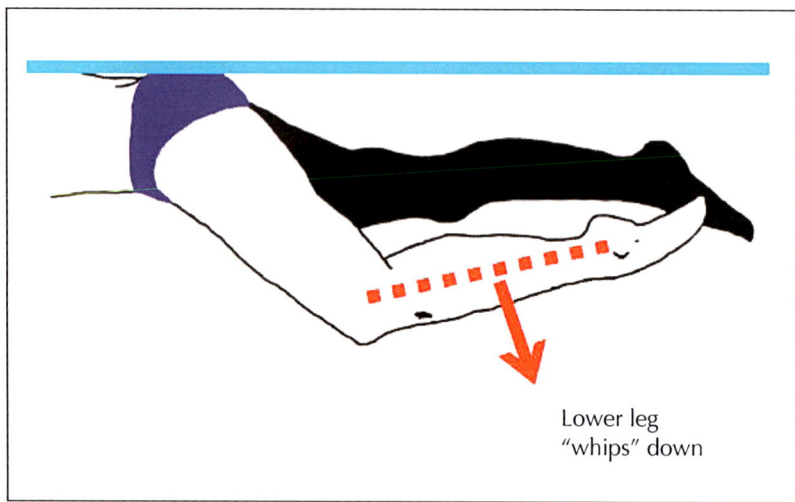

Figure 6.7b
The 'whip' down of the lower leg

Lower leg "whips" down

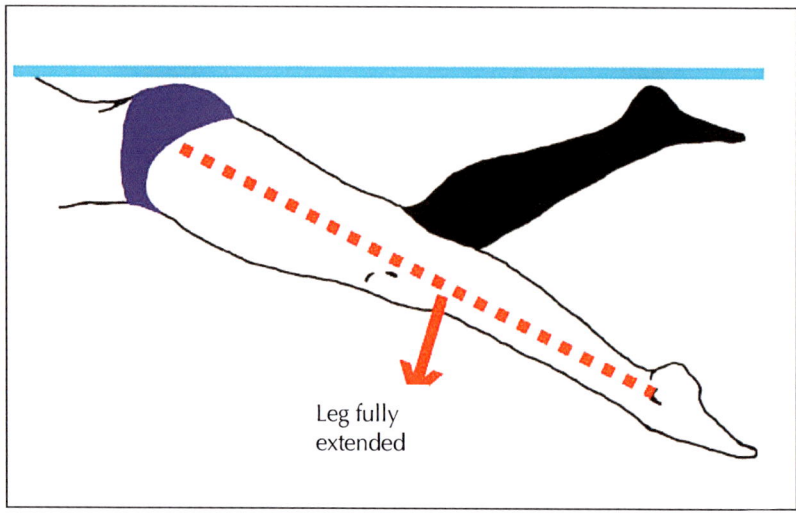

Figure 6.7c
The full leg extension at the end of the downbeat

Leg fully extended

Figure 6.7
The downbeat phase of the front crawl leg kick

Discussion on the leg kick

What is its function?

The basic movement is straightforward. It is a simple action and because it is simple, there is a danger that teachers become complacent about it. They think of the action as nothing more than just 'kicking up and down'.

The kick, however, has several important functions:

- To balance and stabilise the stroke.
- To maintain the body in a streamlined horizontal position.
- To add to forward propulsion.

Throughout the movement the ankles should be kept loose.

What is the effect of the body roll on the leg kick?

As the swimmer rolls around the long axis, some of the kicking action occurs in the vertical plane. However, as the swimmer rolls onto either side in time with the breathing and alternating arm action, some of the leg kicks become a **diagonal** up and down motion.

Look for:
• A diagonal action when the body rolls onto either side. • A vertical action when the swimmer is mid-way through the roll from one side to the other.

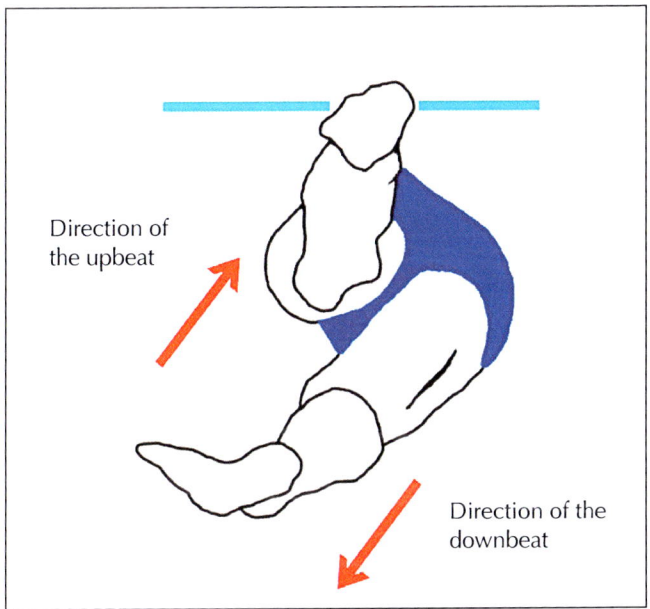

Direction of the upbeat

Direction of the downbeat

Figure 6.8a
The diagonal action when the body rolls onto its right side.

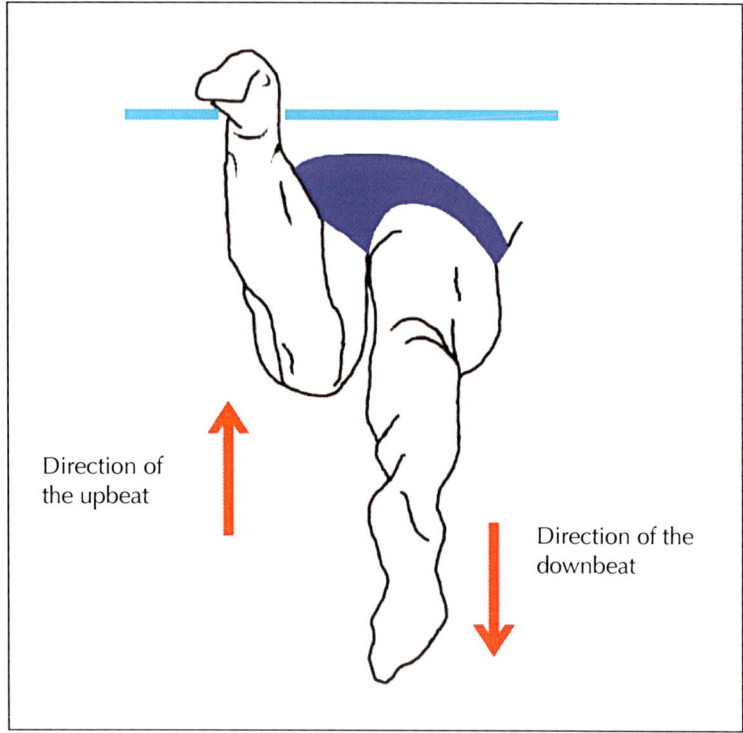

Figure 6.8b
The vertical action when the swimmer is mid-way through the roll from one side to the other.

Direction of the upbeat

Direction of the downbeat

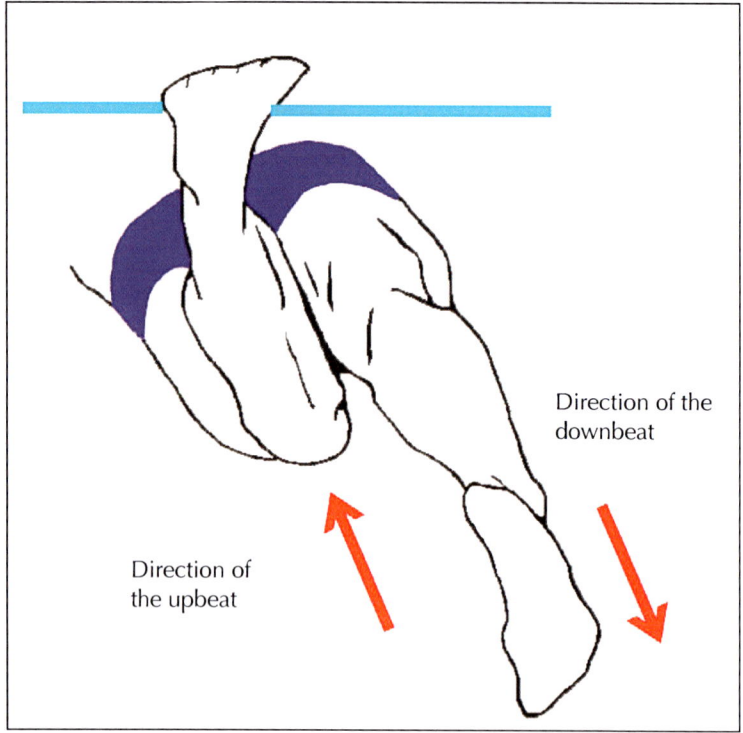

Figure 6.8c
The diagonal action when the body rolls onto its left side.

Direction of the downbeat

Direction of the upbeat

Figure 6.8
The effects of the body roll on the front crawl leg kick

This diagonal movement is the reaction that occurs when the complete stroke is performed. It is a natural reaction and is not something that should be initially taught. Why not?

If the teacher demonstrates the action with diagonal movements, the pupils may attempt to copy this. The result is invariably an over-exaggerated action, with excessive sideways movement, often with the legs wide apart. Therefore the demonstration that the teacher gives must still be in an up and down plane.

This is a classic example of teaching one thing knowing that something a little different may be achieved.

What is the depth of the kick?

The depth of the kick is often thought of as a precise measurement, for example thirty centimetres. Such a measurement is meaningless because the depth has to be **relative to the length of the leg** (that is, the size of the pupil). The depth of the kick also depends on the flexibility of the ankles and the strength of the legs. Good ankle flexibility and strong legs results in a deeper kicking action. This adds to forward propulsion as well as balancing and stabilising the stroke. A shallow flutter-type leg action is much less effective.

Arm action

The arm action is the power house of the front crawl stroke as it provides the main source of propulsion. In our description, we are going to break the action down into six specific phases because this makes the stroke easier to analyse and teach.

Entry

Look for:
• The hands entering the water between the centre line and the shoulder line at a point well in advance of the head. This is best viewed from above.

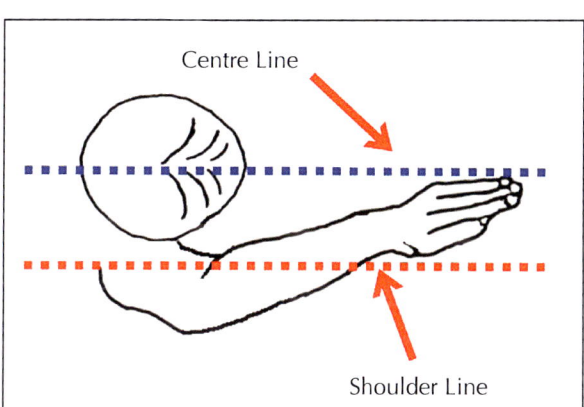

Figure 6.9
Entry position viewed from above

175

From the side

Look for:
• The entry being made fingertips first with the palm facing down or slightly out. • The arm being slightly flexed (not fully extended), so the elbow is higher than the wrist.

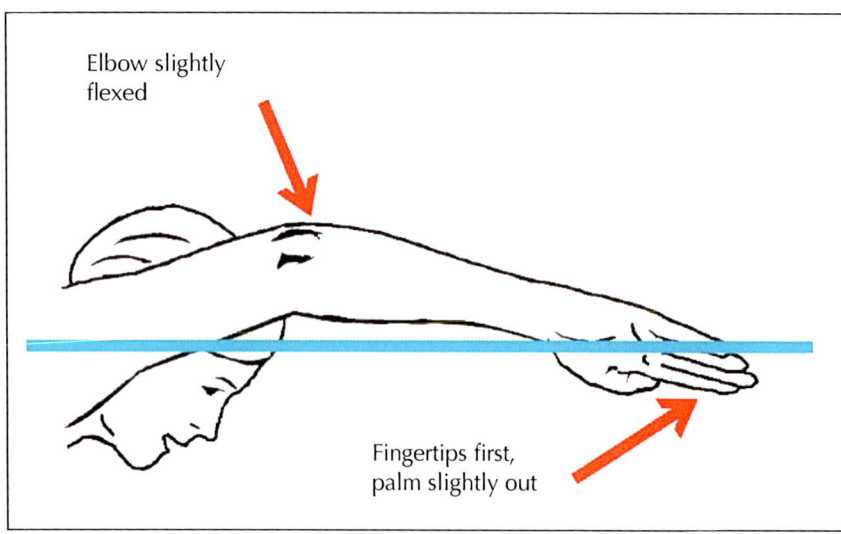

Elbow slightly flexed

Fingertips first, palm slightly out

Figure 6.10
Entry position viewed from the side

Stretch

Look for:
• The hand stretching forwards just under the surface of the water with the palm facing down.

Hand stretches forwards after entry – palm faces down

Figure 6.11
The stretch forward after entry

Point of catch

Towards the end of the stretch the hand begins to press down and the palm starts to face increasingly backwards to gain a real purchase on the water. The point at which this occurs is called the **catch point**. The catch point is reached at about 30 to 45 centimetres below the surface.

Look for:
• The elbow starting to bend as the hand starts to move downwards.

Elbow starts to bend

Figure 6.12
The catch point in front crawl

 With novice swimmers, the catch point is likely to be much deeper. As the stroke improves, the teacher needs to encourage this point to be reached earlier in the stroke.

Pull phase

The pull phase of the arm action consists of two sweeping movements:

- A down-sweep.
- An in-sweep.

Down-sweep

The hand continues to exert a downward and backward pressure on the water. This takes the hand mainly down in a curved pathway. As a result, this phase of the stroke is referred to as the **down-sweep**.

Look for:

- The hand pressing mainly down in a curved pathway.
- The wrist remaining firm and the elbow high. It is the lower part of the arm that performs most of the pull down.

Figure 6.13
The down-sweep in front crawl

 The pressure of the water also causes the beginning of the down-sweep to curve slightly outwards and the end to curve slightly inwards.

In-sweep

As the hand approaches the deepest point, its path changes. The lower arm pulls in under the chin towards the centre line. This part of the pull is referred to as the **in-sweep**.

Look for:

- The elbow bending as much as 90 degrees giving the appearance of a 'boomerang' shape when viewed from the front.

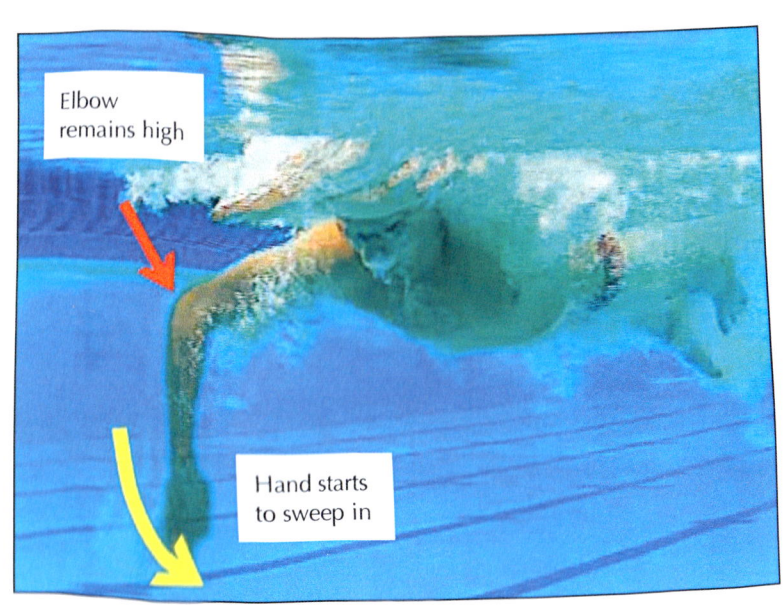

Figure 6.14
The start of the in-sweep in front crawl

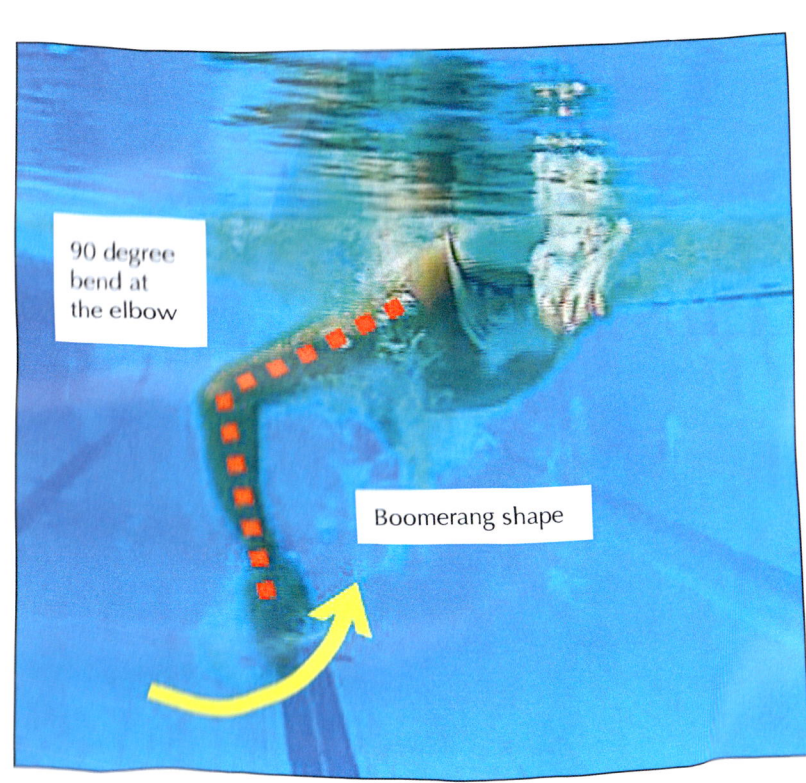

Figure 6.15
The 'Boomerang' shape during the in-sweep in front crawl

Push phase

The hand continues to push back towards the thigh, trying to maintain a backward pressure on the water. As the elbow extends, this also sweeps the hand up towards the surface of the water. This phase is therefore sometimes referred to as the **up-sweep**.

Look for:
• The elbow extending as the hand pushes back towards the thigh.

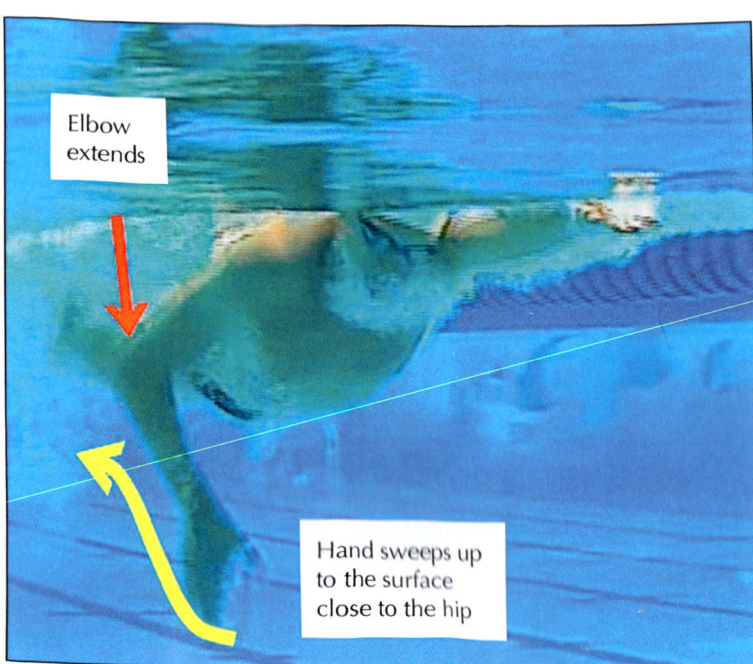

Figure 6.16
The push phase in front crawl

 The natural extension of the elbow during this movement also sweeps the hand up towards the surface.

Recovery

The transition from the push to the recovery phase should be as smooth and continuous as possible.

Look for:
• The arm lifting from the water with the elbow leading.

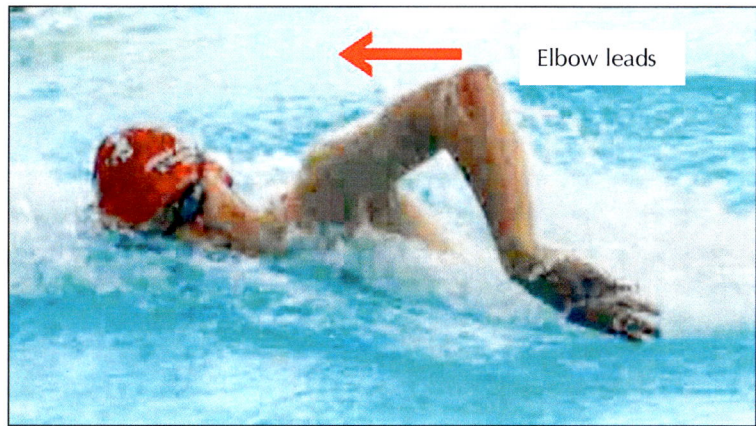

Figure 6.17
The recovery in front crawl as viewed from the side

Look for:

- Once the hand is lifted clear, look for a low, semicircular path over the water passing close to the head.

Figure 6.18
The recovery in front crawl as viewed from behind

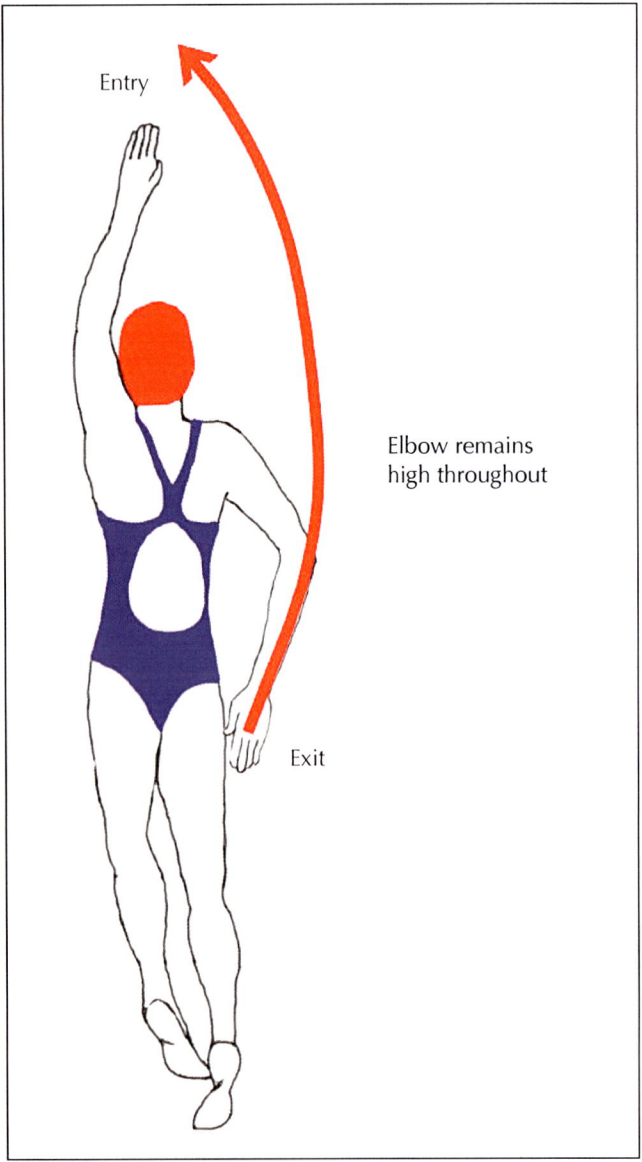

Entry

Elbow remains
high throughout

Exit

Figure 6.19
The low semi-circular pathway of the
recovery in front crawl

Throughout the recovery the elbow always remains higher than the hand. It is important that this high elbow position is achieved.

Discussion on the front crawl arm action

The nature of the recovery

Although we have just broken the arm action down into six specific phases, it is also useful to think of the stroke more simply in terms of two main phases:

- An underwater phase.
- A recovery phase.

The underwater phase is clearly concerned with propulsion and as such, tends to receive most of our attention. The recovery phase often receives much less attention but is important because it does have an indirect effect on propulsion in two ways:

- The recovery phase sets the arm up for a correct entry position. If a correct entry position is not achieved, the rest of the underwater phase of the stroke is likely to be less effective.

- A poor recovery is almost certainly going to have an adverse effect on the limb track of the opposite arm as it pulls through the water. If the arm is recovered too high, then the opposite arm pulls too deep. If the arm is recovered too low, the body does not roll sufficiently to allow the opposite arm to pull under the body (action/reaction).

The recovery also gives the stroke its appearance. It is the phase of the stroke that is most easily seen. If the recovery is not right, the stroke looks 'funny' and the teacher may jump to all kinds of conclusions about what is wrong.

The nature of the recovery depends on a number of factors:

- **Flexibility**: The recovery takes place in an area where the range of movement is limited. The more flexible the shoulder girdle, the easier the recovery.

- **Buoyancy**: If a swimmer's buoyancy is poor, they are going to have more difficulty getting their arms clear of the water.

- **Extent of the push back**: If the arms are pushed back too far at the end of the underwater phase, the recovery tends to be carried out with a straight arm swinging low over the water.

- **Timing of the breathing**: If the breath is taken late into the stroke, the body is still on its side during the early part of the recovery. This often results in a high circular recovery, again with a straight arm.

 Some individual variations must be tolerated but take care to ensure that both the entry position and the limb track of the opposite arm are not adversely affected.

The underwater limb track

The track of the limbs during the underwater phase leads into the second main area of discussion on the arm action.

- The **'S' shape pull** takes place under the body in a fairly well-defined area between the centre line and the shoulder line.

- Throughout the movement, the hands continually change their pitch, starting with thumbs down on the down-sweep, changing to thumbs up on the in-sweep, back to thumbs down during the up-sweep.

During the early stages of learning, it is not necessary to emphasise the 'S' shape pathway or these subtle changes in hand pitch. It is enough just to encourage the children to maintain a backward pressure on the water throughout the pull. Some children adopt the 'S' shape pull quite naturally and clearly this should be encouraged. Others have to be taught the pathway more specifically once their skill and confidence has reached a certain level.

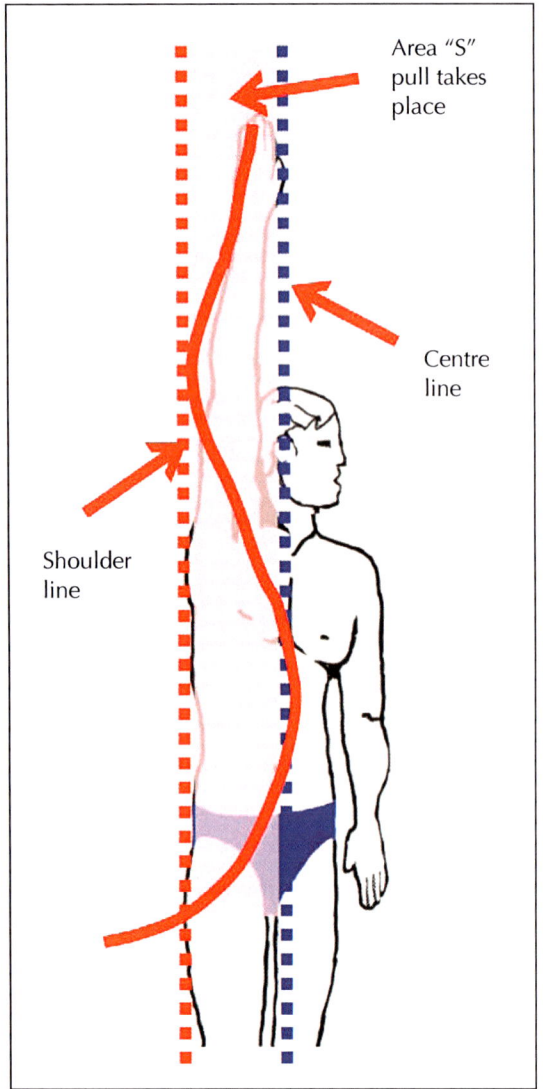

Figure 6.20
The underwater pulling pattern in front crawl

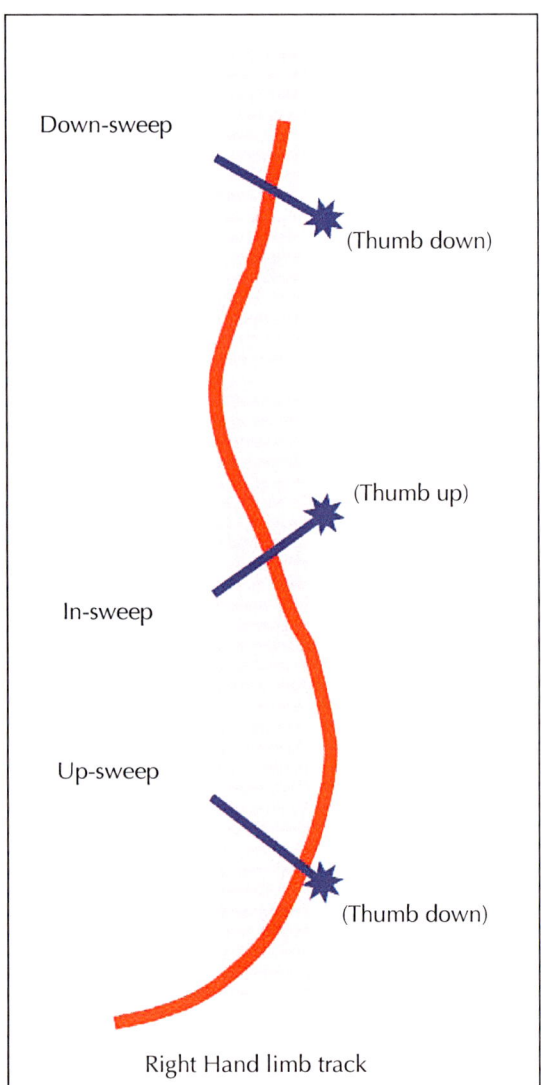

Figure 6.21
Changes in hand pitch during the 'S' pull

What the teacher must look for during the early practices is that the pull takes place within the well-defined area outlined above. No wide movements out to the side or movements across the centre line (particularly on the non-breathing side) should be visible.

If the following checkpoints are achieved, the foundations for a good 'S' shape pull are laid down:

- **An entry position between the centre line and the shoulder line.**
- **The hand under the chin at the end of in-sweep.**
- **A push back to the thigh during the final part of the underwater phase.**

Breathing

The whole action must be smoothly integrated into the stroke with the head kept in line with the body.

When is the breath taken?

The breath is taken as one arm is just about to leave the water to start its recovery and the opposite arm is reaching forward to the catch position.

Look for:
• The head turning just enough for the mouth to clear the water, without undue lifting.

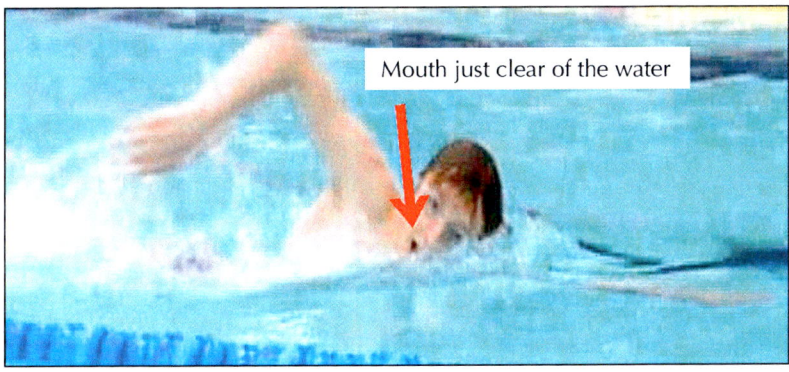

Mouth just clear of the water

Figure 6.22
Side view of the breathing position in front crawl

🔑 It is essential that the action is smoothly co-ordinated with the alternating arm action and body roll.

Types of breathing

There are two types of breathing:

- **Trickle breathing**: Air is inhaled when the face is turned to the side and the mouth is clear of the water. It is exhaled gradually through the nose and mouth while the face is submerged.

- **Explosive breathing**: When the face is submerged, the breath is held. As the face turns to the side, the breath is blown out hard (exploded) before the next intake of air.

Patterns of breathing

There are two basic patterns to the breathing:

- **Unilateral**: Breathing to one side only, every stroke cycle.
- **Bi-lateral**: Breathing every three arm movements (every one and half stroke cycles) making the head turn to alternate sides.

Discussion on the front crawl breathing

The key to developing the stroke is the breathing . . . and yet this is an area which teachers often shy away from. They rarely develop this aspect of the stroke much beyond 'blowing bubbles'.

It is vital that **time** is taken to develop the breathing correctly and link it with the arm action.

Learners often experience difficulties with the breathing simply because they do not breathe out sufficiently. They gasp air in, but do not have time in the stroke to fully breathe out. As a result, they very quickly become breathless and the stroke breaks down.

Once again, what the pupils basically need is **time** . . . time to inhale sufficient breath to take them onto the next phase of the stroke and time to exhale sufficiently to take in more air. During the building block programme this can be achieved if the pupils are encouraged to breathe in time with the leg kick.

A practice recommended for developing the breathing is:

Practice
Breathe in for three leg beats with the face turned to the side and breathe out for three leg beats with the face in the water.

This is a tremendous exercise to help slow everything down to give the swimmer time to breathe correctly.

Two minor points to consider with regards to breathing:

- Firstly, some descriptions of the breathing refer to the head being turned into a trough or 'bow wave' caused by the swimmer as they move through the water. The simile is of a bow wave visible at the front of a boat. Teachers must be aware, however, that beginners will not perform the stroke quickly or smooth enough to create such a bow wave and so reference to this is of little use to either the teacher or the pupil.

- Secondly, in an attempt to get the child to swim at any cost, teachers are tempted to encourage beginners to 'breath hold' during early practices. The danger with this is it can create bad habits that become difficult to correct later. Also, avoiding an area of the stroke which they find difficult to develop is a negative way to teach. *This clearly is not the answer.*

Timing and co-ordination

The co-ordination of the stroke depends on the integration of the following three components into one smooth action:

- The number of leg kicks per stroke cycle.

- The timing of the propulsive phases between the left and right arms.

- The turning of the head to breathe.

With a continuous, strong leg action, the natural timing is for six leg kicks for each complete arm cycle. However, there can be considerable variation to this. Highly skilled swimmers may perform the stroke with either two or four kicks per arm cycle. It is sometimes argued that using two beats per cycle uses less energy and is therefore something that would benefit a distance swimmer. For the learner however, it is vital to encourage them to work towards establishing six beats to each arm cycle. It helps balance the stroke and is the most effective timing to aid propulsion.

The overall objective for the arm action is to create propulsion in a smooth and continuous manner. As one arm finishes its propulsive phase, the other arm completes its recovery and is ready to start its own propulsive phase. Any delay is often seen as a 'glide' on entry while one arm catches up with the other. During this glide phase the swimmer slows down, there is an over reliance on the leg kick and the rhythm is seen as 'pull, slow down, pull, slow down'. These pauses need to be avoided.

The head must turn to the side to breathe and return to the water using an action which is smooth and in time with both the roll of the body and the end of the underwater arm pull on the breathing side. Most swimmers adopt a unilateral breathing pattern (breathing to one side only), choosing their favoured side quite naturally. Nevertheless it is good teaching to encourage pupils to also practise bi-lateral breathing to improve balance and symmetry in the stroke.

THE BUILDING UP OF THE TEACHING PROGRESSIONS

Pre-requisite to learning the front crawl

Before teaching the front crawl, it is essential that pupils can:

- Place their face down in the water and breathe out slowly and confidently.

- Push from the side in a front glide position and regain their feet.

When the teacher introduces these early practices into their building programme, is really a matter of preference. Some may prefer to develop them on their own as a specific introduction to the front crawl stroke. Others may include them when first building up the learner's confidence during early practices on the backstroke.

⚷ What is important, however, is that the teacher is fully aware that the front crawl cannot be developed very far until this level of 'waterman ship' has been acquired.

BUILDING BLOCK 1

Introducing the leg kick

The first building block for the front crawl is straightforward. It introduces the swimmer to the movements of the leg kick. During these first three practices, the head may be held either up or down. It is not necessary for the teacher to emphasise the position of the head at this stage, as the pupil has enough to concentrate on with the leg action.

Practice 1	Teaching points
Holding on to the rail, lift the legs up to the surface by pressing the elbows against the wall and kick the legs in a front crawl action.	• Kick up and down. • Point the toes.

Reason To ensure the pupils understand the instruction. There is no other value to this practice so make it a very short one.

With this first practice, teachers often demonstrate to the class a kicking action with their hands. Take care that the hand movements do not show a flutter-type movement indicating a shallow kick. Teachers should aim to develop a strong action and demonstrate a movement of at least 30 to 45 centimetres deep. The demonstration should be performed both facing the class and side on.

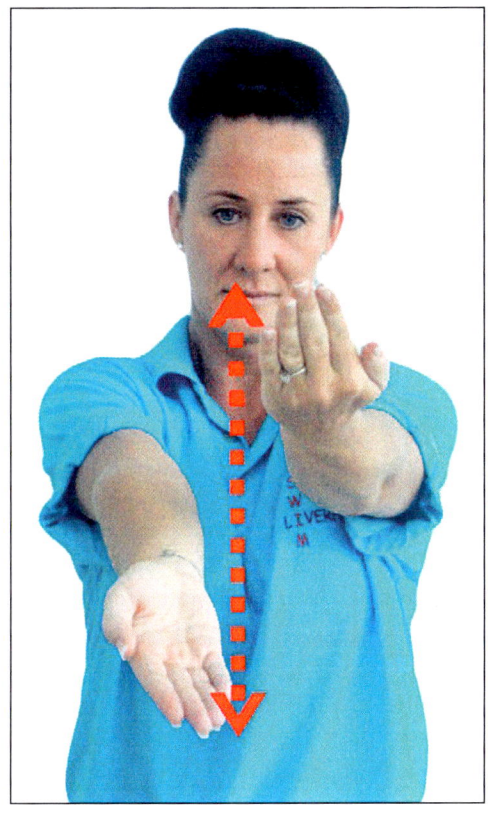

Figure 6.23
Front view of teacher demonstration of the front crawl leg action

Figure 6.24
Side view of teacher demonstration of the front crawl leg action

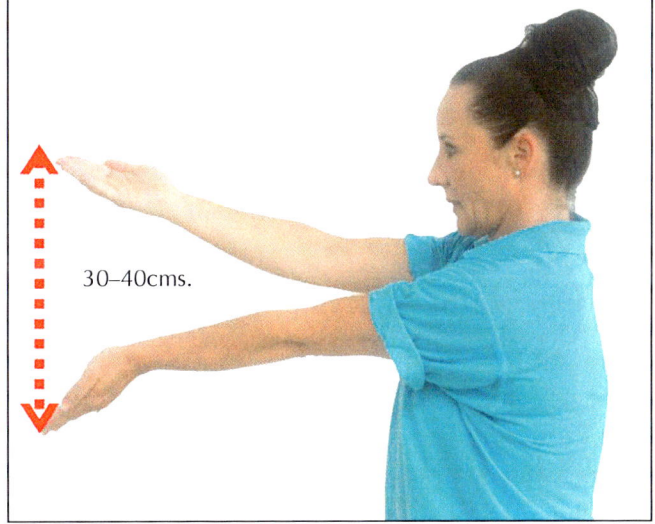

30–40cms.

Practice 2	Teaching points
Holding two floats, one under each arm, push and glide from the wall and start kicking.	• Keep the action continuous. • Keep the legs close together.

Reason	The two floats stabilise the body position. They give the pupil plenty of support so they are not fighting for survival and can concentrate on the leg action.

With nervous pupils, the teacher may use an assistant in the water. They stand facing the pupil at eye level and support the float that the pupil is holding.

Practice 3	Teaching points
Using one float, kick from the push and glide position.	• Keep the legs long. • Keep the ankles loose. • Make the surface 'bubble'.

Reason	Using one float still gives some support whilst the leg kick is practised.

 A teaching point frequently used is 'kick from the hip'. At this stage, we are reluctant to use this because in our experience this tends to produce a 'rocking' effect with real novices. The pupil tries to kick *at* the hip rather than *from* the hip causing the whole body to rock.

We have also deliberately avoided using the word 'straight' when giving a teaching point. Instead we have described the legs as 'long'. Remember the language you use for children is very important because they often take any instructions literally. If we ask for the legs to be straight, the result is often a very stiff action.

BUILDING BLOCK 2

Introducing the breathing

It is vital that the breathing is introduced early in the learners' programme for the reasons outlined earlier. We cannot stress too strongly that *not* mastering these early breathing practices limits severely the progress during later building blocks. It is also quite a natural progression at this stage to combine the first front crawl breathing practices with further leg kicking practices.

Practice 4	Teaching points
Facing the teacher, standing in shallow water, lift the face up with mouth open and breathe in. Slowly lower the face down into the water and blow out through the mouth.	• Lower your face 'slowly' into the water and blow out. • Open your eyes underwater. • Raise the head slowly.

Reason	To make sure the pupils are opening their mouths and breathing in when their faces are above the water. By the evidence of air bubbles, also make sure they are breathing out when their face is down.

The teacher should face the class and talk them through Practice 4 demonstrating the slow lowering of the face in the water and the blowing out through the mouth.

Practice 5	Teaching points
Repeat Practice 4, this time lower the face slowly into the water with the mouth closed and blow out through the nose only.	• Blow out through the nose and mouth. • Listen for the sound of bubbles as blow out.

Reason	To make the pupils aware they can blow out through the nose as well as the mouth.

The word 'slowly' is carefully used when asking the pupils to lower their face into the water because the slow movement prevents water splashing on the face and rushing up their noses. This is often a genuine fear for beginners. It also stops them from 'screwing' up their faces, which constricts their breathing and prevents them from opening their eyes underwater. It is equally important to raise the head slowly from the water to teach them control.

Practices 4 and 5 can be developed easily into a fun situation by asking the pupils to alternate going under the water and . . .

- Holding their nose while blowing out through their mouth.
- Holding their mouth while blowing out through their nose.
- Submerging and blowing out through both.

The teacher can demonstrate the two methods of breathing as shown in Figures 6.25 and 6.26.

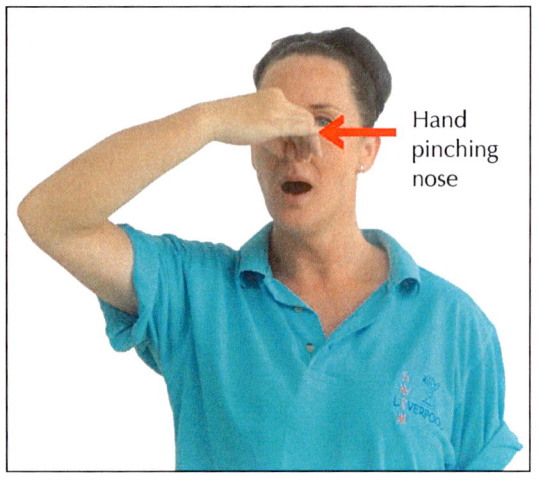

Figure 6.25
Teacher demonstrates breathing through the mouth

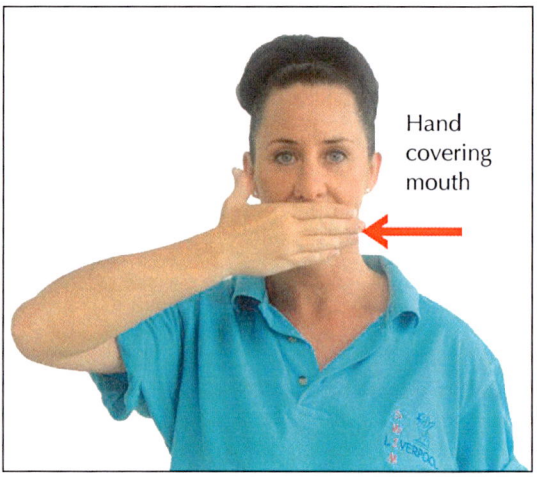

Figure 6.26
Teacher demonstrates breathing through the nose

BUILDING BLOCK 3

To establish the correct body position

The third building block is related to the body position. This is emphasised during the following practice:

Practice 6
Using two floats, one under each arm, practice a push and glide with the head down in the water.

Teaching points
• Face completely in the water. • Ears in the water. • Show the 'nodules' on the back of your neck.

Reason   To encourage the correct head and body position with the face completely submerged.

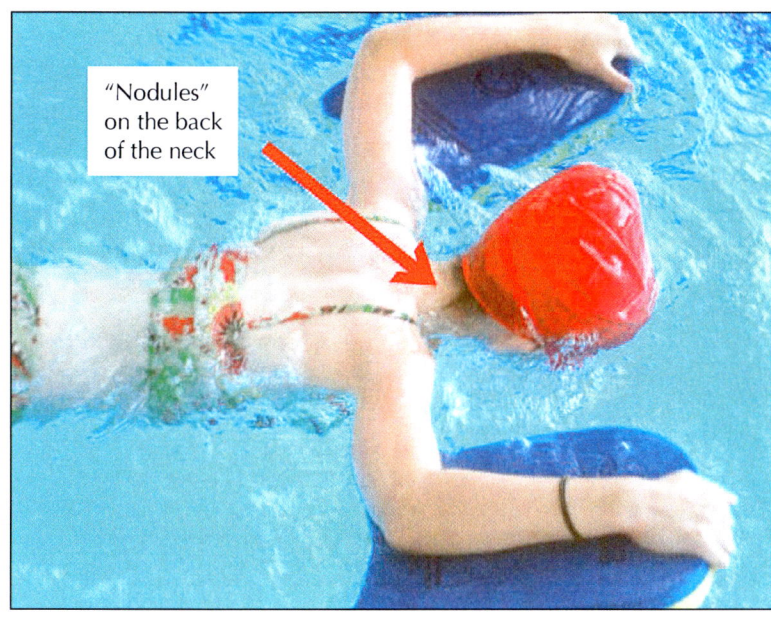

"Nodules"
on the back
of the neck

Figure 6.27
Pupil holding two floats
and performing a push and
glide

The nodules on the back of the neck are the small bony protrusions that the pupils can feel if they bend their head forwards. Once they know where these are, they can achieve the correct head position easily. Ask the pupils to show them when they put their face in the water. Pupils are often unaware of where the actual water line cuts their head and therefore teaching points referring to this are not used.

BUILDING BLOCK 4

Linking the leg action, breathing and body position together

Now is the time to link the leg action, breathing and body position together.

Practice 7	Teaching points
With two floats, one under each arm, breathe in, lower head and push off the wall. Blow out while face is down and start kicking. Lift mouth to breathe in. Then lower face slowly back into the water and breathe out again.	• Keep the leg kick continuous. • Keep the breathing even. • Breathe in when the mouth is clear of the water. • Blow out when the face is in the water.

Reason   To practise linking the leg action, breathing and body position together.

Remember, learners often experience difficulties with the breathing simply because they do not **breathe out** sufficiently. The natural reaction of novices is to gasp air into their lungs in an attempt to survive but in doing so, they do not blow sufficient air out. The result is their lungs continue to fill more than they empty until they reach what must seem close to bursting point. They then have to stop swimming to regain their breath before they make another brave attempt. To avoid practices breaking down in this way, it is essential this skill is mastered early in the building programme.

BUILDING BLOCK 5

To introduce the timing

At this stage, what we basically need is **time**. Pupils need sufficient time to:

breathe in . . . and to breathe out.

So with this in mind, we have set up a rhythm to the breathing. This is achieved by asking the pupils to:

'breathe in for a count of three' **while the head is up and**

'breathe out for three' **while the face is in the water.**

By asking the pupils to count, *'one – two – three'* as they breathe in and again *'one – two – three'* as they breathe out, they are forced to adopt a **pattern** to their breathing. Most of all this slows everything down and gives the swimmer **time** to complete the breathing cycle.

Practice 8	Teaching points
With two floats, one under each arm, practise kicking and lifting the head to breathe in for three, *'counting 1,2,3'* and lowering the head to breathe out for three, *'counting 1,2,3'*.	• Count: *'1, 2, 3 . . . 1, 2, 3'*. • Lower the head gently. • Make sure you blow out when the face is in the water.

Reason   To introduce the co-ordination of the breathing with the leg kick in a way that gives the swimmer time to breathe in and out correctly.

BUILDING BLOCK 6

Introducing the arm action

The next building block involves the arm action. By introducing the dog paddle, the first half of the front crawl pull can easily be woven into the same rhythm and timing developed in the previous practice.

Practice 9	Teaching points
The teacher demonstrates the dog paddle action. The pupils, standing in the shallow water with their feet apart and leaning forward, copy the teacher.	• Stretch forward. • Pull the hands down and back under the chin. • Stretch forward again.

Reason   To make sure the pupils understand the exact movement required by the arms.

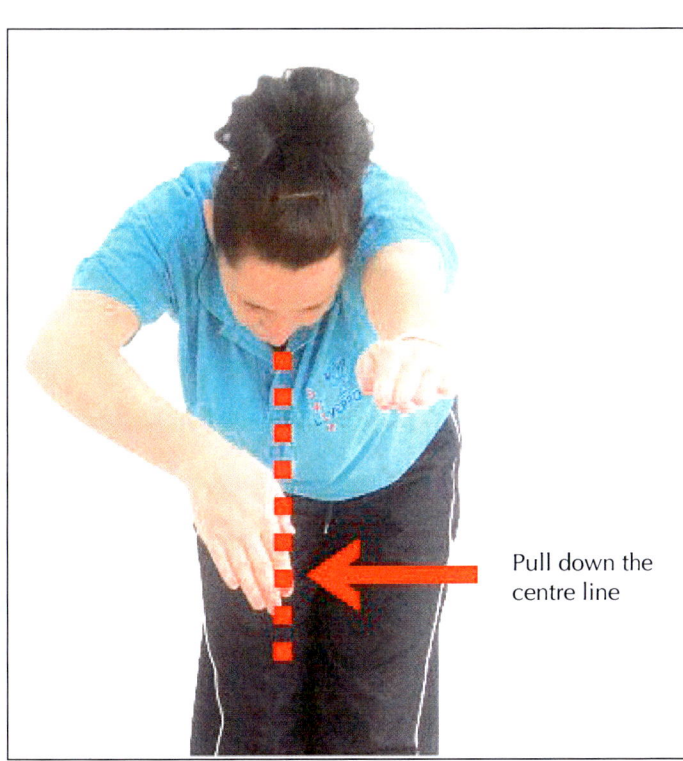

Pull down the centre line

Figure 6.28
Teacher demonstration of the dog paddle facing the class

Figure 6.29
Teacher demonstration of
the dog paddle side view

Pull back
under
the chin

 Remember it is important for the teacher to demonstrate the dog paddle action to the class from both the front and side views so the pupils fully understand the movement required.

Practice 10	Teaching points
Wearing arm bands, start with a push and glide then practise the dog paddle arm action with the leg kick.	• Reach forward. • Pull back under the chin.

Reason The arm bands give the pupils confidence and support.

Practice 11	Teaching points
Wearing arm bands and kicking hard, perform a dog paddle action adding the rhythm of the breathing by *'inhaling for three kicks'* with the head up and *'exhaling for three kicks'* with the head down.	• *'Blow the hands away'* (this forces the pupils to exhale). • Pull back under the chin. • Breathe in and count: 1, 2, 3, breathe out and count: 1,2,3.

Reason To introduce the rhythm of the breathing into the arm and leg action.

Practice 12	Teaching points
When a pupil's confidence is established, then repeat Practice 11 without the arm bands on.	• Keep the leg kick going. • Pull with the hands.

Reason   A progression from Practice 11.

BUILDING BLOCK 7

Teaching the recovery

At this stage the pupils are working with both their arms and legs. To continue the progression, the arm recovery must be taught.

Practice 13	Teaching points
The teacher demonstrates the complete arm action. The pupils copy the arm movement while standing in the shallow water. (This should be done on the side of the pool if the water is too deep.)	• Pull down until the hand is under the chin. • Push back to the thigh. • Lift the elbow out of the water and try to touch the ceiling with it. • Reach forward with the hand.

Reason   To make the pupils aware of the complete arm movement.

After the above practice, the teacher should quite simply let the pupils 'have a go' over a short distance. This is best achieved by working through the following two progressive practices (Practices 14 and 15).

Practice 14	Teaching points
Standing facing the wall, 2–3 metres from the side, push and glide towards the wall and attempt two complete strokes.	• Pull under the body. • Recover over the water. • Enter in front of the head.

Reason   By attempting two strokes towards the wall, the feeling of security is maintained.

Practice 15	Teaching points
Push and glide from the wall and swim with a dog paddle action for three quarters of a width. Then lower the head and finish the width by attempting several complete strokes with the arms recovering over the water.	• Keep the leg action continuous. • Keep the alternating arm action going.

Reason A progression on from Practice 14 once the pupils are happy leaving the security of the wall.

Practices 14 and 15 must be built up gradually, increasing either the number of strokes or the distance covered while attempting the complete stroke.

BUILDING BLOCK 8

To introduce the breathing to the side

Now it is time for the pupils to choose which side they are going to turn their head to breathe. This is determined by returning the pupils to standing in shallow water and taking up a position as shown in Figure 6.30. The teacher must check to see that:

- The head is turned to the side with the ear resting in the water.

- That the head is in the correct position.

- That the mouth is open to breathe in.

Ear resting in the water

Figure 6.30
A teacher demonstration of breathing to the side

The teacher can draw attention to the opening of the mouth to breathe by specifically pointing to their own mouth during the demonstration as shown in Figure 6.31.

Clearly pointing to
the open mouth

Figure 6.31
Teacher emphasises an open
mouth

Practice 16	Teaching points
Starting from the position described above, the pupils roll the face down into the water and blow out, then roll the head up to the side to breathe in. This practice needs to be performed several times breathing to both sides.	• Roll the face down slowly. • Roll the face up and open your mouth.

Reason   To give pupils an understanding of the correct head movement and to practise breathing on both sides.

Once Practice 16 has been attempted several times on each side, the teacher asks the pupils which side they prefer to breathe towards. It is now important to develop this awareness while moving through the water.

Practice 17	Teaching points
With one arm outstretched, supported by a float (non-breathing side) and the other arm down by the hip, kick with the head down, roll the head to the side to breathe. Maintain the rhythm by breathing in for three kicks and out for three kicks.	• Breathe in when the head is rolled to the side. • Breathe out when the face is rolled down in the water. • Count 1, 2, 3 while rolling the head to the side. • Count 1, 2, 3 while rolling the face back into the water. • Keep the whole movement smooth.

Reason   To introduce the turning of the head to the side to breathe with a rhythm that is in time with the leg kick.

BUILDING BLOCK 9

Linking the breathing to the arm action

We now come to the **most important building blocks** in terms of laying the foundations for a good front crawl stroke. Up until now, the breathing has been soundly developed and linked to the rhythm of the leg action. It is inevitable, however, that the breathing must at some time be linked to the arm action. With this in mind, we need to work through a series of practices which will enable the pupil to:

- Identify the specific phases of the arm action.

- Decide at what point in the arm pull they must start to turn their head to breathe.

What point during the arm action is the head turned to the side to breathe?

During the first part of the arm pull the hand is pressed down and back to a point some 45 centimetres under the chin and the elbow starts to bend to reach approximately 90 degrees. Throughout this part of the pull, the elbow remains high (higher than the hand) and this creates what is described as a 'boomerang' shape with the arm.

Once the pupils know what to look for, this shape can easily be seen under the water.

⚷ Looking for this shape is vital for this is the key to linking the breathing with the arm action. When the swimmer sees the boomerang shape, they turn the head to the side to breathe.

Practices 18 and 19 introduce the link between the breathing and the arm action and must be taught **before** the specific phases of the arm action are built up.

Practice 18	Teaching points
After a demonstration by the teacher, the pupils stand in shallow water, bent forward, face down with both arms outstretched. Incorporating the breathing, they practise the arm movement on the breathing side looking for the boomerang shape when the hand is under the chin.	• Pull down the centre line. • Look for the boomerang shape under the chin. • Turn the head smoothly to the side to breathe. • Push back to the hips. • Roll the face down as you recover over the water.

Reason	To make sure the pupils are aware of the shape required when the hand is under the chin.

Using a float in Practice 18 is not advisable at this stage as the float gets in the way of the face going down into the water.

Practice 19	**Teaching points**
Push and glide from the wall, start kicking with arms extended and the non-breathing arm supported by a float. Press the hand on the breathing side down and back under the chin to take a boomerang shape, and then turn the head to the side to breathe.	• Open your eyes and look for the 'boomerang' shape. • Rest your ear in the water when you turn to the side to breathe. • When the head is turned to the side, breathe in.

Reason   To practise the timing using a single arm exercise.

 Another description which we have found useful is . . . *'pull your beard'*. By getting the pupils to imagine they are pulling a long beard, this places the hand in the correct position under the chin.

Why is the boomerang shape so important?

To co-ordinate the breathing with the arm action, the signal to turn the head to the side must come **early** in the arm pull. The boomerang shape is the ideal signal as it occurs early in the stroke. When the pupils see this shape, they must start to turn the head to breathe. By the time the breath is taken, the hand has moved further back towards the hip and is now out of the way.

How to develop the specific phases of the arm action?

Once the breathing has been linked with the arms, we can progress onto developing each specific phase of the arm movement.

All the following exercises start with a push and glide from the wall. The pupils start kicking with both arms extended and the non-breathing arm supported by a float. Unless otherwise stated, the rhythm of turning the head to the side to breathe when the boomerang shape is first seen is maintained throughout.

Teaching points are listed with each practice as they are specific to that particular exercise.

Entry

Practice 20	Teaching points
Pull the arm on the breathing side down and recover over the water. Keep the head up and watch for the hand entering the water at the back end of the float.	• Reach for the float. • Enter finger tips first. • Keep wrists high.

Reason   To develop an awareness of where the hand should enter the water.

Entry close to back end of the float

Figure 6.32
Teacher demonstration of the entry position

Stretch

Practice 21	Teaching points
Repeat the above exercise but with the head down. Enter and stretch forward towards the front of the float.	• Touch the front end of the float with the forefinger.

Reason   To keep the entry in line with the shoulders.

Stretch towards the front end of the float

Figure 6.33
Teacher demonstration of the stretch forwards

Pull

Practice 22	Teaching points
After the stretch forward, press the arm down and back to make a boomerang shape under the chin. Again, emphasise that this is the point at which the head starts to turn to the side to breathe.	• Press the hand down and back under the chin. • Look for the boomerang shape.

Reason   To remind the pupils of the correct pathway followed by the hand during the first part of the pull.

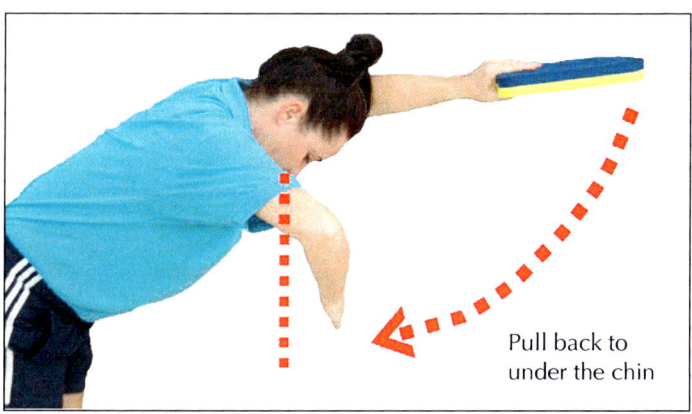

Pull back to under the chin

Figure 6.34
Teacher demonstration of the pull down

It is important that the teacher takes the time to demonstrate the pull down from both the side and the front so the pupils can visualise both the pull back under the chin and the boomerang shape of the arm.

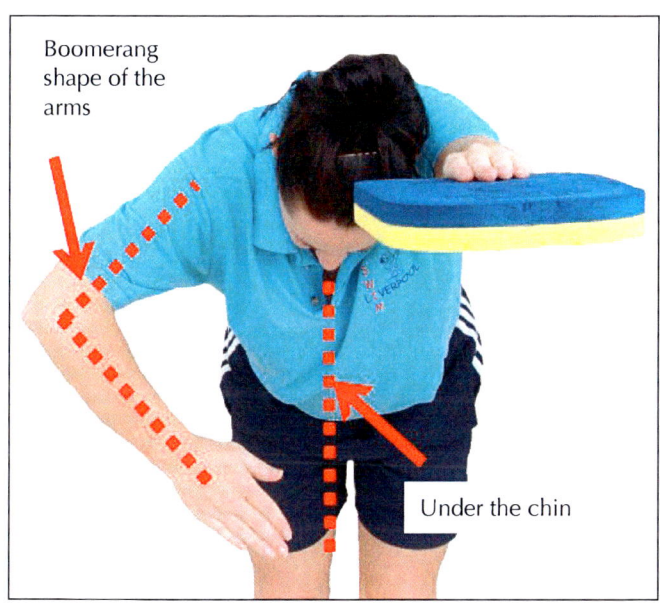

Boomerang shape of the arms

Under the chin

Figure 6.35
Front view of the teacher demonstration of the pull down

Push

Practice 23	Teaching points
Repeat Practice 22, but now as the head is turned to the side to breathe, push the hand right back to the thigh.	• Brush the thigh with the thumb.

Reason To develop the final part of the underwater arm movement.

Push back to the thigh

Figure 6.36
Teacher demonstration of the push back

Recovery

Practice 24	Teaching points
From the thigh, lift the elbow out of the water and take the hand over and back to the entry point. Roll the head back down as the hand goes forward to the entry point.	• Make the elbow touch the ceiling.

Reason To clear the arm over the water and place it back to the entry position.

Elbow lifted.

Figure 6.37
Teacher demonstration of the start of the recovery

Figure 6.38
Teacher demonstration of the recovery action

Figure 6.39
Teacher demonstration of preparation for entry

BUILDING BLOCK 10

Attempting the complete stroke

To tie together all the elements outlined in Building Block 9. There is a choice of two routes:

Route 1

The first route is to work through Practices 20 to 24 on **both** arms individually before the whole stroke is attempted from a push and glide. In this way the various phases of the arm movement are systematically developed for both arms.

It is necessary to change the breathing side during these practices but this itself is valuable because although the pupils have already chosen which side they prefer to breathe on, they do not always choose correctly. Giving the pupils the chance to breathe on the other side helps them decide which they find the most comfortable.

Route 2

The second route is quite simply to attempt the whole stroke from a push and glide immediately after completing Building Block 9 (that is, working through the Practices 20 to 24 on the favoured breathing side only).

Why eliminate the practices on the non-breathing arm?

The reason for this is because the non-breathing arm nearly always **mirrors** automatically the arm action on the breathing side. Some may find this second route surprising, but it works. If the arm practices have been carefully perfected on the breathing side, the non-breathing arm follows the same pattern of movement. It is simple and effective. Try it!

Most pupils are successful when following Route 2. If the pupil still has difficulty with the precise arm action on their non-breathing side, they need to follow Route 1.

 Before the pupils do attempt the whole stroke, the teacher needs to demonstrate the complete arm action again.

When asking the pupils to attempt the whole stroke, the teacher should give a brief resumé of the following teaching points:

- Take the stroke . . . **SLOWLY.**
- Keep the legs . . . **KICKING.**
- Breathe at the . . . **BOOMERANG.**

At this stage the teacher should be looking for a long, slow movement with the breathing woven into a co-ordinated action.

PROBLEMS AND SOLUTIONS

In some cases, one problem will produce many.

This is often the case with front crawl because the alternating arm and leg action, combined with the turning of the head to the side to breathe are intrinsically linked. A problem with the one invariably causes problems in a number of other areas.

For example,

If the head is too high:	• The back arches. • The legs sink. • The arm action becomes difficult. • Increase in frontal resistance.
If the head is too low:	• The hips pike. • The legs rise. • The legs come out of the water on recovery. • Increase in frontal resistance.
If the head is turned late in the stroke to breathe:	• The body will roll onto its side late. • This in turn causes the pulling arm to cross the centre line. • This in turn upsets the rhythm of the stroke and the direction of the kick.

It is therefore important that teachers can recognise this kind of chain reaction.

🔑 Stroke faults are obvious at the extremes, but there are many possibilities in-between.

 One of the major difficulties for novice teachers is to identify correctly what is *actually* causing the problem. It is easy to mistake the cause so take time to look carefully at the stroke as a whole and avoid 'homing in' on the first thing you see.

Arm entry

Problem 1: Arms crossing over the centre line on entry

Cause/effect	Solution
This is due to either: • The head being lifted too high and swung from side to side to avoid putting the face in the water. • A weak leg kick which fails to support the arm action.	Return to the breathing exercises to build confidence to place the face down in the water. If the legs are weak, they need to be strengthened by returning to the early leg practices.

207

Problem 2: Entering the water too wide

Cause/effect	Solution
This results in little more than a paddling action out to the side which is caused by either: • 'Bulky' shoulders restricting the amount of lift that can be achieved during the recovery. • A wide low swinging recovery with the arms straightening too soon before entry.	Exaggerated correction is required, using the teaching points given, to encourage an entry on the shoulder line. Also look at the quality of the leg action because the pupils may not be kicking strongly enough to support the arm recovery.

 Problems 1 and 2 are both the result of a poor entry position. When viewed from the front, (*as the swimmer swims towards you*), they are obvious.

Another clue is the leg action. When viewed from behind (*as the swimmer swims away from you*), they will probably be weaving from side to side as they react from the poor arm movements.

Arm pull

Problem 3: Pulling too deep at the beginning of the pull

Cause/effect	Solution
This is the result of keeping the arm too straight during the early part of the pull and causes the head and shoulders to rise and fall as each entry is made. This gives a 'bobbing' appearance to the stroke.	Go back to the pupils copying a teacher's demonstration while standing in shallow water. Emphasise just one point at a time and ingrain the pulling pattern slowly.

Problem 4: Pulling too wide on the down-sweep or across the centre line on the in-sweep

Cause/effect	Solution
This often causes excessive sideways movement when viewed from behind.	Again, go back to the pupils copying a teacher's demonstration while standing in shallow water. Emphasise just one point at a time and ingrain the pulling pattern slowly.

Problem 5: Not pushing far enough back or pushing too far back

Cause/effect	Solution
Not having enough strength to push back far enough or excessive straightening of the elbow taking the hand too far back.	As in Problems 3 and 4, go back to the pupils copying a teacher's demonstration while standing in shallow water. The teacher must emphasise just one point at a time and ingrain the pulling pattern slowly.

Arm recovery

Problem 6: Arm recovery too high or too low

Cause/effect	Solution
In both cases, the elbow does not bend and the arm remains straight: • With a high recovery, the hand is thrown up above the elbow causing the arm to straighten. • With a low recovery the hand is swung around low over the water, while the elbow remains straight.	Emphasise lifting the elbow out of the water first at the end of the pull.

A teaching point which may help is *'point the elbow to the ceiling'*.

Leg action

Problem 7: Excessive bending of the knees

Cause/effect	Solution
The problem is primarily a body position fault and an incorrect kick that is not kicking from the hips. This produces a great deal of resistance and slows the swimmer down.	Return to: • Basic push and glide with the emphasis on stretching the body hard. • Kicking exercises where the main teaching point is *'kick from the hip'*.

Problem 8: Kick too shallow

Cause/effect	Solution
This is often referred to as a flutter kick and results in a weak action. There is too little knee bend and very little movement from the hip.	The solution is again to return to the basic push and glide and develop the kick as outlined in Building Block 1. The focus should be on kicking slower and deeper.

Breathing

Problem 9: Excessive turning of the head

Cause/effect	Solution
A lack of mastery of the breathing technique is caused by: • Turning the head too high to breathe. • Turning the head to look back when breathing. • Turning the head from one side to the other out of the water.	Return to Building Block 2 and work through the breathing practices emphasising *where* in the stroke the breath is taken.

Problem 10: Lifting the head to the front to breathe

Cause/effect	Solution
This problem is caused by fear of putting the face in the water.	To eliminate this fear, return to the confidence building exercises. This is necessary before progress can be made.

Body position

Problem 11: Head too high or too low

Cause/effect	Solution
This increases frontal resistance and can lead to many problems. It is the result of a lack of awareness of where the head should be held to maintain a good streamlined position.	There should be a return to the push and glide practices to establish the correct head position.

Problem 12: Excessive body roll

Cause/effect

This is often the result of one of the following:

- A straight arm recovery with a pathway which takes the hand high over the swimmer's back.
- Excessive turning of the head to breathe.
- Pulling across the centre line.
- Pulling too deep.
- Poor balance due to a weak leg action.

Solution

The teacher must make an assessment to determine the cause.

The solution invariably requires returning to a single arm practice to improve the arm pull. The swimmer must be encouraged to lift the elbow from the water first on the recovery and keep the elbow higher than the wrist.

If the problem is caused by a weak leg action, more time must be given to strengthen the kick.

Summary

It is essential that practices are not rushed or skipped.

Remember, many stroke corrections rely on **slowing** everything down to give the swimmer the **time** to co-ordinate all the components of the stroke.

THE IMPROVEMENT CIRCLE

The improvement circle for front crawl is built around three core skills.

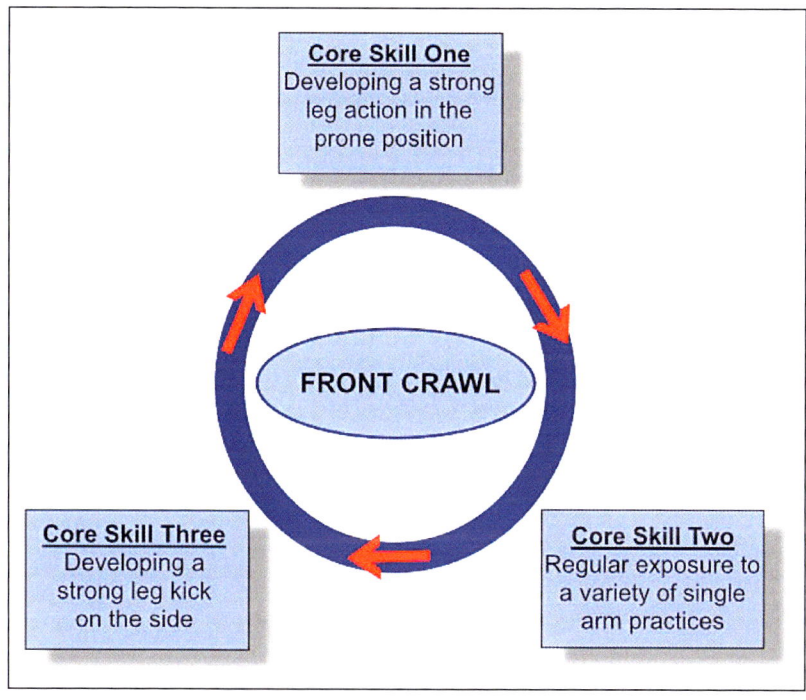

Figure 6.40
The improvement circle for front crawl

Core skill 1: Developing a strong leg action in the prone position

Improvement in the front crawl stroke has to be built around developing a strong and effective leg kick. To emphasise the point, a competent leg action:

- **Helps maintain a stable horizontal body position.**
- **Assists in balancing the alternating arm action.**
- **Adds to overall propulsion.**

It is vital to expose the improver to a range of leg practices to condition and strengthen the movement. Where possible, elements of the arm action and breathing can be integrated into these practices even though the primary purpose is to develop the leg action.

Front crawl kicking practices with support
1. Kicking holding a kick board at the sides with arms outstretched and head raised. This forces the pupil to kick the legs harder. Breathing is also no problem so greater distances can be achieved
2. Kicking laying the forearms over the top of the kickboard so the finger tips grip the front edge. This practice raises the upper torso higher in the water and forces the legs to work even harder than in Practice 1
3. Kicking with one arm outstretched holding a kickboard and the other arm down by the side. This allows regular breathing to the side to occur
4. Holding the kickboard in a vertical position kick pushing the flat surface through the water. The swimmer kicks against the extra resistance with arms outstretched.

Additional kicking can be practised working as a pair or as a team. The activities are limited only by the teacher's imagination. The following are just some examples:

- As a pair, the swimmers perform a team relay with number one kicking across the width, passing the float to number two who in turn kicks across the width.
- In teams of three or four, holding onto a woggle, the team kick across the pool competing against other teams.

The ability to kick without support is an important skill as it not only develops the leg action but also forces the pupil to work harder at maintaining a good horizontal body position. Without the support of a small float, there is an increased fatigue effect so in the first instances the distances attempted need to be kept short to ensure the skill does not deteriorate quickly. With practice, however the pupil's skill will improve.

Front crawl kicking practices without support
1. Kicking without a float, face down between outstretched arms and one hand on top of the other (as in the front glide position). 2. Kicking without a float, both arms down by the side and face in the water 3. Kicking without a float, one arm outstretched and the other arm down by the side.

As the swimmer gets more proficient, kicking under water can be introduced. When the swimmer is submerged they are able to feel the down beat of the kick more easily.

Core skill 2: Single arm practices

Once a strong leg kick is established and a good horizontal body position can be maintained, a variety of single arm practices can be devised either with or without support to develop and co-ordinate the arm action and the breathing with the leg kick. Single arm practices also allow the swimmer to concentrate on one arm at a time and to perform ever increasing distances without the skill level deteriorating.

The two body positions normally used are:

- **With the supporting arm out in front.**
- **With the supporting arm down by the side.**

There is benefit in practising both.

When the supporting arm is out in front, the swimmer's body is extended and more stable in the water and it is easier for the swimmer to enter and stretch out before the catch position is reached. If the supporting arm is placed down by the side, the upper torso and hips are forced to work together to rotate as one and balance the stroke.

With the supporting arm out in front, a small float can easily be held. The teaching practices can be set up in a variety of ways – some examples are presented below:

Single arm practices with the supporting arm out in front holding the back end of a small float
Note: These practices are performed holding the 'back end' of a small float in order to create enough space for the swimmer to perform the action correctly and stretch out underwater after the entry is made.
1. Holding the back end of a float with the supporting arm, perform one width using the right arm only then change arms and perform a second width using the left arm only. 2. A variation of Practice 1 is to perform a set number of single arm strokes (for example, five strokes) with one arm, then change and perform the same number with the other arm. 3. Combine full stroke into the practice by first performing one width right arm only followed by one width left arm only, then two widths full stroke. 4. Work across the width alternating one stroke left arm only followed by one stroke right arm only. This is a 'catch-up' exercise with support.

The same Practices 1 to 4 listed above can be performed without a float.

As the swimmer becomes more competent, the practices can also be performed with the supporting arm down by the side. This is, however, more difficult as the front support is now removed.

 Remember:
- Give equal practice to both the left and right arms so the stroke is developed in a balanced way. There is also great benefit in practising breathing to both sides.
- For variety also perform the single arm practices pulling with a pull buoy or perform the practices with the fingers closed in a 'fist' position. This practice encourages the forearm to be used to pull the swimmer through the water.
- The teaching points can be any of those highlighted in the building programme or shown in the summary list of what to look for in a good front crawl stroke.

Core skill 3: Developing the leg kick on the side

The pupil must become competent at kicking in a variety of positions, particularly on their side. When performing the front crawl stroke, the body roll which occurs naturally causes the legs to kick diagonally as described previously. This therefore needs to be an action which is developed and strengthened.

All too often, the teachers focus is on kicking on the front and kicking on the side is a novelty. Kicking on the side however, is an essential skill to master. Once a swimmer becomes competent at this, many drill progressions can be developed to focus on and improve specific parts of the stroke.

Kicking on the side can be performed in two positions:

- **Kicking with one arm extended.**
- **Kicking with both arms held down by the thighs.**

Kicking on the side with one arm extended is easier. The extended arm can be supported by holding onto a small float and the arm action and breathing can more easily be integrated into the practices.

Kicking on the side with one arm extended

1. Kicking one width on one side, before changing to perform a second width on the other side.
2. Kicking twelve kicks on the side before performing one single stroke cycle (pull and recovery) with the upper arm (arm down by the side). Then hold the side kicking position for another twelve kicks before attempting another stroke cycle.
3. As for Practice 2 but gradually reducing the number of kicks performed on each side until the rhythm is similar to that performed during the full stroke.
4. Starting on the right side and perform a set number of kicks before performing half a stroke cycle (recovery with the left arm, take hold of the float before pulling with the right arm). Having rolled onto the left side, the set number of kicks is performed again before another half a stroke cycle is performed, taking the pupil back onto their right side.
5. As for Practice 4 but gradually reduce the number of kicks performed on each side.

The practices listed above can be performed both with and without support. When practised without support, the freedom gained allows for the opportunity to integrate fuller stroke work into a variety of progressive sequences.

SUMMARY OF THINGS TO LOOK FOR IN A GOOD FRONT CRAWL

Body position

- Position of the head and hips are key factors.
- Hips close to the surface throughout the stroke.
- Water cuts hairline when face is down in the water.
- Head – hips – legs remain in line throughout the stroke.
- Shoulders roll in time with the arm action.
- Hips and legs roll with the shoulders.
- Look for the same degree of roll on left and right sides (45 degrees).
- The horizontal streamline position is maintained throughout while rolling smoothly around the long axis co-ordinated with the arm action and breathing.

Leg kick

- Legs kick up and down close together.
- Kick up with straight legs.
- Leg kick down in a strong 'whip-like' action.
- Feet extended on downbeat.
- Keep the ankles 'loose'.
- Leg action continuous.
- Work the legs to maintain a horizontal body position.
- Direction of the kick continuously changes as the swimmer rolls from a flat position onto their left and right sides.

Arm pull

- Entry is 'soft' and extended – arm is almost straight on entry.
- Hands enter between centre line and shoulder line.
- Finger tips slide into the water.
- Hands sweep under the chin.
- Look for the 'boomerang' shape - 90 degree elbow bend.
- Push back to the thigh is strong and vigorous.
- Elbow remains higher than the hands during the pull.
- Hands trace an 'S' shaped pulling pattern.
- Throughout the 'S' shaped pull the hands continually change their pitch.

Arm recovery

- Hands exit close to the hip.
- Elbow is lifted from water first.
- Elbow remains high throughout recovery.
- Hands sweep in a low semicircular path passing close to the head.
- As the elbow passes the head, it extends in preparation for entry.

Breathing

- Face rolls around slowly in time with the arm pull.
- Head remains in line with the body.
- Lower ear remains close to the extended lower arm.
- Breath taken with mouth just clear of the water.
- Breathe in as the arm starts its recovery.
- Breathe out when the face is in the water.

Timing/co-ordination/rhythm

- Smooth, balanced and continuously flowing.
- 2/4/6 kicks to one arm cycle.
- Breathing once every arm cycle.
- The hand track through the water by both the left and right arms should be symmetrical and balanced.

FRONT CRAWL STROKE ASSESSMENT SHEET

Name of swimmer:		Age:	
Stroke/activity:		Date:	
Analysis carried out by:			

BODY POSITION

Key questions to ask	Teachers observations and comments
• How streamlined is the body throughout the stroke? • What is the hip position throughout the stroke? • How close to the surface is the leg kick? • What is the head position when not breathing? • What is the head position when breathing? • What is the extent of the body roll? • Is the body roll even on both sides? • Do the shoulders, hips and legs roll together as one?	

LEG ACTION

Key questions to ask	Teachers observations and comments
• How strong is the leg kick? • Is the leg kick continuous? • What is the depth of the kick? • To what extent do the feet break the surface? • How close are the legs during the kick? • How strong is the 'whip' down of the lower legs? • Are the feet extended on the down beat? • How does the body roll effect the leg kick? • How many kicks are there per stroke cycle? • What is the rhythm / tempo of the kick?	

ARM ACTION

Key questions to ask	Teachers observations and comments
• Is the entry made between the centre and shoulder lines? • Do the hands enter finger tip first? • How close to the head is the entry position? • Is there a stretch forwards under the surface after entry? • Do the hands pull down under the chin? • Can you see a 'boomerang' shape (a 90 degree elbow bend)? • Do the hands push back towards the thigh? • Do the hands trace an 'S' shaped pulling pattern under the body? • How do the hands change their pitch during the 'S' shape pull? • Does the elbow remain high throughout the pull? • Is the arm action continuous?	

ARM RECOVERY

Key questions to ask	Teachers observations and comments
• Is the elbow lifted from the water first? • Does the elbow remain higher than the hand throughout the recovery? • Do the hands exit the water close to the hips? • Do the hands remain close to the surface throughout the recovery? • Do the hands pass close to the head?	

BREATHING

Key questions to ask	Teachers observations and comments
• Does the head turn to the side to breathe? • How smoothly does the head turn? • Does the head remain in line with the body? • Does the lower ear remain close to the extended lower arm? • When is the breath taken? • How often is the breath taken? • What is the effect of breathing to the side on the overall stroke?	

TIMING AND CO-ORDINATION

Key questions to ask	Teachers observations and comments
• What is the timing between the leg and arm actions? • What is the timing between the breathing and the arm action? • Is there a glide in the stroke? • What is the overall rhythm of the stroke? • Is the arm pull symmetrical? • How smooth and continuous is the overall stroke?	

FINAL IMPRESSIONS AND COMMENTS

Key questions to ask	Teachers observations and comments
• How effective is the stroke? • What contribution do you think the legs make to propulsion? • What contribution do you think the arms make to propulsion? • How flexible do you think the swimmer is? • How strong do you think the swimmer?	

ALTERNATIVE ASSESSMENT SHEET FOR FRONT CRAWL

Name of swimmer:		Age:	

Date of assessment:	

While we favour the previous assessment sheet where the teacher is forced to make their own observations and record exactly what they see, some may prefer a more structured approach where a simple grading system is used. This is presented below:

1 = Poor   2 = Some improvement needed   3 = Good

GENERAL IMPRESSIONS OF THE STROKE

Element of the stroke assessed:	Grade:		
Efficiency of stroke	1	2	3
Continuity of arms and legs	1	2	3
Smoothness of movements	1	2	3
Effectiveness of stroke	1	2	3
Degree of flexibility	1	2	3
Strength of pupil	1	2	3
Comments:			

BODY POSITION

Element of the stroke assessed:	Grade:		
Horizontal (head, hips, feet)	1	2	3
Lateral (side to side)	1	2	3
Body roll around long axis	1	2	3
Degree of buoyancy	1	2	3
General streamlining	1	2	3
Comments:			

LEG ACTION

Element of the stroke assessed:	Grade:		
Action of the kick down (hips, knees, feet)	1	2	3
Action of the kick up (hips, knees, feet)	1	2	3
Depth of action	1	2	3
Width of action	1	2	3
Degree of ankle flexibility	1	2	3
Rhythm/tempo	1	2	3
Effort and quality of action	1	2	3
Contribution to propulsion	1	2	3
Contribution to balancing the stroke	1	2	3
Comments:			

ARM ACTION

Element of the stroke assessed:	Grade:		
Entry position	1	2	3
Action of pull	1	2	3
Action of push back	1	2	3
Action of release and exit	1	2	3
Action of recovery	1	2	3
Hand track through the water	1	2	3
Effectiveness of the sculling action	1	2	3
Degree of elbow bend	1	2	3
Maintenance of high elbow during pull	1	2	3
Maintenance of high elbow during recovery	1	2	3
Level of flexibility	1	2	3
Continuity of action	1	2	3
Effectiveness in generating propulsion	1	2	3
Comments:			

BREATHING

Element of the stroke assessed:	Grade:		
Degree of head movement	1	2	3
Smoothness of movement	1	2	3
When the breath is taken	1	2	3
Breathing pattern	1	2	3
Effect on total stroke	1	2	3
Comments:			

TIMING AND CO-ORDINATION

Element of the stroke assessed:	Grade:		
Timing of leg and arm actions	1	2	3
Timing of breathing	1	2	3
Continuity of stroke	1	2	3
Overall rhythm of the stroke	1	2	3
Comments:			

Final impressions and comments:

Assessment carried out by:	

FRONT CRAWL

Front Crawl is the stroke that we all like to swim
If we enter a race, we think we can win.
Giving a sense of speed and thrills
It's a streamlined stroke, without any frills.
The body is flat and as straight as can be
The head kept still, the feet, you just see
The legs kick up and down non-stop
Work from the hips, with ankles 'a flop'
The hand goes in, just in front of the head,
Thumb touching the 'centre line', it is said.
The hand travels on, pulling back to the thigh,
That's fine! But how do I breathe? You sigh.
Your eyes see the hand just under the chin,
Your brain says 'turn your head and breathe in'
If you breathe at this point, you have to blow out
And breathe in! Explosively - no doubt.
Put all together and when this is done,
You'll see the Front Crawl can really be fun.

Pat Parkes

Chapter 7

Breaststroke

Main Focus:

- Why is breaststroke the slowest of the four strokes?
- Why is the breaststroke difficult for some pupils?
- How wide is the breaststroke leg kick?
- What pathway do the hands follow through the water?
- How do the hands change their pitch during the arm pull?
- When is the breath taken?
- How is the timing best described?
- What is the rhythm of the stroke?
- A 5 stage building programme
- The identification of 6 main problems
- An improvement circle built on three core skills
- A summary of what to look for in a good stroke
- Usable stroke assessment sheets
- A summary poem by Patricia Parkes

Chapter 7

Breaststroke

INTRODUCTION

The importance of breaststroke

It is essential that pupils are taught to swim the breaststroke because the skills used to perform this stroke have many uses, such as:

- **Leisure swimming**: Adults frequently use this stroke to exercise at a leisurely pace.

- **Competition**: It is one of the four recognised competitive strokes.

- **Survival**: Children like to work for and gain survival badges and breaststroke plays a large part in the survival awards.

- **Life saving**: The skills are used in various ways such as towing and approaching a difficult subject.

- **Water polo**: The breaststroke leg action is used when marking opponents and while carrying out many throwing skills.

- **Synchronised swimming**: The execution and linking of figures and set pieces often involve the use of breaststroke skills.

Learning breaststroke

The problem is that teachers may find they do not achieve a very fast rate of success when first teaching this stroke. Many children do not learn the stroke quickly because:

- The movement is totally different from the other strokes.

- The leg action is not a natural movement and can be a difficult skill to master.

- Teachers themselves may not be proficient performers in the stroke and so feel less comfortable teaching it.

Breaststroke is the slowest of the four strokes because:

- **Resistance is greatest** as all the arm movements including the recovery take place in the water.

- It is the **least streamlined** of the four strokes since the upper torso is lifted above the water every stroke to allow the breath to be taken.

- The alternating pull and kick makes **continuous propulsion difficult**.

Therefore because the stroke lacks speed and 'excitement', children may be less willing to learn the stroke.

These difficulties too often tempt the teacher to teach another stroke where they may get success more quickly. This is particularly true if they adopt a 'swim at any price' approach or are under pressure to move children on quickly through a learn-to-swim programme.

Conversely, there are some pupils who find the stroke quite natural to perform. They find they can soon achieve a turned-out foot position during the leg kick and once mastered, they gain success quickly. This often results in a definite split in ability among a class of children with some learning more quickly than others.

 The teacher must be careful not to hold back those pupils who show a natural ability for the stroke or to move on too quickly those who take longer to pick up the skills. The teacher must be prepared to split a class into ability groups and make valuable use of any assistant teachers or water helpers.

WHAT TO LOOK FOR IN A GOOD STROKE

Body position

In breaststroke, the body position is continually changing due to the nature of the stroke.

From the side

The body position alternates between the two positions; the angled position as the breath is taken and the streamlined position at the end of the kick.

The body position as the breath is taken

Look for:
• The upper body (the shoulders and chest) rising as the head is lifted to the front to breathe. • The hips and legs sinking lower in the water (action/reaction). • An inclined body position from the head down to the knees with minimum flexion (bending) at the hips as the legs recover.

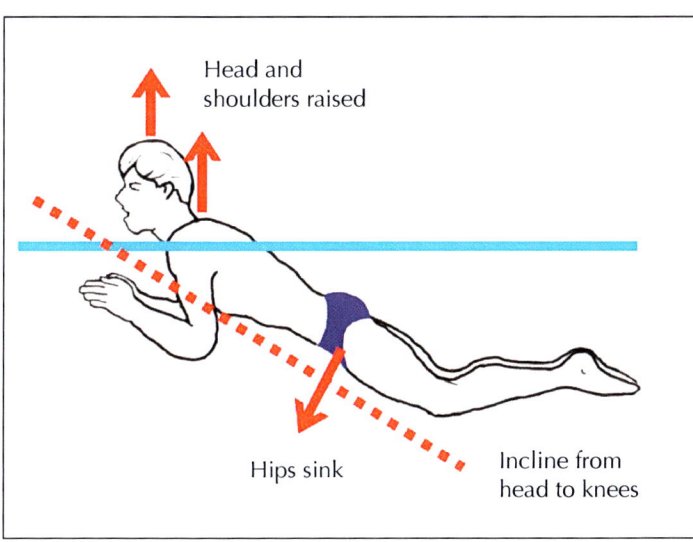

Head and shoulders raised

Hips sink

Incline from head to knees

Figure 7.1
The body position in breaststroke as the breath is taken

 The horizontal body position in breaststroke is more angled at this point than for any other stroke.

The body position at the end of the leg kick

Look for:
• A streamlined position as the head drops back into the water and the legs drive back.

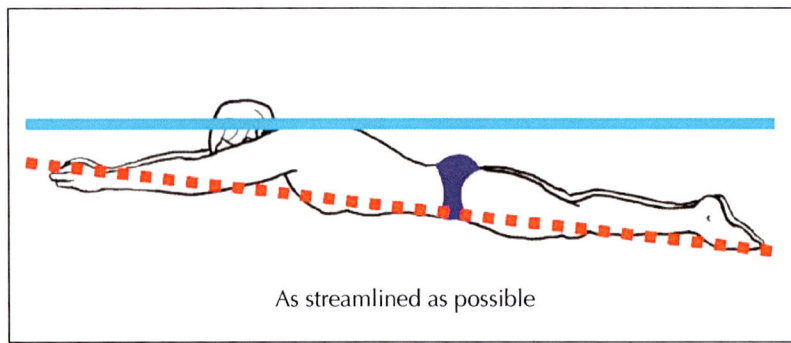

Figure 7.2
The body position at the end of the breaststroke leg kick

As streamlined as possible

From the front

Look for:
• The shoulders remaining level throughout the complete stroke cycle.

Shoulders level

Figure 7.3
The shoulder position in breaststroke as the breath is taken

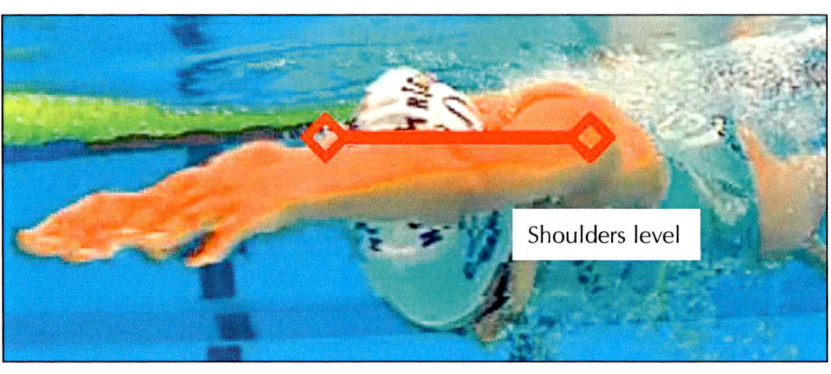

Shoulders level

Figure 7.4
The shoulder position in breaststroke at the end of the leg kick

Discussion on the body position

The need to raise the head and shoulders vertically up above the water surface during every stroke to take a breath creates a continually changing body position. The degree of lifting of the shoulders will vary among pupils. Some will only raise the shoulders sufficient to allow the mouth to just clear the water, while others will raise the shoulders much higher so that the head is completely clear of the surface.

If the first part of the arm pull is fairly narrow and performed with a strong sweep down, this will lift the shoulders high due to an action/reaction effect. The shoulder lift will not be so high with pupils who use a wider arm action where the sweep down is less during this first phase of the pull.

🔑 It is important that there is no 'conscious' lifting of the head up and down to breathe but that the head remains still and is raised above the water naturally as the shoulders are raised.

The raising of the upper body will increase frontal resistance, but a good stretched position during the glide phase will help to reduce this.

Leg action

The recovery and propulsive phases of the leg action must be performed with both legs working **simultaneously and symmetrically**.

Recovery

Look for:
• The heels being drawn up towards the bottom.   • The heels and knees being close to hip width apart.

Legs start extended

Figure 7.5
The start of the breaststroke leg recovery

233

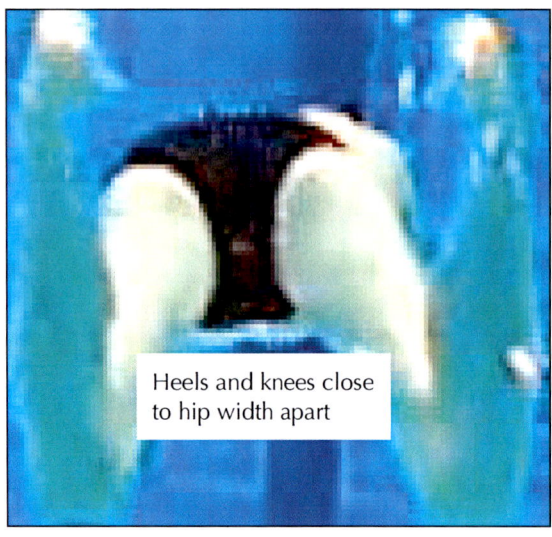

Figure 7.6
An end of the breaststroke leg recovery

Heels and knees close
to hip width apart

At the end of the recovery

Look for:
• The feet turning out ready for the start of the propulsive phase.

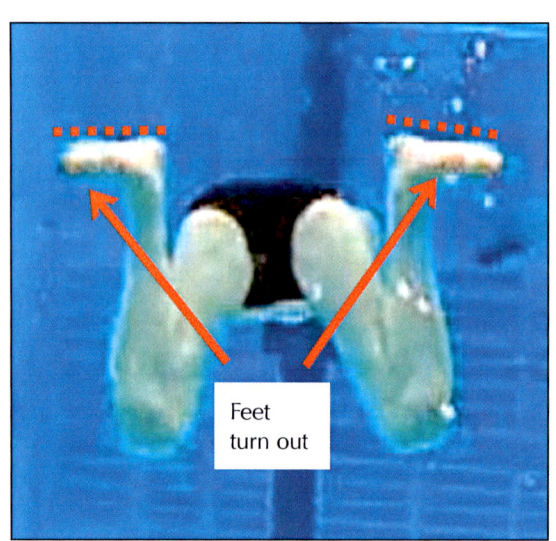

Figure 7.7
The end of the recovery phase of the leg kick
in breaststroke

Feet
turn out

Look for:
• An angle between the upper leg and the trunk of between 110 to 140 degrees. • The lower leg being at a near right angle to the surface of the water.

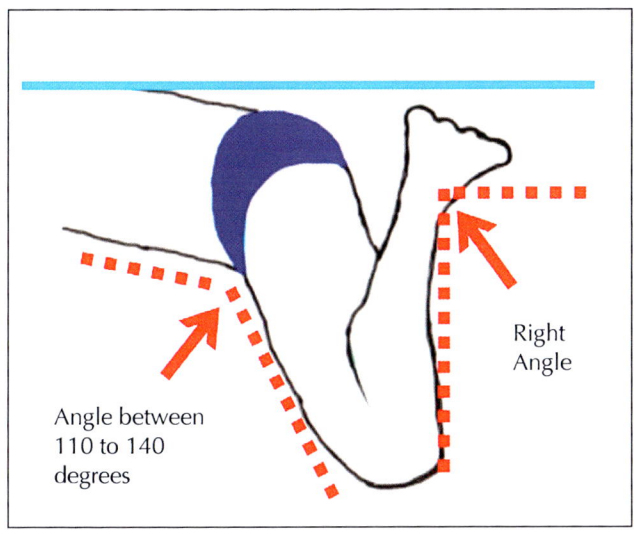

Figure 7.8
The two checkpoints to look for at the end of the recovery

From behind

Look for:
• The legs forming a 'W' shape.

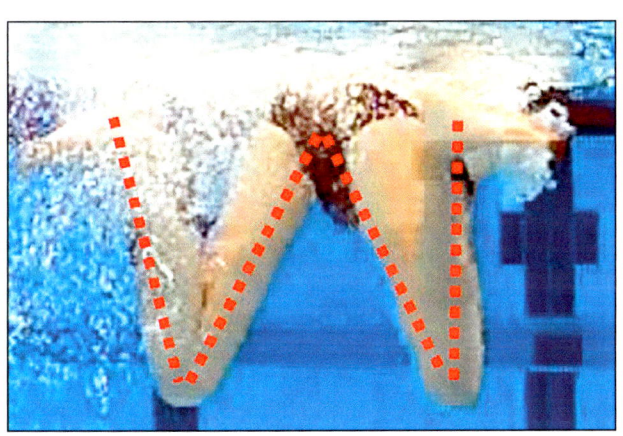

Figure 7.9
The 'W' shape of the legs during the recovery

The 'W' shape can also be seen from the front.

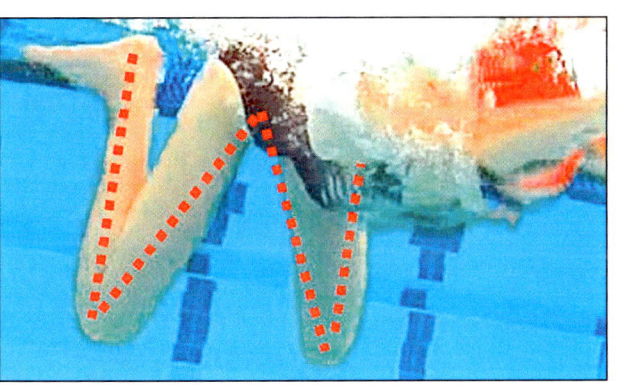

Figure 7.10
A front view of the 'W' shape of the legs during the recovery

The width of the knees may vary, from being fairly close, to a position just outside the body, depending on the flexibility of the swimmer.

During the recovery, the feet turn out to achieve a dorsiflex position. In an ecclesiastical sense, you could say . . . *'the toes point east and west and the soles to heaven.'*

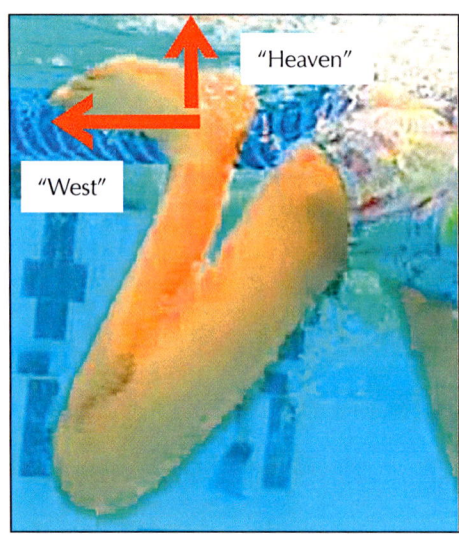

Figure 7.11
The feet turning out at the end of the breaststroke leg recovery

Propulsion

There are two phases to the propulsive movement.

Phase 1

Look for:
• An initial drive back by the feet and lower leg following a curved pathway sweeping outwards and backwards.

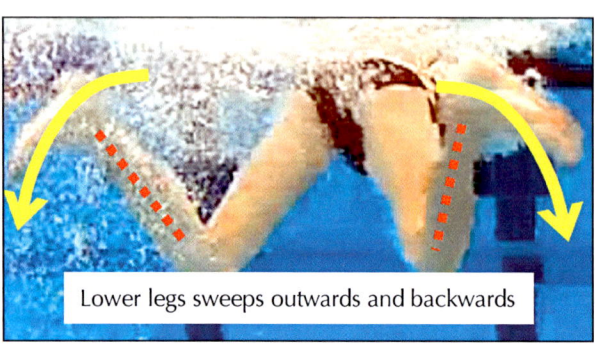

Figure 7.12
Initial kick out and back

236

Phase 2

Look for:
• An extension of the knees, as the feet complete their drive back and come together.

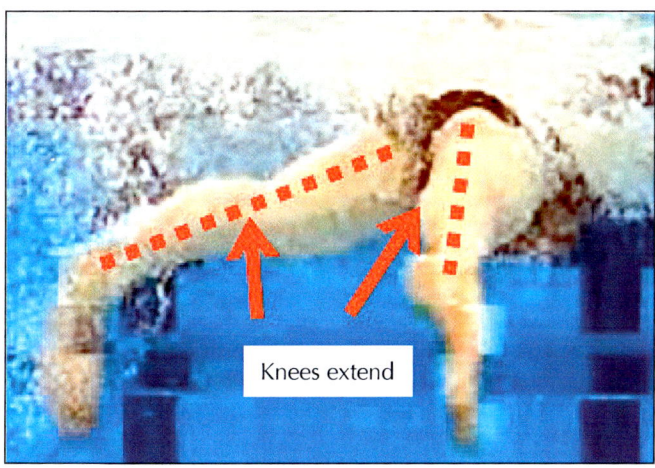

Knees extend

Figure 7.13
Extension at the end of the kick

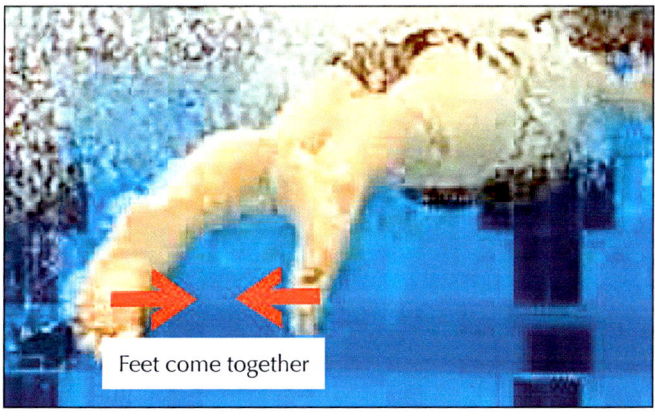

Feet come together

Figure 7.14
Feet coming together at the end of the breaststroke kick

 During this movement the feet are rotated from their dorsiflex position to a toes pointed position (plantar flexion).

Discussion on the leg kick

Types of kick

It is surprising that many authorities still talk about two styles of leg kick:

- The **wedge kick**
- The **whip kick**.

Novice teachers who become familiar with these terms often fall into a trap when observing the leg action. They see a narrow leg action as a whip kick and a wider leg action as a wedge kick.

Even more blinkered is the frequently held belief that competitive swimmers only use a narrow whip-like leg action. As a result they teach novices a wide, wedge-type kick, frequently reinforcing this by issuing the following instructions to guide the pupils through the movement:

'*Up – out – together*' .

This 'up - out - together' concept is easy and they think it is going to be the answer to their prayers . . . but this is not the case. What often develops is a leg action involving three distinct movements with a pause between each:

'*Up (stop) – out (stop) – together (stop)*'

This causes a number of problems:

- It produces a very jerky action without any flow to the movement.
- It results in a slow, inefficient action and the novice swimmer invariably ends up struggling to remain on the surface. This in turn, increases the need to use buoyancy aids.
- There is also a tendency to draw the feet up together allowing the knees to part. This makes it even more difficult to turn the feet out in a dorsiflex position.
- The pupils perform the movement in completely the opposite direction so they end up moving backwards.

Teaching a first class kick

It is time to change our thinking and abandon the old labels of a wedge or whip kick, and think in terms of just one kick which is streamlined and effective:

- **Streamlined** – a fairly narrow action working as much as possible within the confines of the body line.
- **Effective** – turning the feet out in a good dorsiflex position and making sure that the lower part of the leg is driven back to perform the propulsive movement.

There will be some individual differences in the ability to turn the feet out in a dorsiflex position and in the width of the **rounding-out** movement but this should not be interpreted as a different type of kick. As with all strokes, there should be some level of tolerance to these differences.

By looking at the stroke as only having one type of kick, we believe the novice teacher will find the stroke easier to teach.

A lot of teachers become confused about which part of the leg action is the recovery phase. They mistakenly think it is the last part of the kick, as the feet are squeezed together. This is incorrect. Remember the recovery is the drawing of the legs up to the bottom.

The leg track through the water

The leg movement in breaststroke is difficult to perform because the limb track required is very different from any of the other strokes. The curved pathway and the dorsiflexion of the feet is something which some children find unnatural to achieve.

The pupils cannot see this fairly complex movement and because of this, the building programme must emphasise helping the children feel the correct movement of the legs. The pupils need to understand the movement as two symmetrical sweeps which viewed from above can be seen in Figure 7.15.

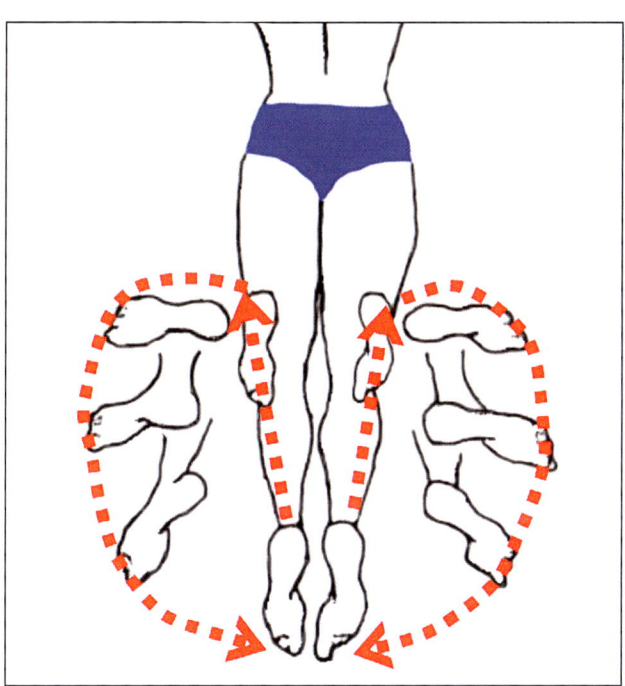

Figure 7.15
The pathway of the feet in the breaststroke leg kick

Remember the limb track of the leg kick through the water is made up of three components. These are shown in Figures 7.16a to 7.16c.

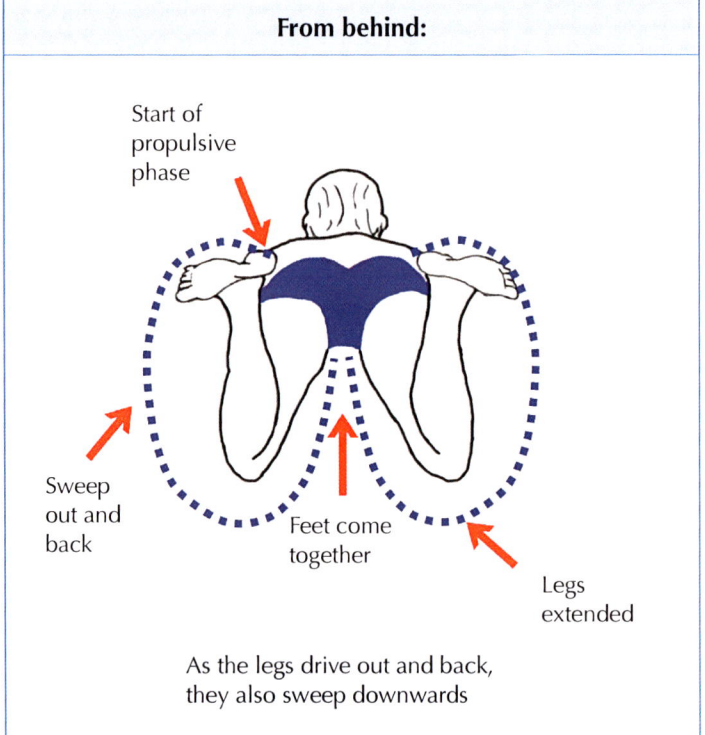

From behind:

Start of propulsive phase

Sweep out and back

Feet come together

Legs extended

As the legs drive out and back, they also sweep downwards

Figure 7.16a
The breaststroke leg track through the water as viewed from behind

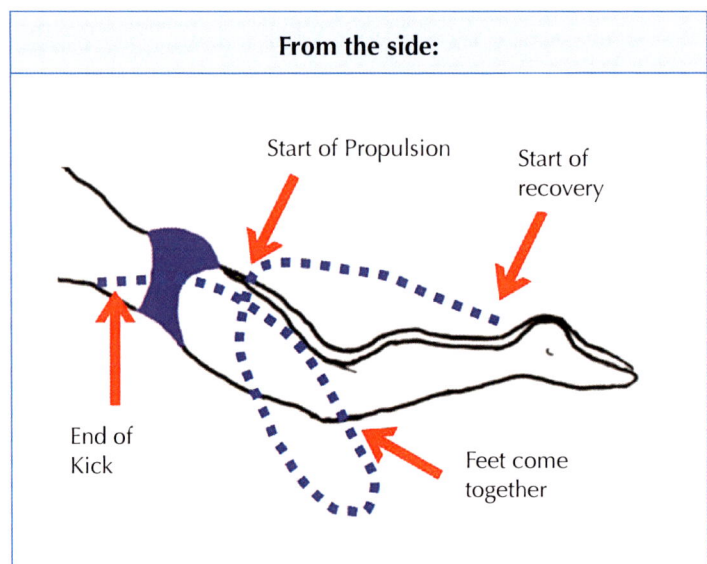

From the side:

Start of Propulsion

Start of recovery

End of Kick

Feet come together

Figure 7.16b
The breaststroke leg track as viewed from the side

Breaststroke

From above:

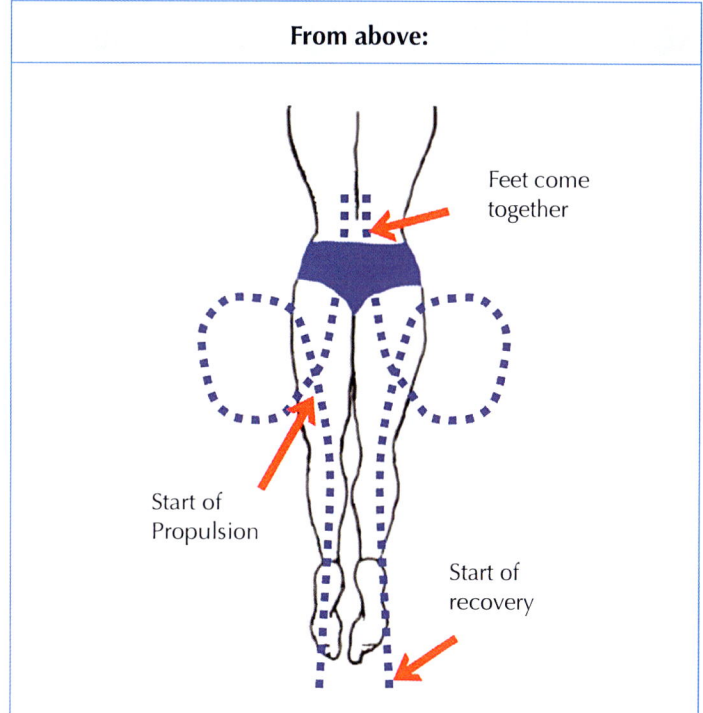

Feet come together

Start of Propulsion

Start of recovery

Figure 7.16c
The breaststroke leg track as viewed from above

Arm action

Movement to catch position

Look for:
• From the extended position, the hands pressing out and slightly down, to gain a purchase on the water.   • The hands being approximately shoulder width apart and about 15 centimetres below the surface of the water as the catch point reached.

Thumbs down on press out

Figure 7.17
Initial press out to the catch position

241

Figure 7.18
Above view of the initial press out to the catch position

Press out to shoulder width

Propulsive phase

The sweep out

Look for:
• The hands sweeping out, down and back in a curved pathway ending in a position just below or wide of the elbows.

Figure 7.19
The start of the sweep out in the breaststroke arm action

Hands sweep out and down

At the end of the sweep out

Look for:
• The lower arms sweeping more downwards. • The hands changing their pitch during the movement, by rotating slightly so the palms end up facing backwards. • The elbows remaining high throughout the movement.

Figure 7.20
The end of the sweep down in the breaststroke arm action

Lower arms sweep down

Elbows high

Hands facing backwards

Figure 7.21
An above view of the end position of the sweep down in the breaststroke arm action

The sweep in

After the sweep out, the hands must be brought in. This is achieved by a 'rounding out' movement where the hands change their pathway and sweep in towards the centre line.

Look for:
• The arms being brought in close to the body. • The hands changing their pitch again, rotating so the palms face in and the thumbs turn up as they sweep towards each other.

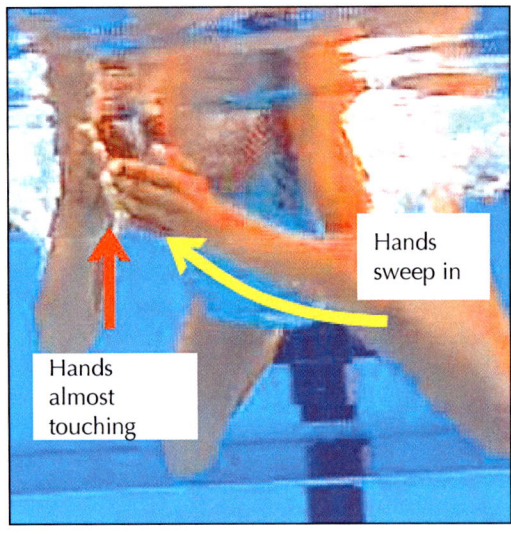

Figure 7.22
The in-sweep in the breaststroke arm action

At the end of the sweep in

Look for:

- The hands are almost touching just under the chin.
- The elbows tucked in close to the body.

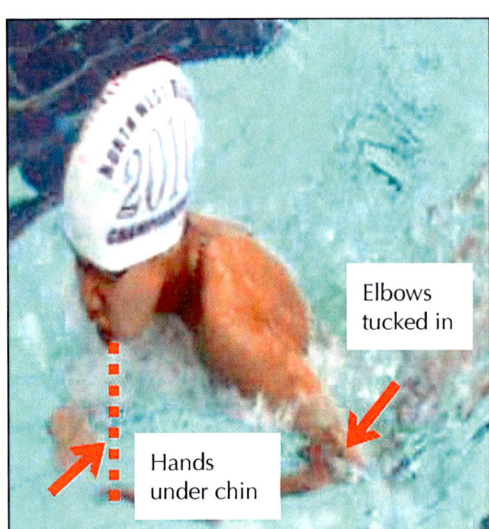

Figure 7.23
The position at the end of the in-sweep

Recovery

Look for:
• The hands being pushed forward with the palms down, on or just under the surface of the water. • At the end of the recovery, the arms reaching full extension.

Hands palms down

Arms extended

Figure 7.24
The end of the arm recovery in breaststroke

Discussion on the arm action

Breaststroke is often thought of as a leg dominant stroke with the arm action playing a much lesser role in terms of propulsion. This is just not true.

The arm action is a major source of propulsion and needs to be taught with the same amount of care as other strokes, identifying the specific areas throughout the movement.

Swimmers should also think of the stroke pattern followed by their hands as tracing two elliptical circles. These are shown in Figure 7.25.

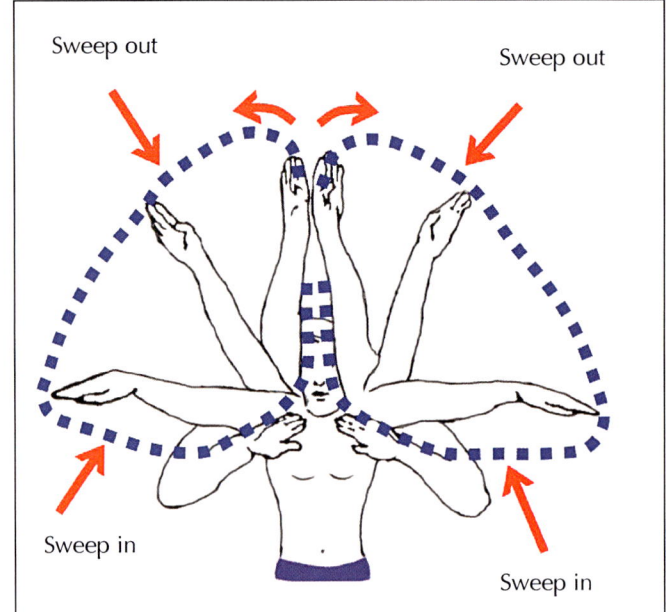

Figure 7.25
The pupils view of the pathway of the hands during the breaststroke pull

This is the hand pattern which the teachers need to encourage the pupils to visualise.

Teachers should look for this and compare what their pupils are doing with the three dimensional hand tracks through the water shown in Figures 7.26a to 7.26c.

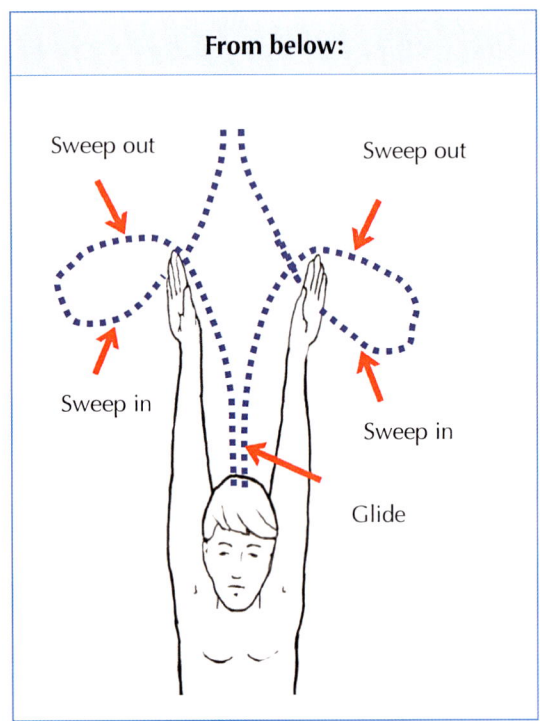

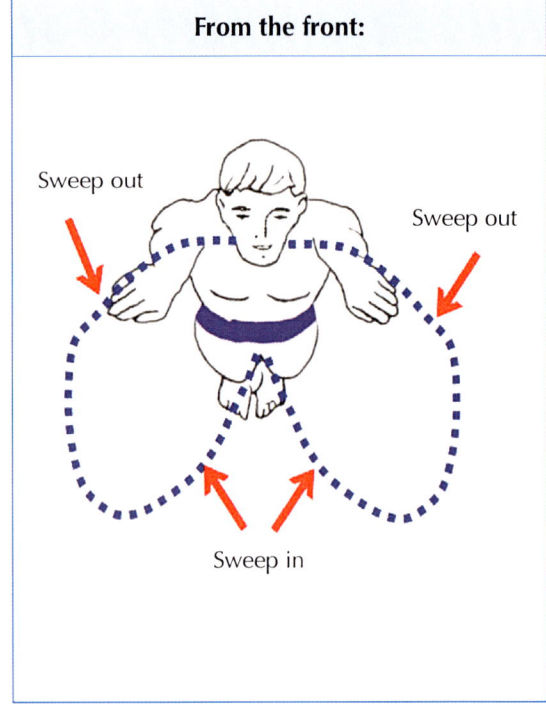

Figure 7.26a
The elliptical breaststroke hand track through the water as viewed from below

Figure 7.26b
The breaststroke hand track through the water as viewed from the front

Breaststroke

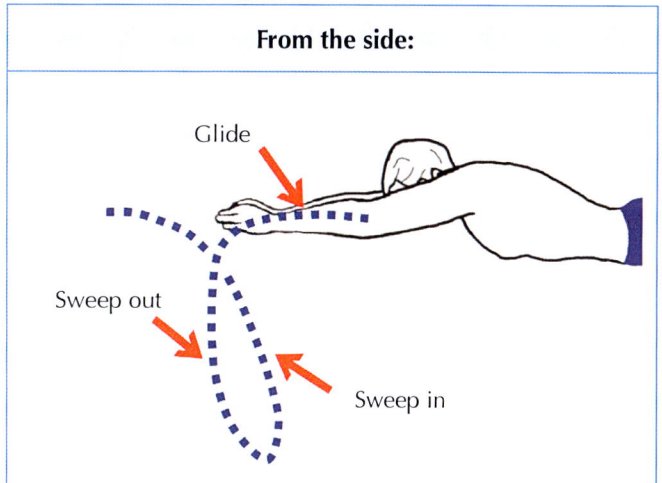

From the side:

Glide

Sweep out

Sweep in

Figure 7.26c
The breaststroke hand track through
the water as viewed from the side

Breathing

In breaststroke, more than any other stroke, the breathing is related specifically to
the arm action.

🔑 The whole stroke is affected by the timing of the breathing.

A normal pattern of breathing

Look for:
• The head beginning to rise at the end of the out-sweep.

Head beginning
to rise

Figure 7.27
The start of the breathing action in
breaststroke

Look for:
• The breath being taken at the end of the in-sweep.

Figure 7.28
The breathing position in breaststroke

Look for:
• The face returning to the water as the arms are pushed forward during the recovery.

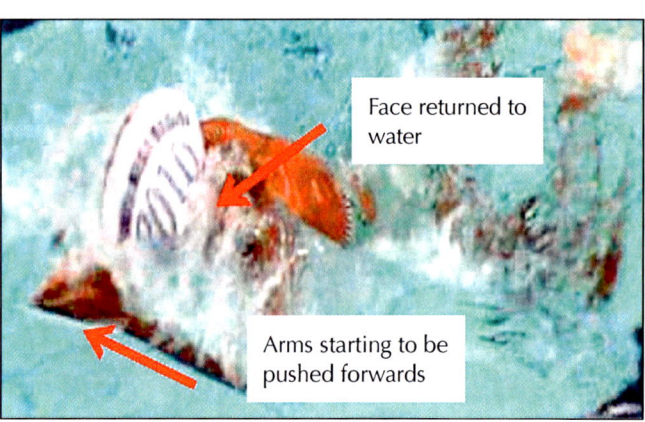

Figure 7.29
The face returning to the water after the breath is taken

Pupils will, however, compensate for their own weaknesses and this will show up in their breathing in the following way:

- If their arm action is weak, the breath will be taken earlier (soon after the arms start the pull to the catch position), relying on the legs to do most of the work.

- If their leg kick is weak, the breath is taken very late (towards the end of the propulsive phase or sweep in), relying on the arms to do most of the work.

Timing

The timing is best described as:

PULL – BREATHE – KICK – GLIDE

There may be some overlap between each of these elements but the basic order must be maintained:

- **Pull**: As the hands pull and complete their out-sweep movement, the shoulders rise, the head raises and the legs start their recovery.

- **Breathe**: The hands continue their movement, sweeping in towards the centre line, the head is at its highest point where the breath can be taken and the legs are just about to drive back.

- **Kick**: As the arms recover forward, the head goes down and the legs kick vigorously back.

- **Glide**: The arms and legs reach their full extension simultaneously and a glide is held for a short time before the sequence is repeated.

 It is important to encourage a short glide phase when first learning the stroke, to slow everything down to give the pupils time to co-ordinate the complete action. As the stroke is developed further, the glide phase is shortened and eventually eliminated.

The rhythm of the stroke

The rhythm of the stroke is based around a **wave-like motion**. This rhythm is the linchpin between the separate elements of the stroke.

A wave reaches its highest point, before falling down and reappearing again further on. When you watch a breaststroke swimmer from the side, you can see this motion. Imagine the top of the wave to be the swimmer's head. The head reaches its highest point, falls down and reappears as another high point further forward. The whole movement is continuous. This is shown in Figure 7.30.

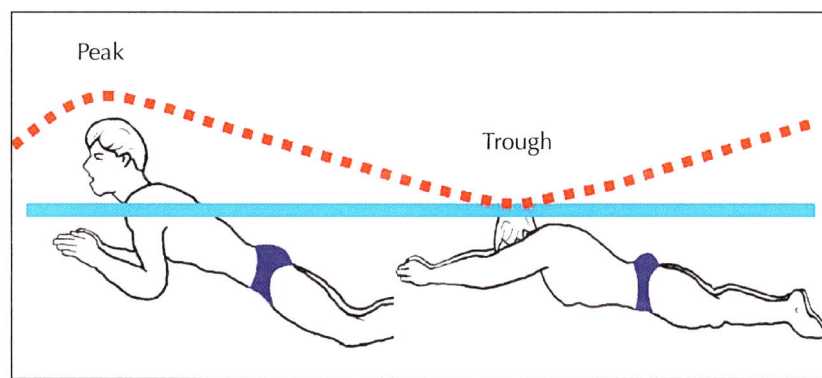

Peak

Trough

Figure 7.30
The wave-like rhythm in the breaststroke

Getting pupils to visualise this wave-like motion can help them set up and feel a rhythm to the stroke. Having taken the breath, they fall 'forward and down' into the trough of the wave, before returning to a peak as the next breath is taken.

THE BUILDING UP OF TEACHING PROGRESSIONS

BUILDING BLOCK 1

Land practice for the leg kick

For this practice, the teacher must sit on a stool or chair facing the group so the demonstration can be shown using both legs.

 Too often a teacher will attempt to demonstrate the leg action using one leg while standing on the other. The demonstration is invariably poor as the teacher struggles to keep their balance and the pupils have difficulty visualising the leg action as a symmetrical one.

The pupils sit on the side of the pool, far enough back so that their thighs are supported and so they are in no danger of overbalancing. They start with their feet down in the water, heels against the wall. The pupils should be encouraged to hold the edge of the pool for balance and support.

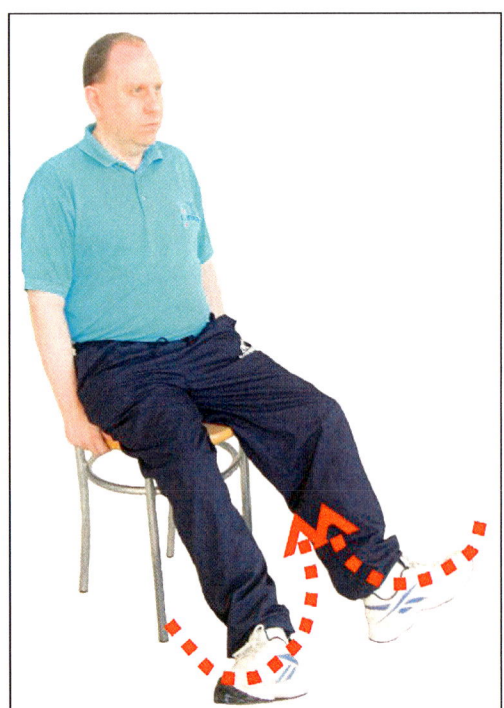

Figure 7.31
The position the teacher takes up in front of the class

Breaststroke

Practice 1

With the teacher and pupils in the above positions, the teacher demonstrates the leg action while the pupils copy the movement.

Reason
- To show the pupils what a dorsiflex position is.
- To ensure that the pupils keep the upper leg still and work the lower leg and foot using knee rotation only.

During the above practice, the teacher talks the pupils through the following descriptive sequence:

Descriptive sequence

- Bring the feet up in front keeping the legs straight, but slightly apart. This is the starting position.
- Pull the feet right up into a dorsiflex position ('square the feet – toes pointing up') as shown in Figure 7.32b.
- Keeping the knees still, drop the lower leg down until the heels actually touch the side of the pool.
- When the heels touch the side of the pool, turn the feet out so the toes are pointing to the side as shown in Figure 7.32c. At this point it is a good idea to ask the children to look down over the edge of the pool to see if their feet are turned out.
- Bring the feet around tracing a circle with the heels and back to the beginning.
- Relax the ankles and point the toes slightly.

It is interesting to note how many children copy the demonstration with their hands as well.

 When the teacher demonstrates this action to the class, it must be accurate because children will copy exactly the movement they see.

At the start, take care that the pupils do not simply draw their knees up higher than their hips in their attempt to demonstrate the movement. This will cause problems on the next practice (the pupils draw their knees up towards their chest and the knees will come high above the water).

It is also a good idea for the teacher to take the pupils through this first practice using three different foot positions: pointed feet, square feet and with the feet turned out. It can be made into a game for small children. This ensures that the pupils fully understand the instructions.

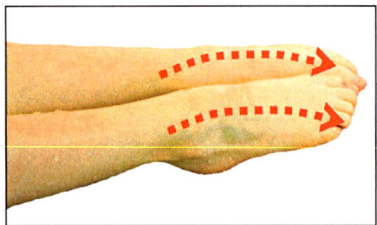

Figure 7.32a
Pointed feet

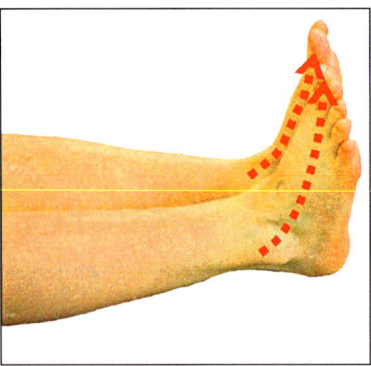

Figure 7.32b
Square feet

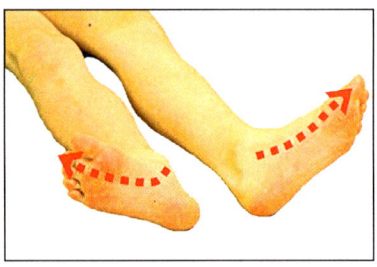

Figure 7.32c
Feet turned out

Figure 7.32
Three different foot positions

BUILDING BLOCK 2

Building up the leg action

Before the pupils attempt the leg kick, it is a good idea to show them a demonstration by an able pupil during which the teacher can point out key points of the movement. Remember visualisation is a powerful tool when learning a new skill.

Practice 2	Teaching points
Lying on the back, one float under each arm, practise the same movement as described in the land exercise.	• Trace circles with the heels. • Keep thighs under the water.

Reason	To practise the movement in the water with plenty of support. This allows the pupils time to concentrate purely on the leg action.

The knees must not come out of the water at any time. It will help if you also ask the pupils to:

- Bring their chin forward a little.
- Look down their body and ask . . . *'Are your knees under the water?'*

This will force the legs to drop slightly and tilt the angle of the body. If they lie too flat, it is very difficult to get a good purchase on the water.

After a short practice on the back the pupils turn onto their front.

Practice 3

Holding onto the bar or rail, extend your legs out behind you, toes pointing. The teacher faces the class and talks the pupils through the following descriptive sequence demonstrating with their arms and hands and emphasising the following teaching points. For greater emphasis, the teacher can place a pair of shoes on their hands as they demonstrate to the class.

Reason   To introduce the pupils to the leg action while on their front.

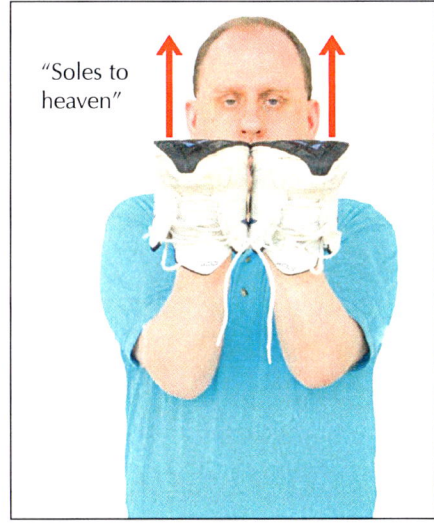

"Soles to heaven"

Teaching points

- Drop the knees down (until the knee is bent at 90 degrees)
- Flatten the feet; make the soles of your feet face the ceiling – 'souls to heaven'.

Figure 7.33
Teacher demonstration of the breaststroke leg recovery

 When the soles of the feet face the ceiling, it is easier to turn the feet out.

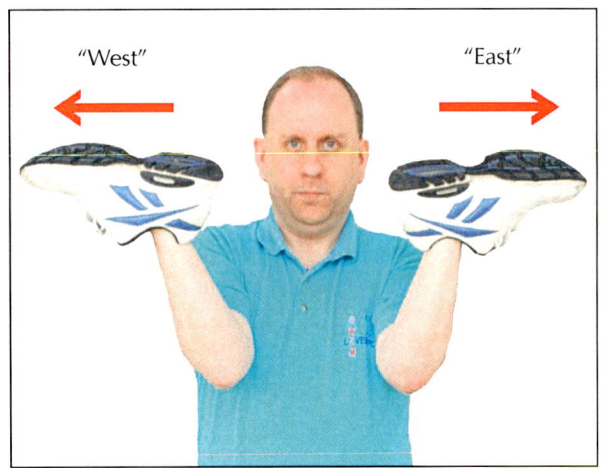

"West"   "East"

Teaching points
• Turn the feet out so they are now in a complete 'W' position.

Figure 7.34
Teacher demonstration of the position at the start of the propulsive phase of the leg kick

 Remember that the best view of this is from behind the swimmer - when they are moving away from you.

Teaching points
• Now make a circle with the heels; keeping the feet turned out.
• Drive back with the inside of the feet.

Figure 7.35
Teacher demonstration of the initial drive back with the inside of the feet

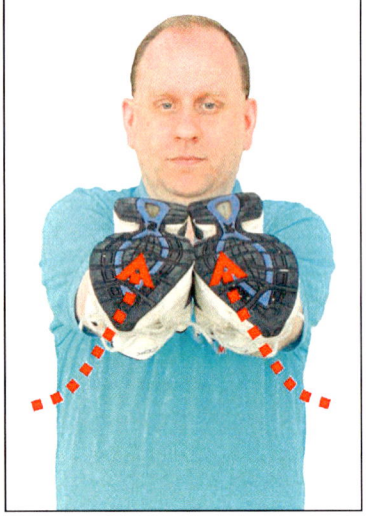

Teaching points
• As you drive back, extend the legs.
• Bring the feet together at the end of the kick with the toes pointed.

Figure 7.36
Teacher demonstration of the extension at the end of the propulsive phase of the leg kick

It may help if during the above practice the pupils press their elbows against the wall as this keeps the body up. Once the pupils have a good idea of the action required, they can have a go at working through the progressive Practices 4 to 6.

Practice 4	Teaching points
With two floats, one under each arm, try the leg action on the front.	• Drop the knees down. • Turn the feet out. • Drive back with the lower leg.

Reason   A natural progression from Practice 3 and using plenty of support.

Practice 5	Teaching points
Turn onto the back and try the leg action holding just one float clasped to the chest.	• Watch the feet and turn them out.

Reason   To work the leg kick on the back with reduced support.

Practice 6	Teaching points
Return onto the front and try the leg action holding one float out in front.	• Turn the feet out. • Drive feet back.

Reason   To practise the leg kick on the front with reduced support.

The teacher must be prepared to talk the pupils through the movement, emphasising specific phases of the kick for the pupils to concentrate on, rather than limiting their description to the all too familiar chant of 'up - out - together'. If not, youngsters will soon 'switch off' and lose interest in the stroke.

The limb track of the leg action is based around getting the pupils to think about what they are doing with their heels, in particular, the idea that the heels kick back in a curved pathway.

An extra exercise which can be introduced at this stage is **treading water**. This is really a breaststroke leg action in a vertical position.

Practice 7	Teaching points
Two floats, one under each arm, practise the breaststroke leg action in a vertical position.	• Press down with the insides of the feet and lower leg.

Reason It makes the legs work simultaneously and as the practice is done in deep water, allows the pupils to feel the pressure against the instep as they work the lower leg.

With confident pupils, this practice can be performed without aids.

Practice 8	Teaching points
Tread water without aids, sculling with the hands.	• Press down with the feet and lower leg. • Use the hands alternating with thumbs down when pressing out and thumbs up when pressing in.

Reason Support is reduced and the sculling movement is a useful introduction into the arm action.

A variation of this theme is 'Chinese dancing'. Standing in shallow water, one leg is picked up and the foot averted so the sole of the foot is facing outwards. This is then pushed onto the floor and the other foot is lifted into the same position. This movement is in effect an 'alternating treading water' action.

Gradually the pupils can progress to deeper water where they can perform the same movement while using their hands to scull.

This is a valuable exercise. It is fun and it makes the legs work hard, developing a skill which can be used later for activities such as water polo. The skill of treading water is described in more detail in Chapter 9.

BUILDING BLOCK 3

Introducing the arm action

By this stage the pupils should have picked up the leg action sufficiently for the teacher to see that they have understood what is required and that they can propel themselves across the width.

It is now time to introduce the arm action. With breaststroke, however, you cannot build up the arm action using one arm practices for this creates an unbalanced and incorrect movement. Neither can you practise pulling arms only for this drill is too strenuous for the learner. Therefore, it is essential to weave the complete arm action in with both the breathing and the timing.

Practice 9
The teacher demonstrates the arm action facing the class and talking the pupils through the action isolating the important areas. The pupils stand in shallow water facing the teacher and copy the movement.

Reason   To give the pupils time to understand and experience what is required.

During the demonstration, the following teaching points are emphasised.

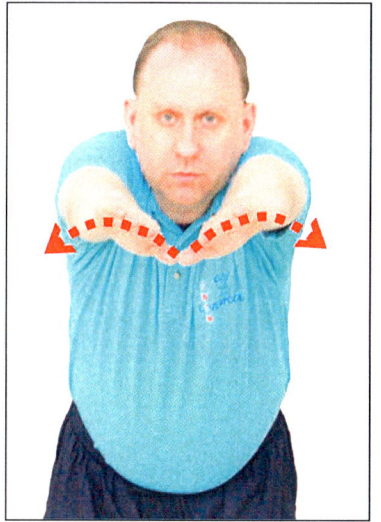

Teaching points
• Lean forward. • Arms extended and fully stretched. • Thumbs slightly down.

Figure 7.37
Teacher demonstration of the starting point

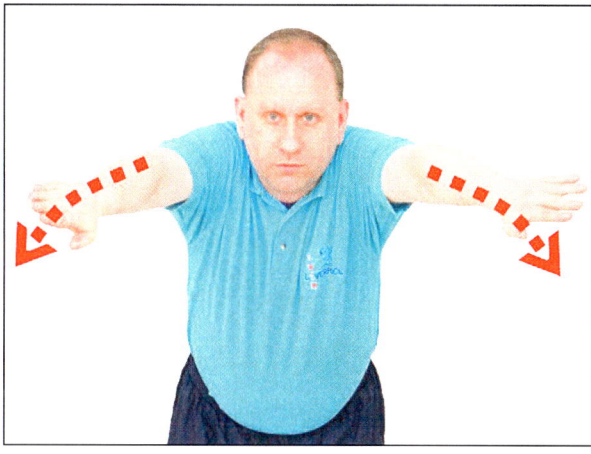

Teaching points
• Press the hands apart to the width of the shoulders.

Figure 7.38
Teacher demonstration of the starting point

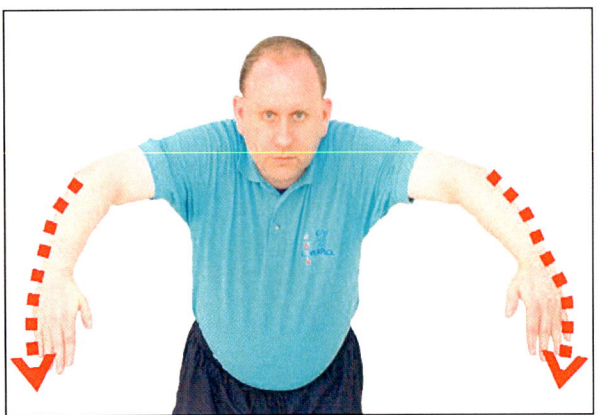

Teaching points

- Pull the hands back, down to a position under the elbows.

Figure 7.39
Teacher demonstration of the sweep out

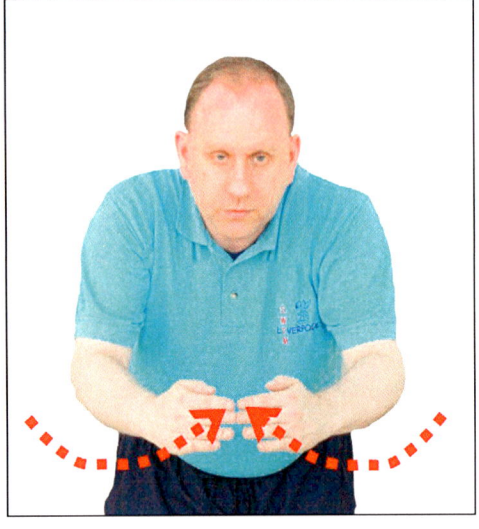

Teaching points

- Sweep the hands in and up under the chin. At this point the arms form a double boomerang shape.
- As the hands come together, bring the elbows in to the side.

Figure 7.40
Teacher demonstration of the sweep in

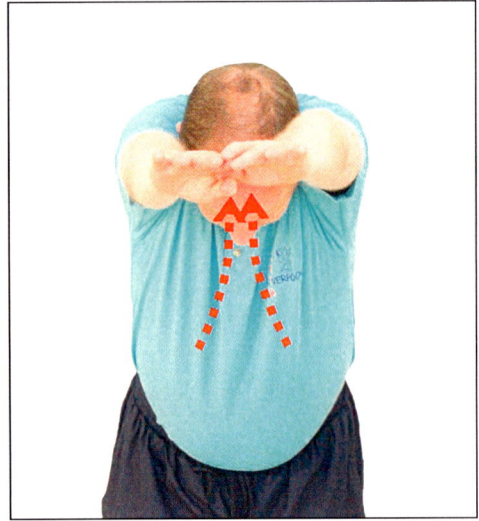

Teaching points

- Pull the hands up and drive them forward.
- Reach for a full stretch position.

Figure 7.41
Teacher demonstration of the arm recovery

In Figure 7.39, the teaching point emphasises that the hands *'sweep out to a position under the elbows'*. When practising, they will sweep out to a position wider than this. This is ac tually what is required but if the pupils were ask to sweep down and out to a position outside the elbows, they invariably pull too wide. This is a good case of asking for one thing but in practice getting something else.

BUILDING BLOCK 4

Developing the timing

Before an attempt at the complete stroke can be made, the timing of the arms and legs must also be introduced using a standing practice. By standing in a more upright position, the timing of the leg action is woven into the arm action.

Practice 10	Teaching points
Similar to Practice 9, the pupils stand in shallow water, arms out in front but with head down between the arms. They pull their arms through the movement and at the widest point bring one knee up to start the leg action. As the arms come in, the feet turn out and the leg drives around and back to the bottom of the pool.	• Focus on the following: PULL BREATHE KICK GLIDE

Reason | To show the pupils exactly where in relation to the arm stroke they are going to kick and to lay the foundations of the 'wave-like rhythm' to the stroke.

The teacher demonstrates Practice 9, talking through the action while the pupils copy the movement.

 Most children have no idea how the leg action links in with the arm action. It is essential to give them the feeling of this timing before the complete stroke is attempted. The teacher must also emphasise that one leg is used just to demonstrate the timing and the other leg is used to stand on.

Practice 11	Teaching points
The pupils stand a few feet away from and facing the wall. With their shoulders level with the water, they lean forward, arms outstretched and perform one complete arm stroke. As the arms sweep around, they complete one leg kick and glide into the wall in the stretched position.	• Start with arms outstretched. • Lean forward. • Perform one arm pull. • As the arms reach their widest point bring the legs up and kick around and back hard. • Hold a full stretched position into the wall.

259

Reason	To show the pupils where in relation to the arm pull, the kick is made. This practice also gives the pupils plenty of time to think about what is required of them.

 Throughout Practices 9 to 11 arm bands may be used to give the weaker pupils extra support. They will still be able to perform the basic movement. Be cautious when using rubber rings because although they free the arms, they give the support in the wrong place; lifting the bottom up out of the water and tipping the swimmer forward.

BUILDING BLOCK 5

Introducing the breathing

At this stage we have not been concerned about the breathing. What we have been concentrating on is a correct arm action plus the kick and glide into the side. Once the pupils have grasped the basic movement, the timing of the breathing can now be added to the building programme.

 At this stage, it is necessary for the pupils to consciously raise their head to breathe as they do not have the strength to raise the body high enough to lift the head out of the water.

Practice 12	Teaching points
Return to standing position as described for Practice 9, but the pupils start with their face in the water and at the widest part of the pull, lift their head to breathe, lowering again as the arms stretch forward.	• At the widest point in the pull, lift the chin forward and up. • Breathe in. • Blow your hands forward. • Return the face to the water. • Look at the bottom of the pool.

Reason	To ensure the pupils know exactly when to lift the head to breathe.

When do you breathe in?

Figure 7.42
Teacher demonstrating when to breathe in

From the front

Breathe in when the head is up and the mouth is clear of the water

When do you breathe out?

Figure 7.43
Teacher demonstrating when to breathe out

From the side

Breathe out as the hands are pushed forwards and the face is returned to the water

Practice 13	**Teaching points**
Now work once again through Practices 10 and 11	• Focus on the following: PULL BREATHE KICK GLIDE

Reason   To emphasise the timing of the breathing with the arm action.

⚷   Breathe in at the mid-pull stage
Breathe out as the hands are pushed away

The teacher must watch carefully for any pupils who are not breathing out as the arms push forwards. As with other strokes, if the pupils only breathe in or breath hold, they will quickly tire and their stroke will break down.

Practice 14	Teaching points
Gradually the number of strokes towards the wall can now be increased to two, then three, then four. When the pupil is ready, they can attempt a complete width of the pool starting with a push and glide.	• Blow out during the glide phase. • Keep the action smooth and continuous.

Reason To gradually build up the pupil's confidence and skill before the complete width is attempted.

It is important to realise that the breaststroke has to be built up in a slightly different way to the other strokes. It does not lend itself easily to an intermediate stage between the part practices and the complete stroke as seen in the other three strokes, for example:

- The dog paddle action used in front crawl.

- A single arm practice used in the butterfly.

- The sculling practices outlined in the backstroke.

In the breaststroke, you have got to teach the pupils the leg action first and then almost push them into the full stroke.

For most pupils this is a big jump and **time** must be taken to develop the arm action and timing.

A good arm action will also improve the leg action as well, since this will help to keep the swimmer up and propel them along until the leg kick can be strengthened and improved. Therefore teachers must ensure that their pupils are given regular practice at the complete stroke rather than just . . . *'legs, legs and more leg work'*.

Once they can perform the complete stroke competently, a good practice is to ask the pupils to swim across the width with the least number of strokes (*or with the least number of kicks while holding onto a kick board*). This encourages a full stretch and glide and improves the efficiency of the arm action and leg kick.

PROBLEMS AND SOLUTIONS

Leg action

Problem 1: The screw kick

Without any doubt, this is the main problem with the breaststroke. A screw kick is any difference in the symmetrical and simultaneous nature of the kicking action or its stroke pattern. Any one of the following may cause this:

Cause/effect	Solution
• One foot turned in instead of out. • One foot pointed instead of a dorsiflex position. • One knee drooped lower than the other. • One knee brought up before the other. • The head turned to the side to breathe.	Go right back to the beginning and start with the preliminary exercises outlined in Building Block 1. **There is no short cut**. The reason why this problem occurs is because the pupils cannot see or feel what is happening to their legs. The only solution is to return to the leg practices to make them more aware of what is required.

Even by going over and over these early leg practices, a teacher may conclude that they are not having much success in correcting the screw kick. We suggest this may be due to a lack of motivation on the part of the pupil who may find the stroke boring and uninteresting and would rather concentrate on the faster strokes.

It is sometimes not until the pupils require this stroke to achieve an award that they become motivated to correct this problem. Nevertheless, the teacher must persevere and we can only emphasise once again that there are no short cuts.

Any solution must be based around trying to make the pupils feel what it is like to perform the correct movement. With individuals who are experiencing particular difficulty, it may be necessary to take them out of the water and try the following practice.

Practice
Lying on the floor or bench, the pupils place their feet in the recovery position. The teacher places their hands on the insteps of the feet and provides slight resistance as the legs kick out, back and down to the floor.

Reason   Resistance is provided so the pupils can feel the movement.

Figure 7.44
Teacher guiding a pupil's legs
through the movement

Where the problem is caused by the face turning to the side to breathe, the reason is fear of the water on the face. To cure this, the teacher must go back to some confidence work (such as submerging the face, blowing bubbles, etc) to eradicate this fear and develop the breathing.

Problem 2: Bringing the knees too far under the body on the recovery

Cause/effect	Solution
If during the recovery the knees are brought to a vertical position under the hips, the thighs present a large profile to the water and considerably increase frontal resistance, slowing the swimmer down.	A greater focus needs to be placed on bending the knees during the recovery. Revert back to the early practices against the wall to emphasise the correct movement.

Arm action

There are two main problems which the teacher may observe with the arm action:

Problem 3: An uneven arm pull with one arm leading the other

Cause/effect	Solution
• Pulling much wider or deeper with one arm compared to the other.	Practise the arm action while standing in shallow water. If necessary, a single arm practice, working only on the problem arm will give the pupil time to focus on the correct movement.

A word of warning, however, for this problem may be caused by the leg action not being strong enough to support the pupil or to give them time to perform the arm action simultaneously. The uneven arm pull is the result of the pupil's 'instinct for survival'. Remove the need to survive and you often remove the problem.

Problem 4: Pulling the hands too far back beyond the shoulder line

Cause/effect

- This much longer pull disturbs the timing and co-ordination of the stroke and the subsequently longer recovery underwater causes a considerable increase in resistance.

Solution

Return to the standing demonstration and emphasise a narrower movement where the hands are kept in view at all times. Be prepared to use a woggle under the armpits asking them not to pull past the woggle.

Timing

Problem 5: Incorrect timing

Cause/effect

- At the early stages pupils may push off the wall and kick first before they then try to get the pull and breathing in. This is often because they learn the kick first and much time is spent on developing the kick so it becomes ingrained.

Solution

Return to Building Block 4.

Problem 6: Lifting the head too early

Cause/effect

- If the head is lifted during the initial out-sweep, the propulsive phase of the in-sweep is less effective and there is a delay before the leg kick starts their kick back.

Solution

The focus needs to be placed on encouraging the pupil to keep their face in the water until after they start the in-sweep.

THE IMPROVEMENT CIRCLE

The improvement circle for breaststroke is built around three core skills.

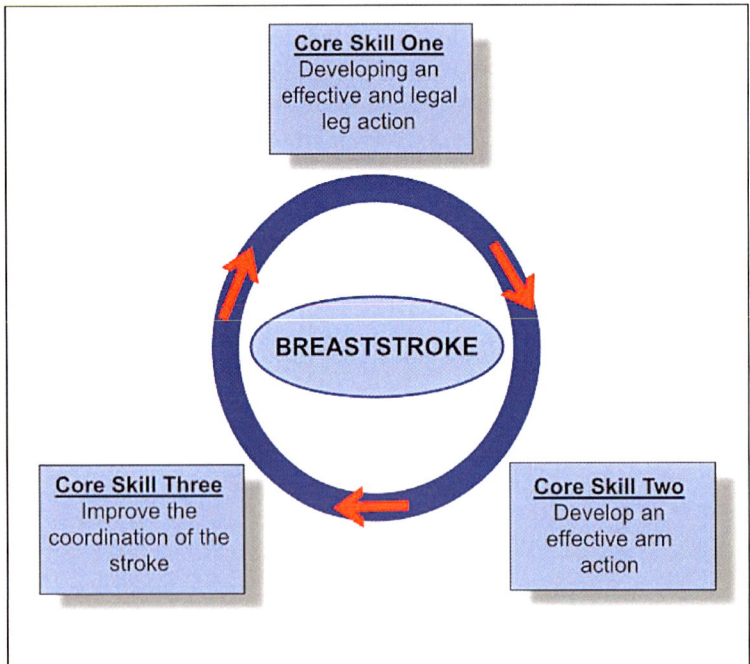

Figure 7.45
The improvement circle for breaststroke

Core skill 1: Developing an effective and 'legal' leg action

The breaststroke leg action contributes significantly to propulsion. It is therefore essential that the improver develops an effective and legal leg action. As a result, the teacher needs to spend more time improving the leg kick.

Regular exposure to a range of leg practices will help condition and strengthen the movement but priority must always be given to performing the action correctly and legally. The teacher must show patience and be willing to revert back to earlier practices to reinforce the correct movement. Never sacrifice quality for quantity; for example a desire to achieve distance badges.

Breaststroke kicking practices with support

1. Holding a kickboard with the arms outstretched and the head raised. Breathing is no problem so greater distances can be covered and the inclined body position is stable.
2. Laying the forearms over the top of the kickboard with the finger tips over the front edge will create a more inclined body position than Practice 1.
3. Holding the kickboard by its back edge, kick while integrating the breathing by raising of the head to breathe during the recovery and lowering the head down between the arms as you kick back.
4. On the back, hold a float to the chest and perform a breaststroke leg kick.
5. On the back, hold a float over the thighs and perform a leg kick.
6. Holding a kickboard in a vertical position so the flat surface is pushed through the water. Kicking against this extra resistance helps strengthen the leg action.

These practices can be performed with a pull buoy between the thighs to prevent the pupils from using the top part of the leg, therefore limiting the movement to the lower leg only. The only problem is the child is then concentrating on holding onto the pull buoy rather than on the leg action required.

Kicking without support should also become a key feature in the improver programme. It not only strengthens and conditions the movement, but also encourages the pupils to improve their streamlining as they assume a front glide position at the end of each kick. As with front crawl, once the float is removed, the practice becomes more fatiguing so distance must be kept short to ensure the skill does not deteriorate.

Breaststroke kicking practices without support

1. Kicking face down between outstretched arms and raising the upper torso to breathe each kick.
2. Kicking on the back with both arms down by your side.
3. Kicking on the back with both arms stretched out behind the head.
4. Kicking on the front with both arms down by the side and again raising the upper torso to breathe each kick.
5. Kicking underwater from a push and glide position.

 The teacher needs to make sure that the pupils do not start to lift their knees from the water when they are practising the kicking exercises on the back. The focus must be on dropping the lower leg down before the heels trace a circular pathway, driving the swimmer backwards.

Core skill 2: Developing an effective arm action

The arm action is strengthened and conditioned through isolated practices and development drills.

 Arms only practices with a pull buoy held between the legs are very strenuous. Care should be given when using this with distance practices.

Breaststroke pulling practices with support

1. Pull arms only, holding a pull buoy between the legs, keeping the head up.
2. As for Practice 1, but with the head down, lifting the head every stroke or every other stroke to breathe.
3. Pull arms only, holding a pull buoy between the legs, using a small dolphin leg action as the arms recover.
4. Pull arms only, holding a pull buoy between the legs, with the hands closed into a fist shape.

As the breaststroke arm action becomes stronger, more drill work without support can be introduced to the improver.

Breaststroke pulling practices without support

1. Pull breaststroke arms using a small dolphin leg action as the arms recover.
2. As for Practice 1, using fins for added momentum.
3. A variation is to work Practices 1 and 2 with either the head up or the head down.
4. Breaststroke arms with two dolphin leg kicks and breathing each stroke. Kick once into the stretch and again during the glide.
5. As for Practice 4 but with fins for added momentum.

To further improve the arm action, we can also think of the arm pull as one large sculling movement. The sudden change from the out-sweep to the in-sweep in the breaststroke arm action helps generate propulsion. This ability to change from a thumbs down (on the out-sweep) to a thumbs up (on the in-sweep) during the arm pull is a major feature of the stroke.

A range of sculling practices is outlined in Chapter 9. The main ones to benefit the breaststroke arm action are:

Descriptions of the sculling practice with pull buoy held between the legs

1. **Under elbows scull – head first**: Lying on the front with head down, the upper arms are locked into position in front of the chin and out to the side. The hands are placed directly below the elbows, fingers pointing to the bottom of the pool. Keeping the upper arms still, the hands and lower arms press out and in rapidly – thumbs back on press out and forwards in the press in. To breathe just lift the head then place it back down again. This action is similar to the breaststroke arm pull when the hands change from the out-sweep to the in-sweep.
2. **Front scull – head first**: Lying on the front with arms outstretched, chin on the water and fingers pointing towards the bottom of the pool, a small sculling action is practised – thumbs down on the press out and thumbs up on the press in. Throughout the scull the arms remain straight.
3. **Vertical scull – treading water**: A vertical position is maintained by using the hands to scull rapidly – thumbs down on the press out, thumbs up on the press in.

 Although sculling as a main theme would not necessarily be taught in a breaststroke lesson, it can be woven into the building programme as a contrasting activity which is closely linked to the stroke and which benefits its development.

Core skill 3: Improving the co-ordination of the stroke

To perform the complete stroke effectively, special attention must be given to the timing and co-ordination of the leg kick, arm action and the breathing. Remember we are looking for the component parts to link together in a smooth, continuous manner based on the sequence:

PULL – BREATHE – KICK – GLIDE

The aim is to ensure that as the propulsive phase of the arms end, the propulsive phase of the leg kick begins.

Breaststroke co-ordination practices

1. While in a front glide position, perform two breaststroke kicks followed by one arm pull with a breath.
2. Similar to Practice 1 but performing two pulls followed by one leg kick.
3. Alternate three strokes with a super long glide, then three strokes faster with no glide.
4. Combination practices mixing kick, sculling and arm action practices.
5. Build up the size of the pull by starting with a very small front scull, and then gradually make the arm action bigger until the full arm action is performed.
6. Reducing glide sequence – Lap 1 hold glide for six seconds, Lap 2 hold glide for four seconds, Lap 3 hold glide for two seconds, Lap 4 no glide.
7. Count the number of strokes across the width of the pool, then try to improve efficiency by reducing the number of strokes.

 It is important to encourage a glide phase when first learning the stroke to slow everything down and give the pupils time to co-ordinate the complete action. As the stroke is developed further, the glide phase is shortened and eventually in a competitive stroke, eliminated.

We have already discussed how the nature of the stroke causes the upper torso to rise and fall during every stroke cycle. Something to look for in the full stroke is for the body to be as streamlined as possible during the main propulsive phases of the stroke. These are:

1. **During the propulsive phase (down-sweep and in-sweep) of the arm action.**
   The face should remain in the water until the in-sweep of the arms is near completion.

2. **During the propulsive phase (in-sweep) of the leg kick.**
   As the legs drive back and in, the face should be back in the water and the arms nearly extended.

In this way, the propulsion generated by the arms and legs is maximised.

SUMMARY OF THINGS TO LOOK FOR IN A GOOD BREASTSTROKE

Body position

- The upper body rising at the end of the in-sweep.
- No conscious lifting of the head up and down.
- Head remains still and is raised above the water naturally as the shoulders are raised.
- The head drops back into the water by the end of the kick so the body assumes a classic front glide body position.
- The shoulders remain level throughout the complete stroke cycle.
- Shoulders rise sufficiently to allow mouth to clear the water.
- As the breath is taken the body is inclined from the head through to the knees.

Leg kick

- On the recovery, the heels are brought up close together towards the seat.
- At the end of the recovery:
  - The heels and knees are hip width apart.
  - The feet turn out so the legs form a 'W' shape.
  - The angle between the upper leg and trunk is greater than 100 degrees.
  - The lower legs are at right angles to the surface.
- At the start of the drive back, the feet turn out (east and west) and the toes turn up towards the shins ('souls to heaven').
- Strong drive back by feet and lower leg.
- Heels drive back in a curved pathway sweep outwards and backwards.
- The legs kick back to full extension and come together.
- Feet finish the kick with the toes pointed.

Arm pull

- From extended position the hands, press out and slightly down.
- The first part of pull is made with the thumbs down/palms out.
- Hands sweep out, down and back to outside shoulder width.
- During the out-sweep, the elbows remain high.
- At the start of the in-sweep, the hands are rotated so palms face in.
- The hands sweep in close to the centre line.
- At the end of the in-sweep the hands are forward of the chin and may be slightly palms up.

Arm recovery

- Hands drive forwards to full stretch.
- The elbows follow the hands and squeeze in towards the centre line.
- Hands remain close together.
- As the hands drive forwards, the palms rotate palms down.

Breathing

- Start lifting the face at the end of the out-sweep.
- Breath is taken in as arms start their recovery.
- Face lowered into the water during the last part of the recovery.
- Breathe out during the glide.

Timing/co-ordination/rhythm

- One breath every stroke cycle.
- Look for a 'pull – breathe – kick – glide' rhythm.
- Look for a classic front glide position at the end of each stroke.
- The legs remain straight during the first part of the pull.
- The legs drive back as the arms reach their full stretch forwards.

BREASTSTROKE ASSESSMENT SHEET

Name of swimmer:		Age:	
Stroke/activity:		Date:	
Analysis carried out by:			

BODY POSITION

Key questions to ask	Teachers observations and comments
Teachers observations and comments • What is the head position when breathing? • What is the head position at the end of the recovery? • What is the hip position when breathing? • What is the hip position at the end of the recovery? • What is the inclination of the body when breathing? • How streamlined is the body at the end of the kick? • How level are the shoulders throughout the stroke?	

LEG ACTION

Key questions to ask	Teachers observations and comments
Teachers observations and comments • How far do the knees come under the body on recovery? • What is the width of the knees on recovery (relative to the hips)? • What is the degree of hip flexion at the end of the recovery? • How good is the pupil's ability to turn the feet out? • How wide is the circular motion of the kick back? • Is there a strong 'whip-like' action with the lower leg? • How deep are the feet when they finish the kick? • Are the toes at the end of the kick? • Is the kick symmetrical?	

272

ARM ACTION

Key questions to ask	Teachers observations and comments
Teachers observations and comments • Are the thumbs down and palms out at start of pull? • How wide is the initial sweep out? • What is the position of hands at the end of the sweep out? • Do the hands change to face in on the in-sweep? • Do the hands sweep in under the chin? • Do the elbows squeeze into the centre line? • Do the arms extend during recovery? • Do the hands remain close together on recovery? • How effective is the overall sculling action? • Do the arms contribute to propulsion?	

BREATHING

Key questions to ask	Teachers observations and comments
Teachers observations and comments • When the breath is taken? • Is there any deliberate movement of the head? • How high is the chin above water when breath is taken? • Is a breath taken every stroke? • How smooth is the movement? • What is the effect of breathing on total stroke?	

TIMING AND CO-ORDINATION

Key questions to ask	Teachers observations and comments
Teachers observations and comments • What is the timing between the leg and arm actions? • What is the timing between the breathing and the arm action? • Is there a glide in the stroke? • How long is the glide? • What is the overall rhythm of the stroke?	

FINAL IMPRESSIONS AND COMMENTS

Key questions to ask	Teachers observations and comments
Teachers observations and comments • Is the stroke legal? • How effective is the stroke? • What contribution do you think the legs make to propulsion? • What contribution do you think the arms make to propulsion? • How flexible is the swimmer? • How strong is the swimmer?	

ALTERNATIVE STROKE ASSESSMENT SHEET FOR BREASTSTROKE

Name of swimmer:		Age:	
Date of assessment:		Stroke:	

BODY POSITION	Yes	No		LEG KICK	Yes	No
Is the body inclined when the breath is taken?				Do both the feet turn out in a dorsiflex position during the kick?		
Is the body streamlined during the glide phase?				Is the leg action performed without a screw kick?		
Does the head rise and fall naturally to allow the breath to be taken?				Are the heels drawn up to the backside hip width apart?		
Is the head deliberately raised and lowered to breathe?				Are the knees drawn up too far under the body?		
Is the head raised too high when the breath is taken?				Do the feet drive back in a whip-like action?		
Do the hips sink too low when the breath is taken?				Do the legs finish the kick together in an extended position?		
Are the shoulders horizontal throughout the stroke cycle?				Is there a glide phase at the end of the kick?		

ARM PULL	Yes	No		BREATHING	Yes	No
Is the pull for both arms even and simultaneous?				Is there a breath taken every stroke?		
Is the arm pull too narrow?				Is the breath taken when the head is at its highest point?		
Do the hands pull back too far past the shoulders?				Is the chin raised too high when the breath is taken?		
Do the hands face inwards during the in-sweep?				Is the breath taken as the hands sweep in under the chin?		
Do the hands come close together under the chin?				Is the head lowered back into the water between the upper arms?		
Do the hands extend forwards just under the surface of the water?				Is the breathing action smooth?		
Is there a glide at the end of the recovery?				Is the breath exhaled during the glide phase of the stroke?		

TIMING AND CO-ORDINATION	Yes	No		FINAL IMPRESSIONS	Yes	No
Is there a 'pull – breathe – kick – glide' rhythm?				Is the stroke legal?		
Is the stroke leg dominated?				Is the leg action effective?		
Is the stroke arm dominated?				Is the arm action effective?		
Is the glide phase too long?				Does the breathing fit into the stroke smoothly?		
Is the glide phase too short?				Is the overall stroke effective?		
Is there any bobbing of the head during the stroke?				Is the breathing action smooth?aDoes the swimmer have any problems with being too buoyant?		
Is the stroke smooth and continuous?				Is the pupil a natural breaststroke swimmer?		

BREASTSTROKE

Breaststroke is the stroke that we turn to for rest.
Some would say, for them it's the best.
Its origins, we know go way back in time
It is always difficult for teachers to mime.
They stand on one leg to show the path
Which often causes the pupils to laugh!
The key words are 'simultaneous' and 'symmetrical' you know
It's a stroke that appears to be leisurely and slow.
The feet are drawn up, turned out and kicked back,
Awkward to do, if co-ordination you lack.
The timing is 'pull, breathe, kick and then glide'
Take a deep breath, try one full stroke to the side!

Pat Parkes

Chapter 8

Butterfly

Main Focus:

- Why does the butterfly have such a dynamic body position?
- What is the importance of the leg kick?
- How wide is the arm entry?
- What pulling pattern do the hands trace?
- What is the nature of the recovery?
- When does the first kick occur?
- When does the second kick occur?
- How much undulation is there in the stroke?
- A 5 stage building programme
- The identification of 5 main problems
- An improvement circle built on three core skills
- A summary of what to look for in a good stroke
- Usable stroke assessment sheets
- A summary poem by Patricia Parkes

Chapter 8

Butterfly

INTRODUCTION

In most learn-to-swim programmes, butterfly is regarded as the fourth stroke. It is the one to 'have a go at' once the other three have been mastered. It is also known as the hardest stroke because it is considered the most strenuous and it is often thought be difficult for pupils to learn to perform well.

Teachers' attitudes towards the butterfly

Attitudes towards the butterfly are coloured by the fact that:

- It is likely to be the stroke that the teachers themselves find the most difficult to perform. Consequently, they have little feel for the **sculling** motion during the arm pull or the general **rhythm** of the stroke and therefore lack confidence when it comes to teaching the butterfly.

- The stroke does not have a very strong place in many of the swimming badge schemes. Once pupils can swim the backstroke, front crawl and breaststroke, swimming programmes can start to suffer from 'badge-itis' (the need to collect badges . . . any badge at all costs). As a result, there is little time given to developing the butterfly.

Yet butterfly is good fun and young people are always keen and eager to learn the stroke. It is different from the other strokes. It offers them a challenge and is seen as the stroke that all the best swimmers can perform. It definitely has appeal and teachers need to capitalise on this and keep the interest alive.

At this point, many teachers sit back and say:

> *'Ah yes, but you need a lot of strength and stamina before you can attempt to learn the butterfly' .*

To support this argument, they explain that after only a few strokes, the learner's performance degenerates into little more than a thrashing movement as they do not have the strength to raise the body up high enough to clear the arms over the top of the water.

What they fail to see, however, is that this breakdown in the stroke is rarely the result of a lack of strength. It is invariably the result of the learner not having enough time to breathe.

With so much to concentrate on, the need to breathe is often the last thing on the pupil's mind. As a consequence, the stroke breaks down simply because the learner 'runs out of air'.

There is less likelihood of the stroke breaking down in the early stages of learning if the teacher can find a way of:

- **Slowing** everything down to 'buy' the swimmer **time to breathe**.
- **Building up a rhythm** which allows the breathing to fit naturally into the stroke in a smooth, relaxed manner.

WHAT TO LOOK FOR IN A GOOD STROKE

Body position

The butterfly is performed with an undulating body motion. This results in a very **dynamic** body position.

To help the teacher understand this, we need to take a slightly different approach and be more specific about what we mean by 'body position'. We should be looking at the position of the **torso**, (shoulders, chest and hips), as the swimmer moves through the water. By looking at the position of the torso only, it is easier for the teacher to focus on the correct area.

From the side

When viewed from the side, the torso is seen to 'pivot' at the hip area. This creates an overall view of an undulating rhythm in which the shoulders and the chest follow a 'wave-like' pattern.

Look for:
• The rising of the body towards the crest of the wave. • The falling of the body back down towards the trough of the wave.

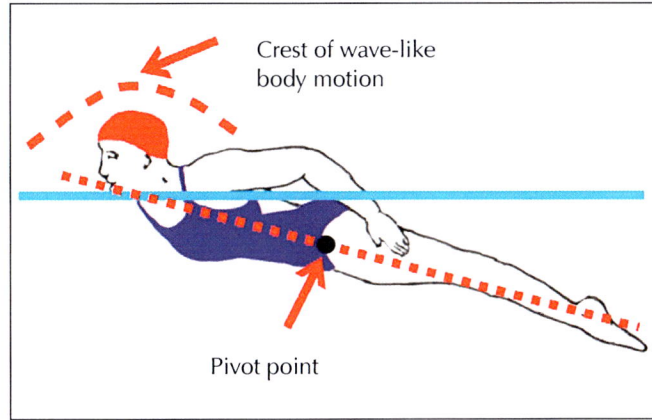

Figure 8.1
The body position at its highest point when breathing

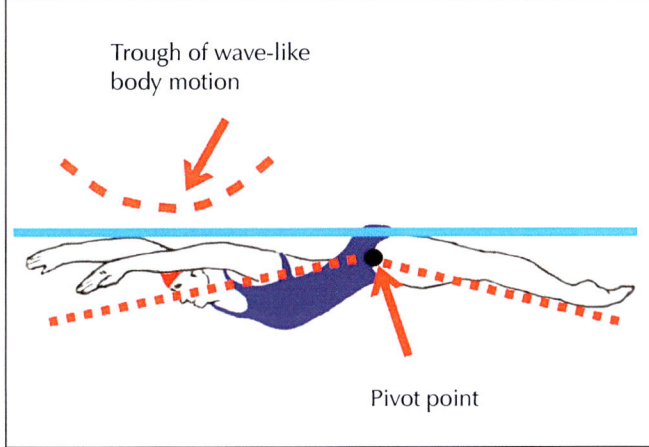

Figure 8.2
The body position at its lowest point.

Throughout, the hips remain very close to the surface of the water and may even appear to rise above it.

From the front

Look for:
• The shoulders lifting clear of the water and the head rising to breathe. • The head and shoulders disappearing under the surface of the water as the torso falls down into the trough.

Shoulders clear of water

Figure 8.3
The body position at its highest point from the front

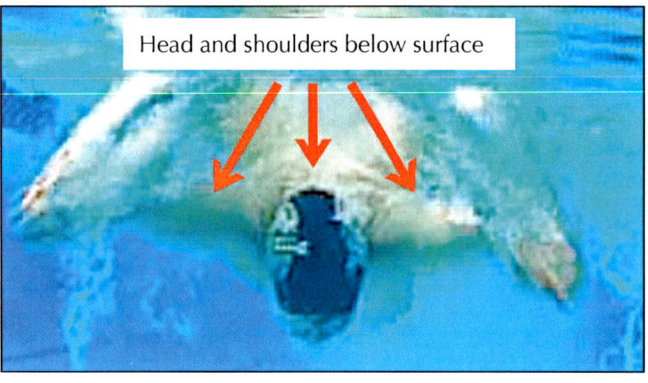

Head and shoulders below surface

Figure 8.4
The body disappearing underwater at its lowest point

Discussion on the body position

It is difficult to outline a set body position because the torso is **continually changing** as it is repeatedly lifted up out of the water, followed by a fall back down under the surface.

The body position is therefore never static. If a comparison is attempted between a front glide body position and the dynamic one that can be observed when swimming the butterfly, some teachers may feel confused.

The amount of undulation varies according to:

- **Body type**: A taller more flexible body type is likely to undulate more than a shorter stockier type.

- **Buoyancy**: Good floaters achieve the action with far less effort than poor floaters.

Therefore, as ever, bodily endowment will ensure success for some swimmers more than others.

Leg action

Both legs move simultaneously up and downwards, balancing the movements of the arms and the upper body. This adds to the undulation. To fully understand the correct movement, the action needs to be broken down into two phases: the upbeat and the downbeat.

The upbeat

The upbeat is the recovery phase of the butterfly leg kick. At the start of the upbeat the legs are extended. The depth varies according to the size of the pupil.

Look for:
• The legs starting to lift upward with no bend at the knees.   • A slight lowering of the hips as the legs rise.

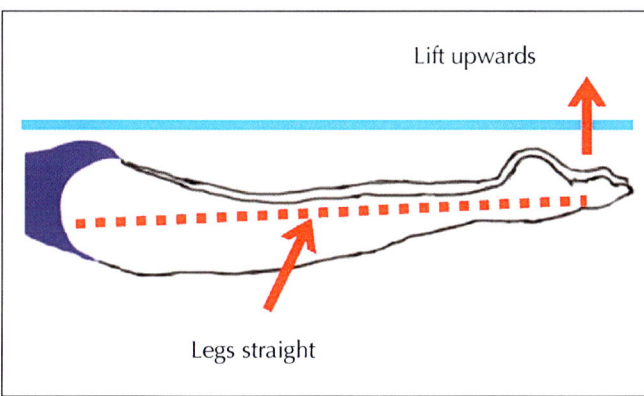

Figure 8.5a
The straight leg lift of the upbeat

The upper leg then starts to move downwards.

Look for:
• The bending of the knees and the continual upwards movement of the lower leg.   • The upbeat ending when the feet reach the surface. At this point the hips are at their lowest level.

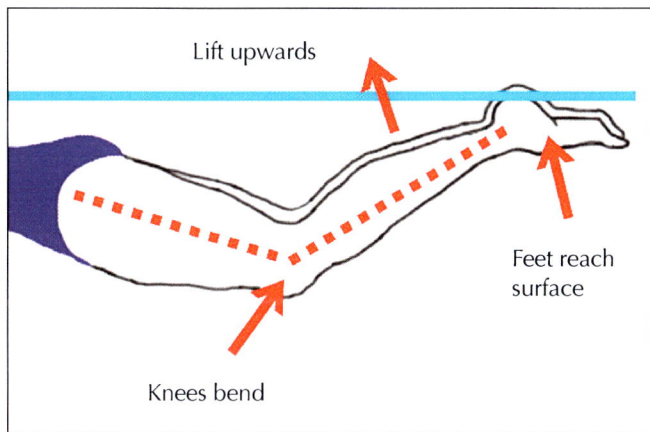

Figure 8.5b
The end of the upbeat

At the top of the upbeat, the knees should reach a flexion of less than 90 degrees. If the legs bend to 90 degrees or more, then the flexion is too great. Then the feet begin to plantar flex (toes pointed) in preparation for the downbeat.

The downbeat

The downbeat is the propulsive phase of the butterfly leg kick.

Look for:
• A vigorous drive down with the lower legs and extended feet. • A full extension of the knees as the feet continue on to the bottom of the downbeat. • The elevation of the hips as a reaction from the vigorous drive down of the legs.

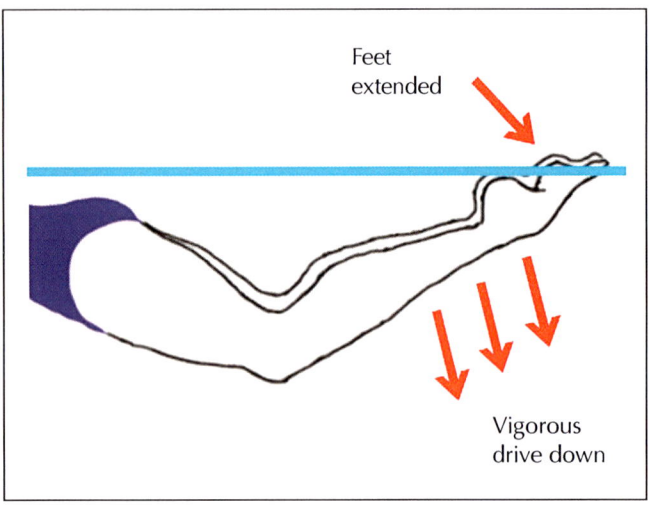

Figure 8.6a
The start of the downbeat in the butterfly kick

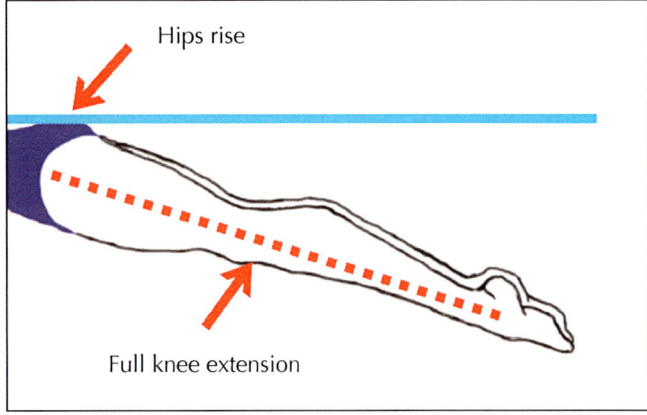

Figure 8.6b
The bottom of the downbeat in the butterfly kick

Discussion on the leg action

 It is vital for an effective leg action that the swimmer is encouraged to use the lower legs during the kick down (propulsive phase).

A propulsive action can only be developed properly if emphasis is placed on:

- Encouraging a full extension of the ankles on the kick down.
- Developing a feel for a whip-like action with the lower legs.

Teachers often mistakenly think that if they get the children to 'wiggle' their hips, this somehow produces the correct leg movement. They may establish an undulation but this is without any real concern or understanding for the propulsion involved. Whilst the leg kick is intrinsically linked to the undulating body action, it is important to realise that no amount of 'wiggling' at the hips will generate propulsion.

Arm action

The arm pull is the main source of propulsion. The arms work simultaneously and symmetrically throughout the complete stroke cycle.

The double arm pull, uses the muscles of the chest and both arms at the same time, resulting in a strong propulsive action. Also, the ease with which the double arm recovery is achieved is dependent on the flexibility of the shoulder girdle.

The butterfly pulling pattern

In Figure 8.7:

- The first part of the limb track, the sweep out followed by the sweep in, is the **pull phase**.
- The last part of the limb track, where the hands sweep slightly out and backwards, is the **push phase**.

The limb track that the hands trace is often likened to a key-hole shape and so the pattern has become known as the **key-hole pull**.

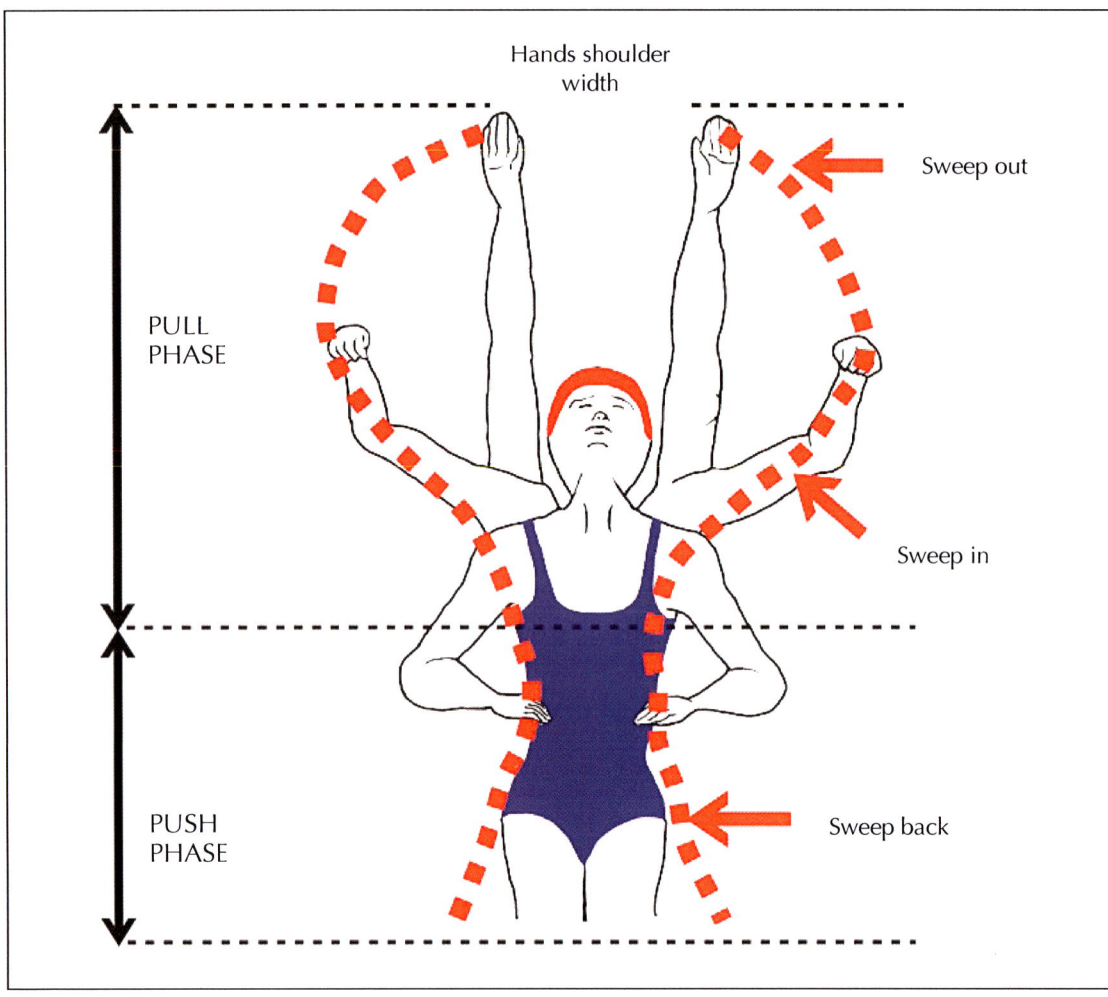

Figure 8.7
The key-hole pulling pattern of the butterfly arm action

Look for:
• The hands starting fairly close together on entry. • As the arm action is performed, the hands tracing a pulling pattern through the water that is similar to a key-hole shape.

With this in mind, we can now move on to look more closely at each phase of the arm action.

Entry

Look for:
• The hands entering the water in front of the head and in line with the shoulders. • The entry being made with the hands slightly angled, palms facing out so that the thumbs enter the water first. • The arms being almost fully extended. Ideally, they should slope slightly downwards, so the elbows are just higher than the wrists.

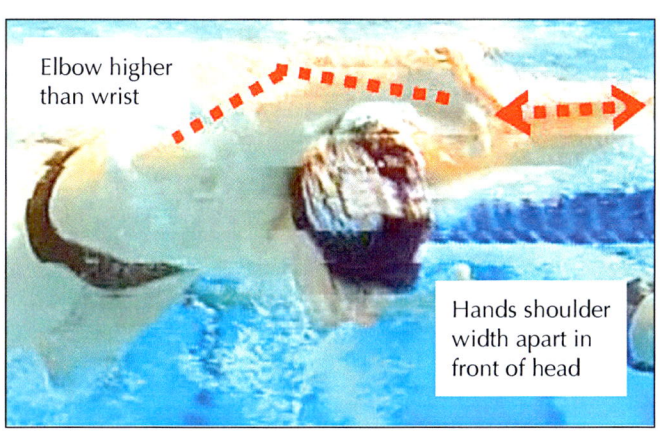

Figure 8.8
The butterfly entry position

 The exact position of the entry may vary slightly with the degree of shoulder mobility.

Point of catch

As soon as the hands enter the water, the catch is made.

Look for:
• The hands making an initial sideways movement very similar to the breaststroke. • A press mainly out and slightly down to reach a point just outside the shoulder line, approximately 15 cms. (6 inches) below the surface.

Figure 8.9
The press out to the catch point in butterfly

Hands make initial sideways movement

Pull phase

From the catch position, the hands continue to trace a curved path outwards then inwards.

Out-sweep

Look for:
• The lower arms sweeping down, so the hands end up underneath the elbow. • The hands changing pitch to face backwards, finger tips pointing down. • The hands reaching their deepest point in the stroke.

Figure 8.10
The start of the out-sweep in butterfly

Lower arms sweep down

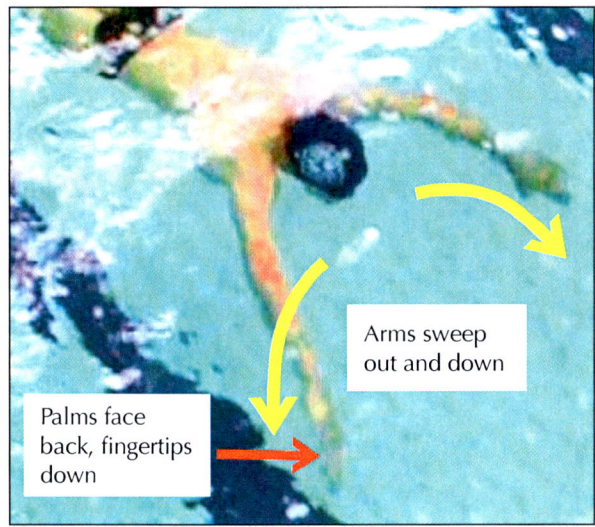

Figure 8.11
The out-sweep as viewed from above

Arms sweep
out and down

Palms face
back, fingertips
down

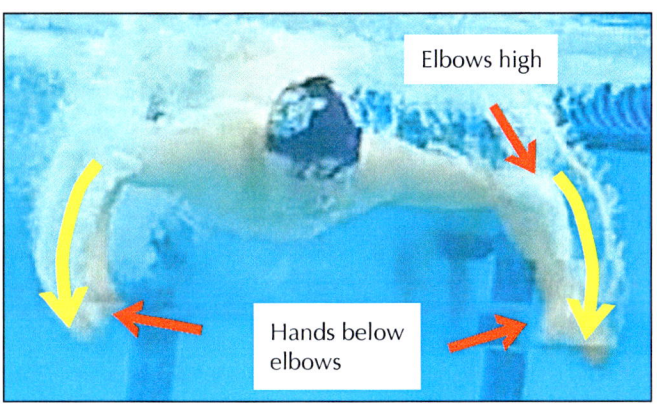

Elbows high

Figure 8.12
The end of the out-sweep in butterfly

Hands below
elbows

🔑 Throughout this out-sweep the elbow remains high.

In-sweep

Look for:
• The hands sweeping in under the chest as the elbows increase their bend to about 90 degrees. • The hands coming within 15 centimetres of each other at their closest point in the key-hole pattern. • The hands changing their pitch so the palms turn in slightly to face each other.

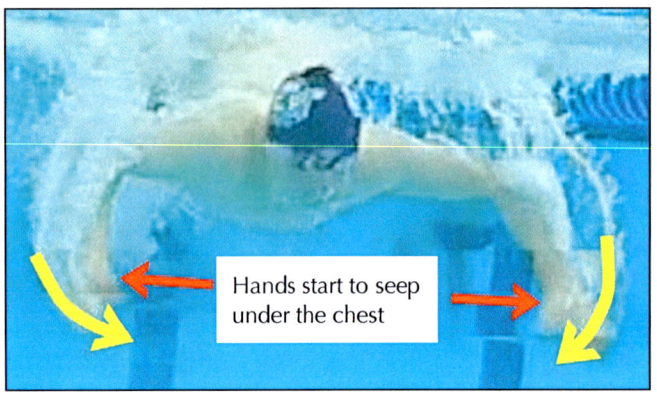

Hands start to seep under the chest

Figure 8.13
The start of the in-sweep in butterfly

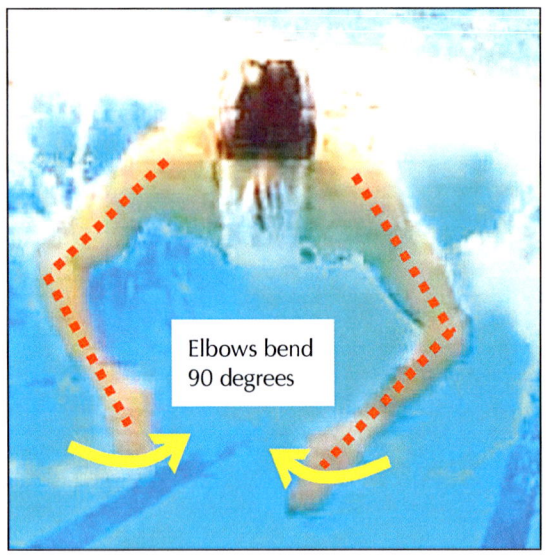

Elbows bend 90 degrees

Figure 8.14
The in-sweep in butterfly

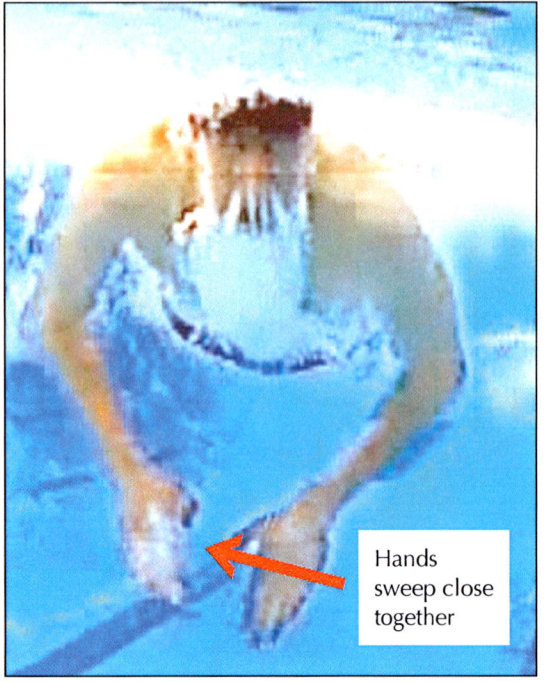

Hands sweep close together

Figure 8.15
The end of the in-sweep in butterfly

Push phase

> **Look for:**
>
> - The pull changing to a pushing action from the moment the hands pass under the chest.
> - The arms straightening as the palms push back towards the thighs, maintaining their purchase on the water for as long as possible.
> - The thumbs almost brushing the thighs before the arms begin their recovery.

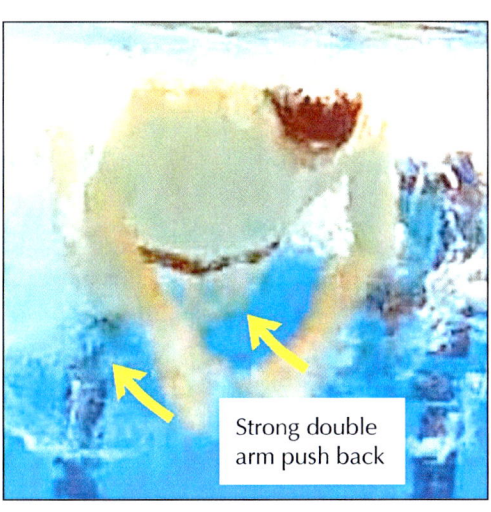

Strong double arm push back

Figure 8.16
The push phase in butterfly

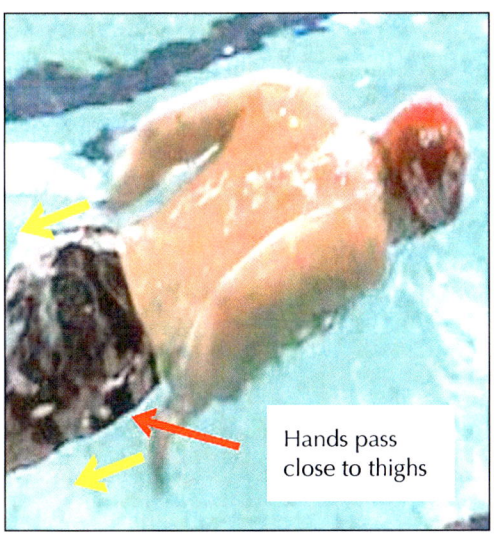

Hands pass close to thighs

Figure 8.17
An above water view of the push phase in butterfly

Recovery

Look for:
• The hands exiting the water, little finger first and swinging in a wide circular movement back to the entry point.

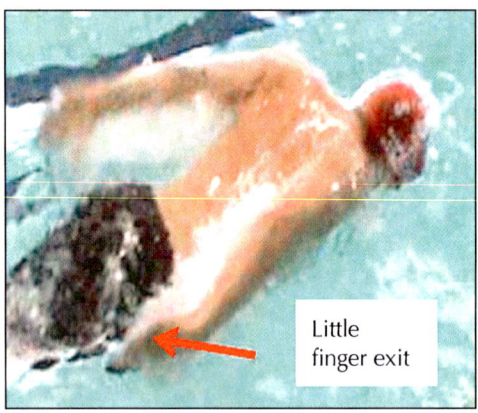

Figure 8.18a
The start of the recovery in butterfly

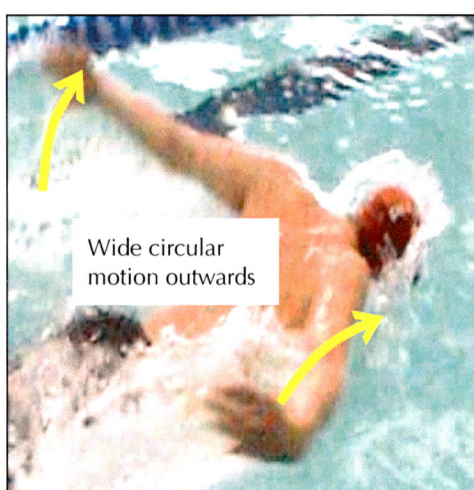

Figure 8.18b
The first half of the recovery in butterfly

Figure 8.18c
The second half of the recovery in butterfly

By exiting the water little finger first and maintaining that position during the first half of the recovery, the muscles of the neck and shoulder are released, enabling the head to drop back into the water more easily.

Although the recovery is made low over the water, it is essential that the whole arm is kept above the surface during the recovery movement for the stroke to be legal and for minimal resistance.

Discussion on the butterfly arm action

Variations in the stroke pattern

Although we have described one accepted stroke pattern, there are other variations depending on an individual's physique, flexibility and buoyancy. The teacher needs to tolerate variations mainly in terms of:

- The underwater limb track.
- The nature of the arm recovery.

Forearm rotation and hand pitch

An interesting point to note is how the forearm rotates to change the pitch of the hand during the stroke pattern.

The ability to rotate the forearms first in one direction and then in the other is a key component of the butterfly action.

We have already seen in the front crawl chapter how this is used during the arm pull. In the butterfly the hands also scull as they follow the key-hole path, by moving the palms:

Outwards . . . inwards . . . then outwards again.

This is achieved by medial rotation.

- **First inwardly**: Starting with the thumb down and the palm facing out, the forearm rotates in towards the centre line ending with the thumb up and the palm facing in.
- **Secondly outwardly**: This is rotation in the opposite direction. Starting with the thumb up and the palm facing in, the forearm rotates away from the centre line, ending with the thumb down and the palm facing out.

This skill plays a vital part in all the strokes. Therefore it is essential that the teacher gives the novice regular practices in sculling.

Breathing

The breathing action is so closely inter-related with the co-ordination of the arm and leg movements, that it is best described as a complete sequence.

Set as table

Look for:
• As the hands push back, the legs kick down and the chest rises so the head can be easily lifted out of the water.   • The chin begins to push forward – in a conscious movement.   • The breath is taken at the end of the push phase and the start of the recovery phase.

Chin and mouth clear of the water

Figure 8.19
The breathing position in butterfly

Look for:
• As the arms recover, the head drops deliberately back into the water before the hands reach the entry position.   • The chin is tucked into the chest as the legs kick down again.

Face back in the water down before hands enter

Figure 8.20
The return of the head to the water after the breath has been taken

⚷ The combination of a strong push back followed by the powerful lift of the body out of the water during the recovery, lends itself to an explosive type of breathing.

Timing

There are two leg kicks to one arm cycle:

- The **first kick down** occurs as the arms enter the water.

- The **second kick down** occurs as the arms push back towards the hips.

☞ Rhythm plays a great part in the butterfly, more than any other stroke. It is essential that the two leg kicks be performed with equal effort to maintain a smooth, well-balanced and continuous rhythm.

The co-ordination and rhythm of the stroke is based on the concept that:

☞ The head leads the way. The head must consciously be lifted and dropped within the stroke. The key is for the head to move before the arms as shown in Figures 8.21 and 8.22.

Look for:
• The head being lifted from the water *before* the arms start their recovery.

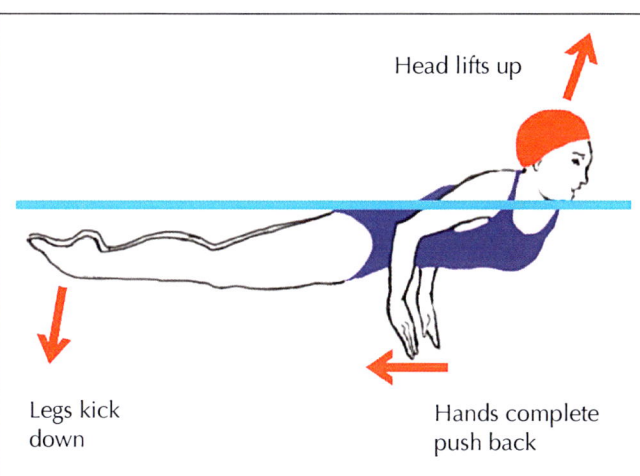

Head lifts up

Legs kick down

Hands complete push back

Figure 8.21
The lifting of the head before the arms start their recovery

Look for:
• The head being dropped back into the water *before* the arms reach their entry point.

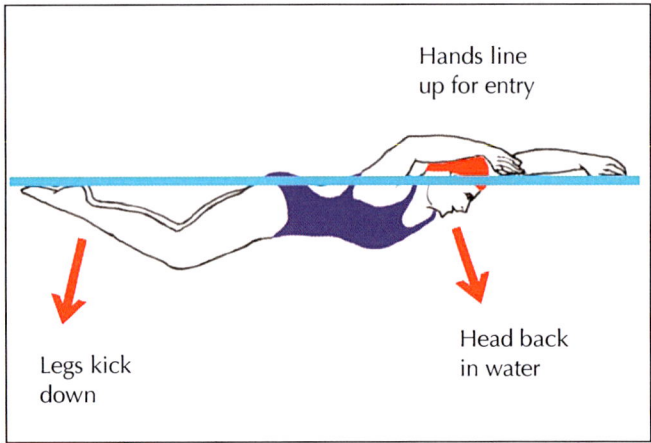

Hands line
up for entry

Head back
in water

Legs kick
down

Figure 8.22
The dropping of the head into the
water before the arms reach their
entry point

The degree of undulation

Teachers sometimes see the movement of the hips as a specific movement which
needs to be taught rather than it being simply a reaction of the arm and leg
movements. This leads them to emphasise pushing the bottom or hips up and down
while teaching the leg action.

This does little to generate the right undulating rhythm to the stroke (*the wave-like
movement travelling down the body, starting at the head and ending at the feet*). As
a result, the teacher falls into the trap of trying to establish an undulation without
any concern for the propulsion involved in the leg kick, particularly the use of the
lower leg.

 It is vital for an effective leg action that the swimmer is taught to use the lower legs
during the kick down (propulsive phase).

An effective, propulsive leg kick can only be developed by emphasising:

- Full extension of the ankles on the kick down.

- Developing a feel for a whip like action with the lower legs.

Note that a lot of work during the early stages is to develop the leg action while
holding onto a small float. This restricts the undulating motion somewhat and
so when the full stroke is completed, the undulating movement has to be
emphasised.

THE BUILDING UP OF TEACHING PROGRESSIONS

By the time the butterfly is introduced to the pupils, it is most likely they have
already grasped some of the fundamentals of the other strokes, so the starting point
is more advanced. We can therefore start straight away to develop the kick. It is

essential that from the start the stroke is built up by developing an effective leg kick that:

- Helps maintain the correct body position.
- Assists in setting up a rhythm to enable the arm action to be smoothly integrated into the stroke.

BUILDING BLOCK 1

Introducing the leg kick

Practice 1	Teaching points
Practice a front crawl leg action while holding onto the rail.	• Kick from the hips.

Reason   To check that the kick is from the hips.

The teacher now demonstrates the difference between the front crawl and butterfly leg action.

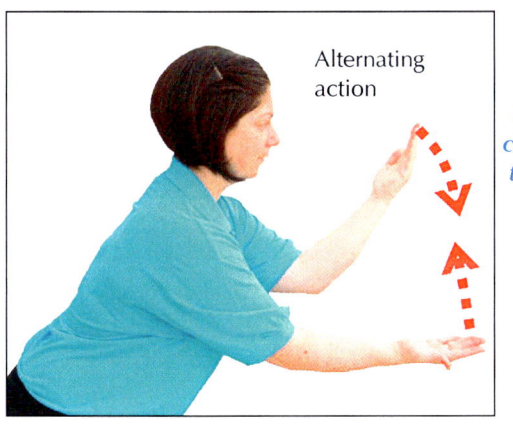

Figure 8.23a
The teacher demonstrating a front crawl leg action

Figure 8.23b
The teacher demonstrating a butterfly leg action

Practice 2	Teaching points
Holding the rail, start kicking front crawl and without stopping, change to a dolphin action when asked to do so.	• Keep the feet together. • Point the toes.

Reason | The legs start working from the hips and this is maintained as the action changes to working both legs simultaneously.

Practice 3	Teaching points
Push and glide with two floats, one under each arm, start kicking front crawl to halfway across the width, then change to a dolphin leg action.	• When changing to butterfly kick, 'glue' the legs together.

Reason | The two floats give maximum support and allow the pupil to concentrate on just the legs, feeling the difference between an alternating action and one where the feet are kept together.

There is little value in spending a lot of time on these practices other than to ensure the correct movement is being performed. The pupils need to be perfectly clear what their legs are doing and to feel what it is like to kick up and down with their legs together. This is a new movement for them.

These initial kicking exercises are must be done over a short distance because the children very quickly become fatigued. For this reason, a number of the leg practices can also be done on the back where breathing does not present a problem.

Practice 4	Teaching points
Repeat Practice 3 on the back, kicking backstroke to halfway across the width, then change to a double leg movement where the feet are kept together.	• Join the legs together at halfway and beat as one.

Reason | This is simply a variation on Practice 3 but the pupil will not experience any difficulties with the breathing.

The teacher now re-demonstrates the butterfly leg action from both the front and side.

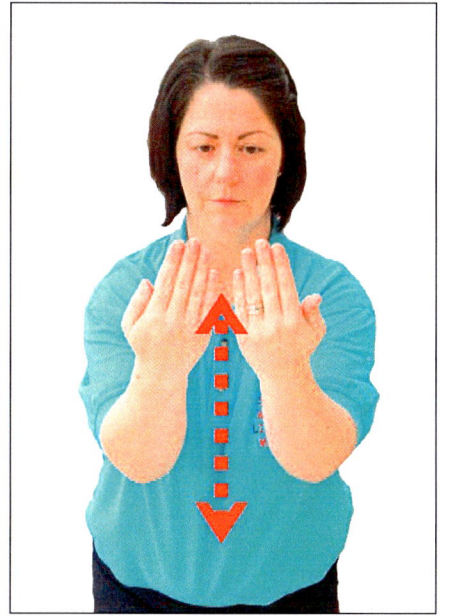 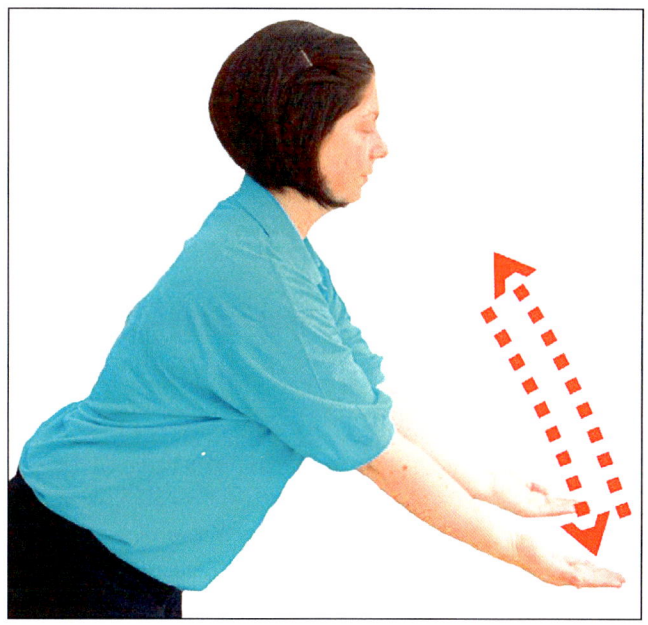

Figure 8.24
The butterfly kick from the front

Figure 8.25
The butterfly kick from the side

Practice 5	Teaching points
Holding one float out in front, kick across the width using a dolphin leg kick.	• Press down with the front of the foot.

Reason   To develop and strengthen the leg action.

Practice 6	Teaching points
Dolphin kick across the pool on the back, with one float clasped to the chest.	• Kick up hard with the legs together.

Reason   A variation on Practice 5.

BUILDING BLOCK 2

Introducing the breathing

So far these practices have been performed with the head either up or down. Our primary concern has been to introduce the action and make sure the pupils understand what is required. Before we can go much further, however, we have got to fit the breathing into our practices. This also allows the pupils to establish a proper body position. Therefore in Practice 7, a pull buoy is used rather than a flat float because it allows more flexibility but still gives some support.

Practice 7	Teaching points
With a pull buoy held in front, push and glide, and lift the head to breathe in every two beats (leg kicks).	*BREATHE IN . . . beat, beat* *BREATHE IN . . . beat, beat*

Reason To introduce the breathing every two leg kicks and start to build up the rhythm.

The teacher demonstrates this rhythm to the pupils as shown in Figures 8.26a to 8.26c.

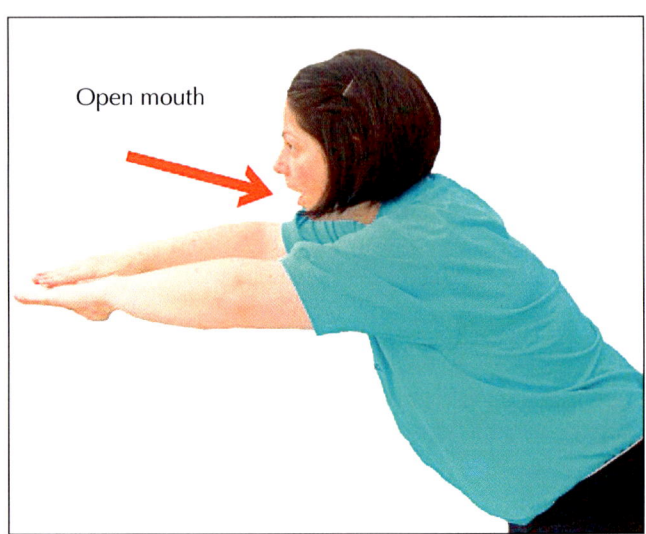

Figure 8.26a
Lifting of the head

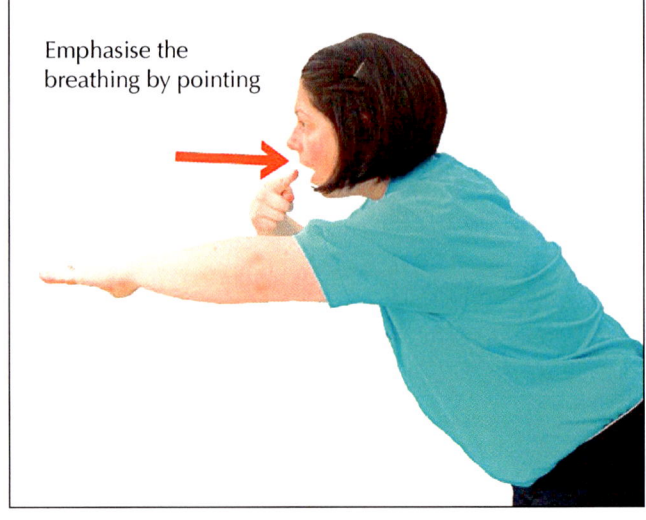

Figure 8.26b
Pointing to the mouth to breathe in

Butterfly

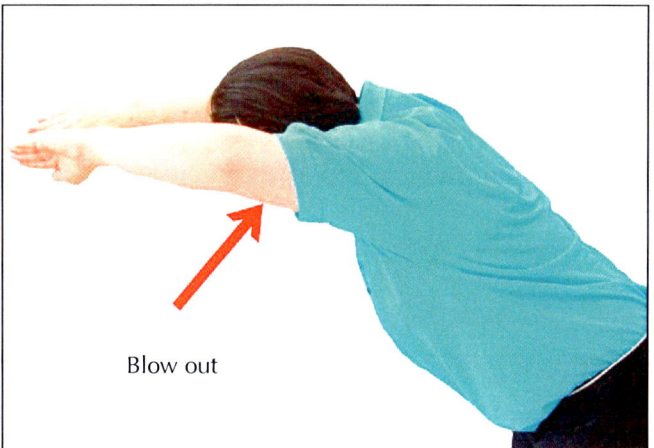

Figure 8.26c
Put head back down and *'beat – beat'*

Blow out

Remember that it is also important for the teacher to encourage the pupils to breathe out by 'explosive' breathing as the head is lifted out of the water, otherwise the practice soon breaks down.

BUILDING BLOCK 3

Introducing the undulation

The undulation does not have to be introduced as a conscious movement but can be woven into the building programme by simply changing the nature of the kicking practice.

Practice 8	Teaching points
Push and glide, pull the arms down to the side and hold them there while kicking to the same rhythm, lifting the head every two beats to breathe in.	• Drop the head. • Round the shoulders

Reason   With no floats to inhibit the movement, this allows the body to undulate more freely while performing the leg action.

Practice 9	Teaching points
If possible, Practices 5 to 8 are repeated using flippers.	• Allow the flippers to do the work.

Reason   To develop ankle extension and get the feel of the undulating movement.

Flippers can be used when teaching butterfly. They help develop ankle movement and give the feeling of strength and speed. Be careful though because a lot of time can be wasted finding the right size, getting cramp in the toes, flippers falling off and so on. The teacher must also be aware that flippers can produce difficulties in timing. The legs propel the swimmer along faster than the arms can keep up. As a result the arms end up performing little more than a 'tracing' movement of the limb track.

BUILDING BLOCK 4

Introducing the arm action

When introducing the arm action it is important for the teacher to break the movement down and link the phases of the pull to the movement of the head. By knowing where the head and arms should be at any given time, the pupils can look for checkpoints that help establish the correct limb track and timing of the arm movement.

To introduce the arm action, it is best to have the pupils standing in shallow water. If only deep water is available, however, the following practice can be performed on the poolside.

Practice 10
If possible, Practices 5 to 8 are repeated using flippers.

The pupils stand in shallow water. The teacher demonstrates the arm action with the pupils copying.

Reason   This is important because they need to understand the pattern the hands trace through the water and how the hand pitch changes along the path.

 The stroke pattern introduced at this stage must be exaggerated to enable the pupils to feel the movement as they stand in the water. The pattern they trace is not the one we ultimately want to achieve. However, similar to the backstroke where the straight arm pull is taught first and the bent arm developed from this, so an exaggerated **key hole** is first introduced for the butterfly and, once learnt, is then modified.

The teacher's instructions
'The hands enter the water.'

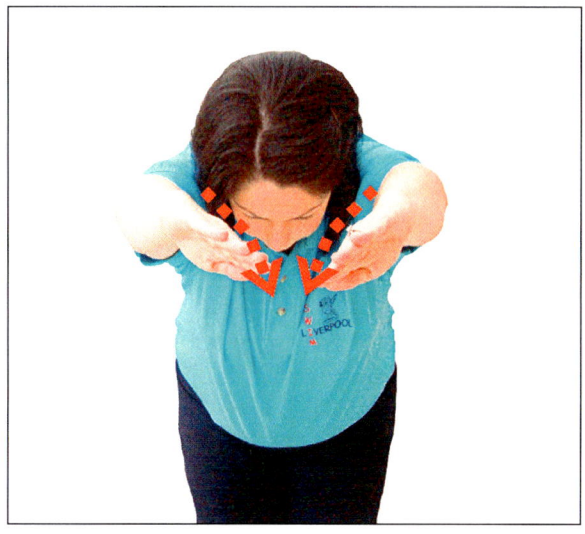

Teaching points

- Thumbs down.
- Backs of hands almost together.
- Arms almost straight.

Figure 8.27
Teacher demonstration of the hand entry

'The hands pull sideways to the width of the head.'

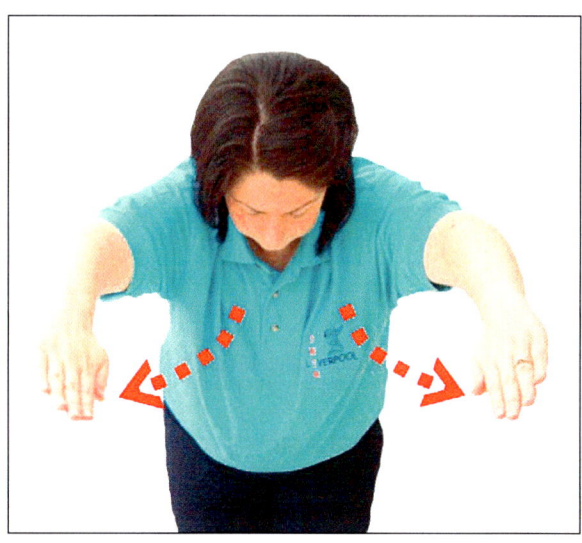

Teaching points

- Palms turn to face back.
- Fingers drop down.

Figure 8.28
Teacher demonstration of the initial pull sideways

'The elbows start to bend and the arms pull down and back.'

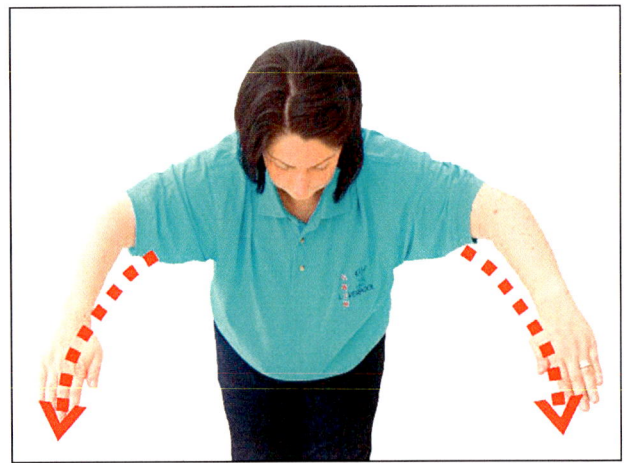

Teaching points

- Hands part further.
- Keep elbows high.
- Head remains down.

Figure 8.29
Teacher demonstration of the out-sweep

'The hands sweep under the body and come together under the shoulders.'

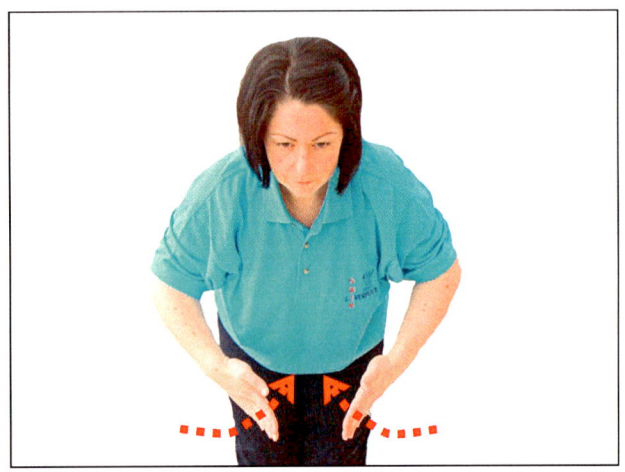

Teaching points

- Finger tips pointing down.
- Palms facing back.
- Hands flat.
- Elbows high.
- The head begins to lift.

Figure 8.30
Teacher demonstration of the in-sweep

'The chin is lifted so breathing can take place.'

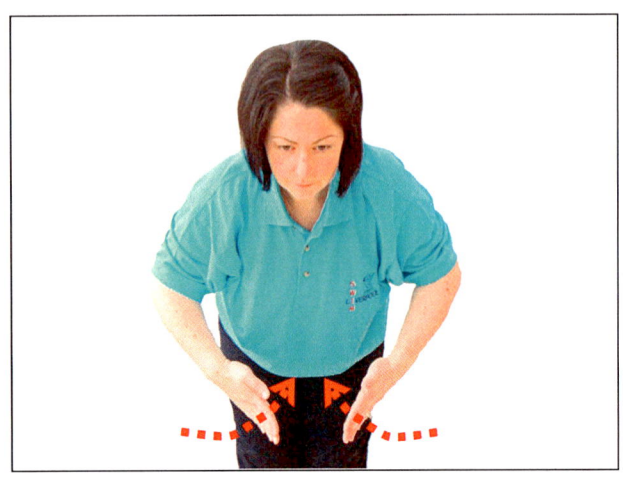

Teaching points

- Push the chin forwards.
- Look forwards.
- Mouth clear of the water.

Figure 8.31
Teacher demonstration the pushing of the chin forwards

'The arms are pushed outwards and backwards towards the thighs and the spine is straightened.'

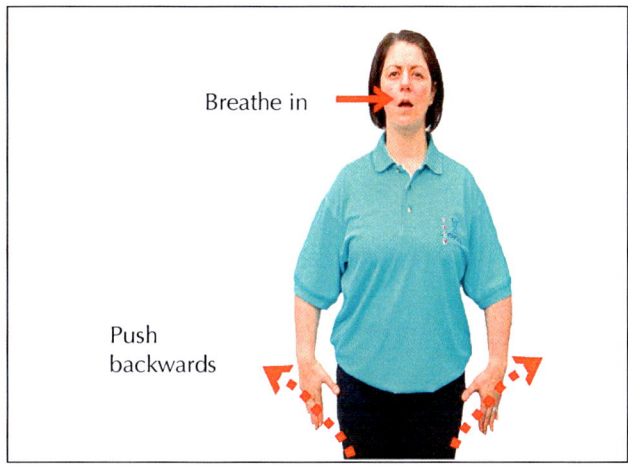

Teaching points
• Thumbs brush thighs. • The hands sweep out to the side. • Breathe in.

Figure 8.32
Teacher demonstration of the push backwards

It may also be useful to show this position from the side to emphasise the straightening of the spine as shown in Figure 8.33.

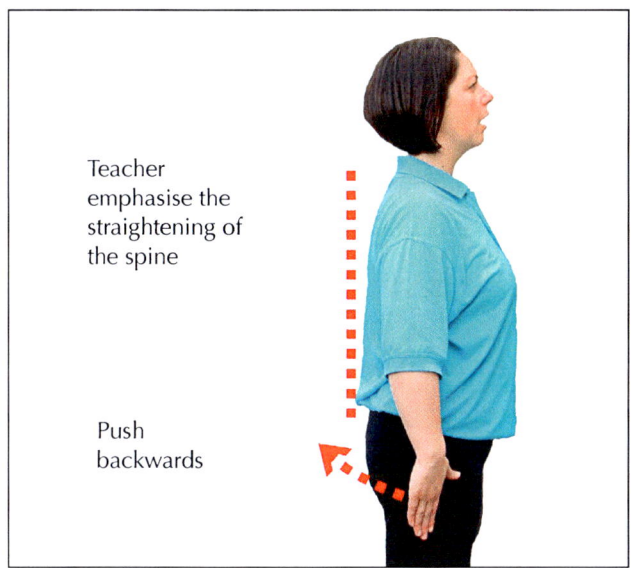

Teaching points
As the head lifts out of the water: • Push the chin forward • Straighten the spine

Figure 8.33
Teacher demonstration of the push backwards from the side

'The arms are then lifted out of the water.'

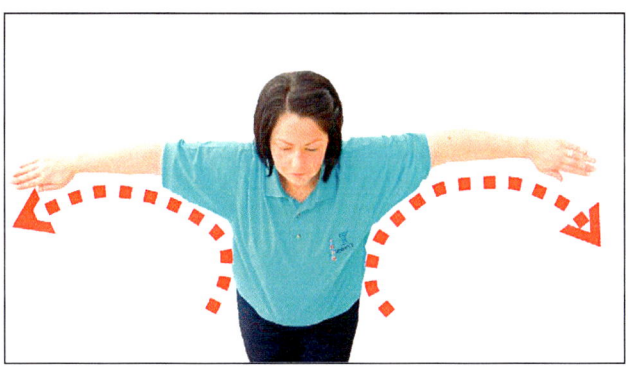

Teaching points
• Little finger first.

Figure 8.34
Teacher demonstration of the start of the recovery

'The arms sweep over the water in a smooth, relaxed manner.'

Teaching points

- Little finger first.
- Little finger high.
- Arms straight.

Figure 8.35
Teacher demonstration of the
recovery over the water

During this sequence one aspect must be emphasised . . . **'the movement of the back'.**

- Instructions in Figures 8.27 to 8.30 are carried out with the pupils standing in the water, bending forward.
- As the head begins to lift during instruction 8.31, the back begins to straighten.
- By the time the thumbs brush the thighs, (Figures 8.32 and 8.33), the pupil should be standing upright.
- Then as the arms recover, the pupil leans forward again.

The whole point of this sequence is that it simulates what happens within the full stoke. It gives the feeling of the undulation and pinpoints the exact time and place when the pupil lifts their head to breathe.

After the standing demonstration and practice, the pupils need to 'get in and have a go' but at this stage they still need some support. So with a pull buoy between the thighs, the pupils are asked to swim the full stroke over a series of widths or short distances.

The teacher gives them one area at a time to focus on. This encourages the pupils to concentrate and also gives them resting time as the teacher describes the next part of the sequence.

Practice 11

Using a pull buoy or small float between the thighs, practice the arm movement across the width or half width. Although the legs have a float between them, kick from the knees.

Teaching points

- Work the arms together.

Reason   The support in the hip area gives the pupil's time to slow everything down and concentrate on the arm action.

Practice 12	Teaching points
Try the whole stroke without aids working through the same sequence and focusing on each area in turn.	• Think about each part of the action

Reason   A progression from Practice 11.

Developing the arm action

To develop the arm action further, the focus should be on the following areas when practising the whole stroke:

AREAS OF FOCUS	REASON
• Concentrate on thumb entry with the hands back to back and pulling sideways.	To gain a streamlined position at the beginning of the stroke and to place the hands correctly for the next phase.
• Watch the hands under water tracing a key-hole pattern.	To keep the head down.
• As the hands come together under the shoulders, lift the chin to breathe and pull shoulders back.	This gives the pupil a specific point in the stroke when to lift the head. The pulling back of the shoulders also helps get a high body position that aids the recovery over the water.
• Push the hands strongly back to the thighs and breathe.	To continue the lift of the body and allow the mouth to be clear of the water.
• As the arms come out of the water, drop the head down and emphasise little finger exit.	To completely clear the water with the arms and rotate the hands to make the exit out of the water easier.

BUILDING BLOCK 5

Improving the timing

To emphasise the two leg kicks per arm cycle, the following teaching points should be frequently used:

As the head lifts to breathe and the arms are under the body, **kick down hard**.

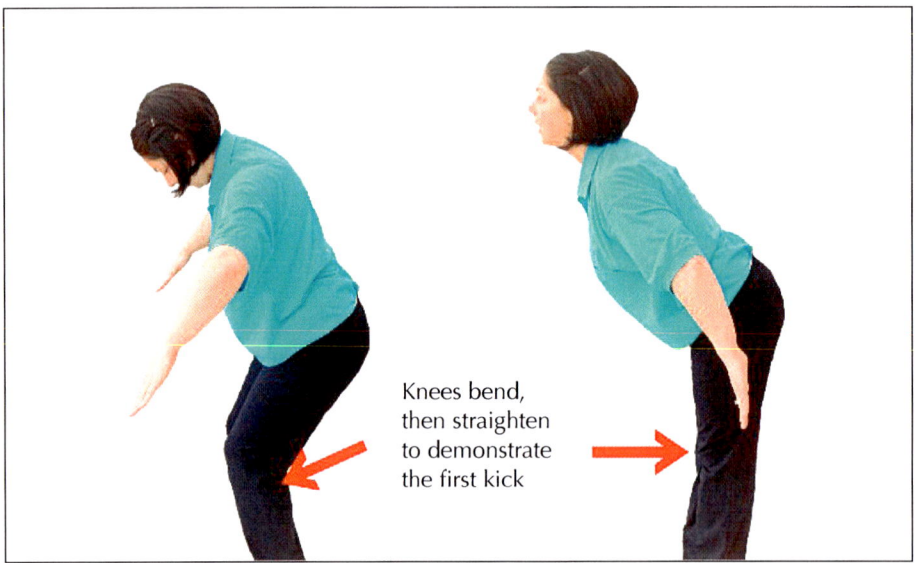

Knees bend, then straighten to demonstrate the first kick

Figure 8.36
Teacher demonstration of the timing of the first kick with the breathing and arm action

As the face is returned to the water and the hands enter, **kick again**.

Knees bend, then straighten again to demonstrate the second kick

Figure 8.37
Teacher demonstration of the timing of the second kick with the breathing and arm action

The key element in developing the timing is to teach the stroke with the breathing.

Improving the rhythm

The butterfly is the most 'fish-like' of all the competitive strokes, imitating the undulating motion of a dolphin. When one watches a good swimmer, the **rhythm** of the stroke is so evident, it looks effortless. To develop this rhythm takes practice. It is unlikely that a novice swimmer be able to perform the stroke over any great distance before the rhythm of the stroke is lost.

Therefore, the stroke has to be broken down so that:

- The timing and rhythm are easier to learn.

- The swimmer can feel what the rhythm is like.

- The swimmer can maintain the rhythm over some distance.

One arm butterfly drills

Improving the rhythm is best achieved by working through a number of butterfly drills, normally associated with the competitive swimmer. The drills which follow are all based around the **one arm butterfly** practice performed in a variety of ways. This breaks the stroke down into an easier skill and because the practice can be maintained over a greater distances, this helps to 'groove' the correct movement patterns before the whole stroke is once again attempted.

Practice 13	Teaching points
<ul><li>Holding a float, push and glide from the side and start the legs working.</li><li>Keeping the left arm in front still holding the float, pull and recover with the right arm only.</li><li>To breathe, turn the head to the side as the hand pushes back towards the hip.</li><li>Return the head quickly before the hand enters the water to start another pull.</li></ul>	<ul><li>Keep the leg kick continuous.</li><li>Kick as the hand pushes back towards the hip.</li><li>Kick again as the hand enters the water.</li><li>Turn the head to the side to breathe as the hand pushes back.</li><li>Return the face to the water before the hand enters.</li><li>Watch for the 'key-hole' pattern underwater.</li><li>Keep the arm straight and low over the water on recovery.</li></ul>

Reason   This drill breaks the full stroke down into an easier skill with some support. This gives the swimmer time to concentrate on one arm at a time. It also schools the swimmer into the rhythm required for the full stroke.

Practice 14	Teaching points
• As for Practice 13, but with no float.	• Focus on the teaching points outlined in Practice 13

Reason A progression on the same theme as Practice 13.

Practice 13 and 14 should be repeated using both arms, working across the width pulling with the right arm only, then back again using the left arm only.

There are a number of variations on this one arm butterfly drill which all help to build up the skill and conditioning required to perform the stroke well. These are:

1. **Variations in the position of the non-pulling arm**

   Practice: Performing a single arm butterfly, keeping the arm that is not in use down by the side.

   Reason: This enables the head and shoulders to undulate more freely, diving under the water as the pulling arm enters. Care must be taken that this undulation does not become excessive.

2. **Variation of the number of strokes used**

   Practice: Instead of performing one width on one arm, followed by one width on the other arm, any combination of stroke counting can be used. For example:

   • Three strokes right arm only, followed by three strokes left arm only, then three right arm only again and so on.

   • Similarly, the single arm practice may also be combined with some stroking on the full stroke. For example:

   • Swim one width right arm only, follow by one width left arm only, then one width full stroke (double arm).

   • Swim three strokes right arm, three strokes left arm, then three strokes full stroke, repeating the sequence until a certain distance is covered.

3. **Variations with the use of swimming aids**

Single arm butterfly drills can be performed using either:

   • A pull buoy between the thighs to give added support to the hip region.

   • Flippers to add strength and speed and increase feel of the body position.

 One of the best ways to use flippers is in combination with a pull buoy held between the thighs. Performing the full stroke in this way reduces the reliance on the legs, but the added speed and strength from the flippers helps lift the swimmer's body up out of the water to breathe.

4. Variation in the breathing position

- **Practice**: An alternative practice which teachers may use is a single arm drill with the head being lifted to the front to breathe, (instead of turning the head to the side), keeping the chin close to the water.

- **Reason**: This imitates more closely the breathing action performed during the full stroke but is slightly less comfortable than turning the head to the side to breathe.

 This practice is not suitable for beginners. The problem is the considerable reduction in power by only using one arm does not lift the upper body high enough to facilitate a comfortable breathing action.

 There is no point in doing drill work if the skills practised are not transferable to the full stroke. For this reason it is vital that all drill work must end with an attempt at performing the whole stroke.

PROBLEMS AND SOLUTIONS

Leg action

Teachers may observe two main problems associated with the leg kick:

- The legs and feet not being kept together resulting in an alternating action.
- Excessive bending of the knees.

Problem 1: Alternating legs and feet

Cause/effect	Solution
Usually the pupil has not grasped the fact that both legs must be kept together and worked simultaneously. In attempting to kick up and down, a front crawl type action is produced with the legs alternating, often in an irregular manner.	Some time must be spent on going over the early kicking practices in Building Block 1, where the difference between the front crawl and butterfly actions are emphasised.

Problem 2: Excessive knee bend

Cause/effect	Solution
This problem is more acute when the pupils adopt a poor body position. They are desperate to lift their head and shoulders up out of the water to breathe and in doing so, their back end (*hips, legs and feet*) sinks. As a result, all they can do is to bend the knees in an attempt to perform a dolphin leg action.	Return to Building Blocks 2 and 3, where the breathing and undulation is introduced.

Breathing

Problem 3: Breathing in the wrong place

This is seen as breathing either too early or too late in relation to the arm pull.

Cause/effect	Solution
Too early: A pause in the arm action is seen after entry, then immediately the pull starts, the head is lifted to breathe. **Too late**: The arms are pulled right the way back to the thighs before the head is lifted to breathe and the head is still up as the arms recover and enter the water.	As the timing of the breathing is linked so closely with the arm action, there must be a return to Building Block 4. The exaggerated key-hole stroke pattern needs to be emphasised again to slow the stroke down, allowing time for the breathing to be brought in at the correct point.

Arm action

- The two most frequently seen problems are associated with the recovery. These are:

- The arms not clearing the water.

- The arms recovering irregularly over the water.

Problem 4: Arms not clearing the water

Cause/effect	Solution
The arms not clearing the water on recovery because the body is not being lifted high enough by the kick.	Start by returning to Building Blocks 2 and 3 to practise the leg action and improve the undulation. From there, progress onto Building Block 5, using the single arm drill to emphasise the feel and timing of the recovery.

Problem 5: Arm recovery irregular

Cause/effect

The arms are not recovering simultaneously. This is due to either:

- The leg action not being strong enough to lift the body high enough for the arms to clear the water.
- The arms tend to trace a poor or almost non-existent key-hole pattern underwater. Both arms do not reach the thighs at the same time and so one arm is 'flung' over the water before the other.

Solution

If the leg action is not strong enough, greater time needs to be spent on developing and strengthening the action using a variety of practices.

With a poor key-hole pattern, a return to Building Block 4 is essential to work through the standing practice to establish an exaggerated and symmetrical action.

Discussion on butterfly

When thinking about the main difficulties that pupils experience with the butterfly, it is too easy to say they simply lack the necessary strength and flexibility to perform the stroke well.

If this were the case, there would be little point in attempting to teach the stroke to young people because clearly they are not going to be very strong. Teachers cannot hope to make any improvement in terms of strength or flexibility during what is often only one thirty minute lesson each week.

We can only re-emphasise what was stated in the introduction – a breakdown in the stroke is rarely the result of a lack of strength – it is usually the result of the learner not having enough time to breathe.

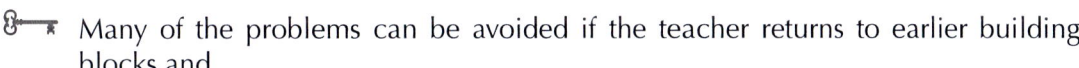 Many of the problems can be avoided if the teacher returns to earlier building blocks and . . .

- Slows everything down to buy the swimmer time to breathe.
- Builds up a rhythm that allows the breathing to fit naturally into the stroke in a smooth, relaxed manner.

THE IMPROVEMENT CIRCLE

The improvement circle for butterfly is built around three core skills:

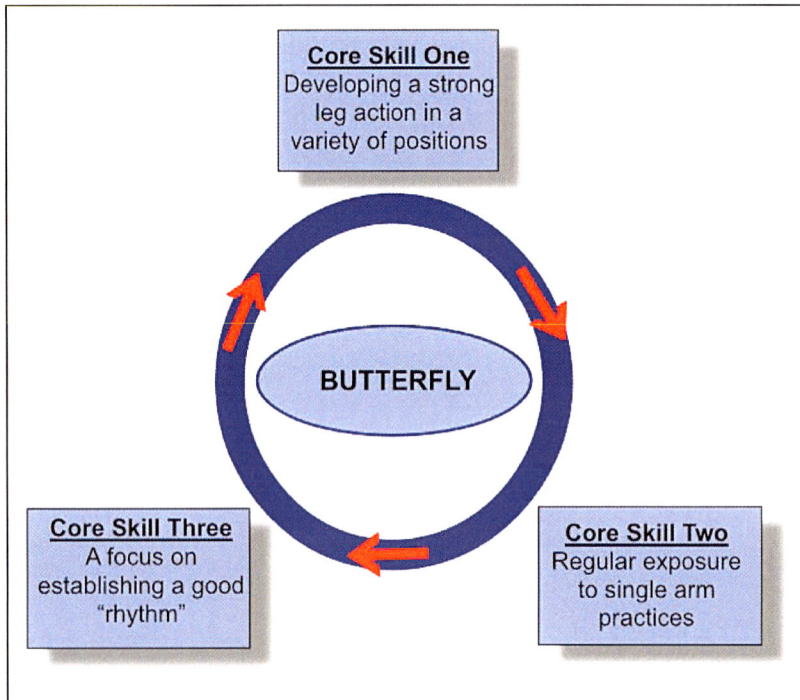

Figure 8.38
The improvement circle for the butterfly

Core skill 1: Developing a strong leg action in a variety of positions

A competent leg action:

- Assists the hips in maintaining a position close to the surface throughout the stroke cycle.

- Adds to overall propulsion as the double 'fishtail action' is a powerful movement.

Above all, a strong leg action performs a vital role in helping the swimmer to establish and maintain a rhythm to the stroke reducing the build-up of fatigue as the swimmer performs the stroke. It is therefore vital to build the improver programme around first establishing an effective leg kick.

Butterfly kicking practices with support

All of the kicking practices with support outlined in the front crawl improvement circle can be performed using a butterfly leg action. These include:

1. Kicking with arms outstretched, holding a board with either the head up or the head down.
2. Holding a kickboard with one arm outstretched and the other arm down by the side, breathing either to the side or the front.
3. Holding the kickboard in a vertical position pushing against the flat surface of the board.

In addition:

- Regular exposure to kicking butterfly on the back while holding a float either across the chest or behind the head with arms outstretched helps to develop the dolphin action further.
- Kicking on the side with the lower arm extended in front holding a kickboard and the other arm down by the side gives the swimmer a further variation to improve the leg action.

 A special note of caution here. When practising butterfly kick with support, **only use a small float**. Using a large kickboard places an increased strain on the lower back.

Even when using a small float it is a good idea to mix up the practices and include a variety of work in different body positions to reduce the potential for any injuries to occur.

Once the pupil has acquired a degree of competency kicking with support, it is important to develop the kick further by improving the ability to kick without support. As with the other strokes, it is important to remember this can be very tiring for the pupil. Keeping the practices short ensures the skill level is maintained.

Butterfly kicking practices without support

1. Kicking without a float, face down between outstretched arms.
2. Kicking with both arms down by the side.
3. Kicking with one arm outstretched and the other arm down by the side.
4. Kicking on the back with arms either down by side or stretched out behind the head.
5. Kicking on the side with the lower arm extended out in front.
6. Kicking on the front, both arms extended and no float.

Core skill 2: A regular exposure to single arm practices

As in front crawl, breaking the stroke down into a single arm practice gives the pupil time to co-ordinate the arm action with the leg kick and the breathing and it enables them to perform the stroke without the skill level breaking down. At first, the practice is often performed with the supporting arm out in front and breathing to the side. Pupils find this helps them to learn the skill and develop the correct timing and rhythm (two kicks to one arm pull) for the stroke.

Single arm practices for butterfly

1. With the supporting arm outstretched in front and holding the back-end of a small float, perform one width right arm only then change to perform a second width with the left arm only – breathing to the side or front.
2. As for Practice one, performing a set number of single arm strokes with one arm, then change and perform the same number on the other arm.
3. Perform the single arm practice with the supporting arm down by the side and breathing to the front.
4. Additional support can be given by holding a pull buoy between the legs while still encouraging a strong leg action.
5. A variation can be introduced by performing these practices with the fingers closed in a 'fist' position.

More advanced is a single arm practice with the supporting arm down by the side enabling easier breathing to the front. This should be encouraged as soon as possible as it is the breathing action used when performing the full stroke. However, this practice is more tiring so distances need to be kept short.

 Once again ensure equal practice is given to both left and right arms so the stroke is developed in a balanced way.

Avoid pulling only with a pull buoy (legs remaining still) especially when attempting a full arm stroke. This places additional strain on the lower back and destroys the timing and co-ordination of the stroke. This practice is used only with advanced swimmers for the purpose of strengthening and conditioning.

Throughout the development of this single arm skill, the same teaching points used in the building programme need to be continually emphasised.

Core skill 3: A strong focus on establishing a feel for the rhythm of the stroke

During our introduction to the butterfly, we highlighted the need to build up a rhythm that allows the breathing to fit naturally into the stroke in a smooth, relaxed manner. In this way the stroke is less dependent on strength and more dependent on timing, co-ordination and rhythm. It is important therefore to focus on a variety of ways to encourage the improver to feel the rhythm of the stroke.

The following Practices 1 to 3 outline how the rhythm can be built up from the leg action.

Butterfly

1. Kicking underwater in a variety of positions, either on the front, back or side.

Kicking underwater improves the feel of the action for the swimmer. Once the swimmer is below the surface, they are no longer kicking in an area that is a mixture of both water and air but are kicking surrounded completely by water. Here the swimmer is able to feel the effectiveness of their propulsive actions more easily.

Starting from an underwater push-off the wall, kicking head first underwater with both arms down by the side allows a free undulating motion to be felt. The head should be encouraged to lead the undulating movement with the hips and legs working a strong dolphin action behind.

2. Kicking 'through' the surface

The same practice can be performed along the surface of the water again encouraging the head to lead the movement with the timing based on the following:

Kick once as the head goes down under the water.

Kick again as the head comes up.

3. Kicking 'through' the surface, adding single arm strokes

The same practice as outlined in Practice 2, but performing six leg kicks to set up the rhythm. Then on the seventh and eighth kicks perform one single arm pull. Gradually increase the number of single arms strokes added to the practice while still maintaining the rhythm.

The single arm practices highlighted in Core Skill 2 also assist in giving the pupil a feel for the correct rhythm of the stroke. When these are combined with full stroke, the objective becomes one of trying to maintain the rhythm throughout the practice.

4. Single arm/full stroke combination

Work five strokes right arm only, then five strokes left arm only followed by five complete double arm actions before either stopping or starting the sequence again.

Butterfly can be performed on the back. While strictly not butterfly it does encourage the pupils to focus on performing two kicks per arm cycle and allows them to breathe without difficulty whenever they choose. This variation is also fun to do.

5. Double arm backstroke with a butterfly leg kick

Perform a double arm backstroke action with two butterfly leg kicks each complete arm cycle.

Remember that teaching butterfly is not about strength and stamina. It is about the teacher finding ways to:

- Slow everything down to buy time for the swimmer to breathe.
- Build up a rhythm that allows the breathing to fit naturally into the stroke in a smooth, relaxed manner.
- Encourage the pupils to enjoy the stroke.

SUMMARY OF THINGS TO LOOK FOR IN A GOOD BUTTERFLY STROKE

Body position

- Hips close to the surface throughout stroke – may even appear to rise above the surface.
- Slight undulation of the hips.
- At the highest point when the breath is taken, the chin should be just clear of the water.
- At entry/catch, the body is as streamlined as possible.
- The body position is continually changing as the position of the torso (shoulders and chest) rise and fall to allow the breath to be taken.

Leg kick

- A simultaneous kicking action with both legs working together to create a vigorous 'whip-like' kick down which is powerful and effective.
- Kick up with straight legs.
- Knees slightly bent at the top of the upbeat.
- Legs kick down in a strong 'whip-like' action.
- As the lower leg kicks down, the feet are extended.
- Legs remain together and the action is continuous.
- The kick down causes the hips to rise slightly.

Arm pull

- Hands enter in line with the shoulders, arms almost straight, thumb first
- Hand traces a 'key-hole' pattern.
- Hands sweep down and out to gain a fix on the water.
- Hands then sweep in coming close together under the shoulders/upper chest.
- Forearms press back vigorously towards the hips.
- Elbows remain higher than hands during the pull.
- The double arm pull is very strong and is the main source of propulsion.
- The left and right arm should be balanced and symmetrical.

Arm recovery

- Arms exit little finger first.
- Arms recover almost straight over the water in a low wide circular motion.
- As they pass the head they swing into the forward extended position in preparation for entry.

Breathing

- Breathe with chin pushed forward.
- Breathe in at the end of the press back.
- The breath is taken with the chin just clear of the water.
- It is vital that the face drops back down in the water before the hands enter.

Timing/co-ordination/rhythm

- Two kicks to one arm pull.
- Kick down as the hands enter the water.
- Second kick down as the hands push back to thighs.
- Breathing once every two strokes.
- Both kicks are hard though the difference in body position causes the first kick to be longer and the second kick to have more knee bend.

BUTTERFLY ASSESSMENT SHEET

Name of swimmer:		Age:	
Stroke/activity:		Date:	
Analysis carried out by:			

BODY POSITION

Key questions to ask	Teachers observations and comments
• When is the head lifted from the water? • When is the head returned to the water? • How high is the head lifted from the water? • What is the position of the hips throughout the stroke cycle? • What is the inclination of the body on entry?	

LEG ACTION

Key questions to ask	Teachers observations and comments
• Is the action of both legs simultaneous? • Do the legs remain close together? • How bent are the knees at the top of the upbeat? • Is there a strong 'whip-like' action with the lower leg on the kick down? • Are the toes pointed on the kick down? • How deep are the feet when they finish the kick? • Is the leg action continuous?	

ARM ACTION

Key questions to ask	Teachers observations and comments
• Where do the hands enter the water? • How do the hands enter the water? • How bent is the elbow on entry? • What hand pattern do the hands trace? • Where do the hands sweep under the body? • Is there a strong push back? • Do the elbows remain high during the pull? • Are the left and right arms balanced and symmetrical?	

ARM RECOVERY

Key questions to ask	Teachers observations and comments
• Where do the hands exit the water? • How do the hands exit the water? • How high is the recovery relative to the surface of the water? • How much elbow bend is there on the recovery?	

BREATHING

Key questions to ask	Teachers observations and comments
• When the breath is taken? • Is there any deliberate movement of the head? • How high is the chin above water when breath is taken? • Is a breath taken every stroke? • How smooth is the movement? • What is the effect of breathing on total stroke?	

TIMING AND CO-ORDINATION

Key questions to ask	Teachers observations and comments
• How many kicks are there per arm cycle? • What is the timing between the leg kick and the arm action? • What is the timing between the leg kick and the head position? • How strong are both the kicks? • What is the overall rhythm of the stroke? • Does the stroke flow? • Is the rhythm smooth and undulating?	

FINAL IMPRESSIONS AND COMMENTS

Key questions to ask	Teachers observations and comments
• Is the stroke legal? • How effective is the stroke? • What contribution do you think the legs make to propulsion? • What contribution do you think the arms make to propulsion? • How flexible is the swimmer? • How strong is the swimmer?	

ALTERNATIVE ASSESSMENT SHEET FOR BUTTERFLY

Name of swimmer:		Age:	

Date of assessment:		Date of Reassessment	

Stroke Observations	Areas To improve	Key practice To use	Re-assessment observations

BODY POSITION

LEG KICK

ARM ACTION

ARM RECOVERY

BREATHING

Stroke Observations	Areas To improve	Key practice To use	Re-assessment observations

TIMING AND CO-ORDINATION

GENERAL IMPRESSIONS

First assessment	Second assessment

AREAS TO IMPROVE IN ORDER OF PRIORITY

	Following first assessment		Following second assessment
1		1	
2		2	
3		3	

BUTTERFLY

This is the stroke that is long and low
Up and down and over we go.
The legs keep together, they work from the hip
As they beat down, the body does tip!
There are two beats per stroke, one small and one strong
A smooth flowing rhythm helps this stroke along.
The hands enter the water, in front of the head,
They trace a pattern, like a keyhole, it's said.
When the hands are in place, just under the chin,
The head lifts up to take a breath in.
The hands continue to press back to the thigh
It all looks so easy. Go on – have a try!

Pat Parkes

Chapter 9

Interesting Water Activities

Main Focus:

- Treading water – breaststroke leg action and alternator kick
- Surface diving – head first and feet first
- Underwater swimming
- Sculling – seven different types of sculling positions
- Floating – various floating positions to improve body control
- Types of entries
- Types of exits
- Partner work
- Game activities
- A summary poem by Patricia Parkes

Chapter 9

Interesting Water Activities

INTRODUCTION

A fundamental principle when teaching swimming is to make pupils aware of how their bodies move in water. This can be described as **body awareness** and is best taught by developing and encouraging a wide range of different water-based activities and skills.

These activities add fun to a class and can often be used as a contrasting activity at the end of a lesson. Teachers are always asking 'what can we do?' Alternatively, they can be used for a series of special lessons as part of a course programme.

> 🔑 It is important for the teacher to remember to teach these activities in a progressive way. They can be woven into a variety of practices for all strokes.

TREADING WATER

Treading water is used extensively in many life saving, water polo and synchronised swimming activities:

- In **survival work**, it allows vision above the water and time to think about the situation.
- In **life saving**, it allows time for a situation to be assessed.
- In **water polo**, it is a vital skill for players to see the game in play and mark opponents while the goalkeeper uses the skill constantly.
- In **synchronised swimming**, the skill is used to hold set positions in the water.

There are several methods of treading water and it is always a good idea to introduce as many as possible. Each variation adds to the pupils body awareness.

Breaststroke leg action method

Look for:
• The body upright (vertical). • The head clear of the water. • The legs kicking down and out simultaneously as in a breaststroke leg action.

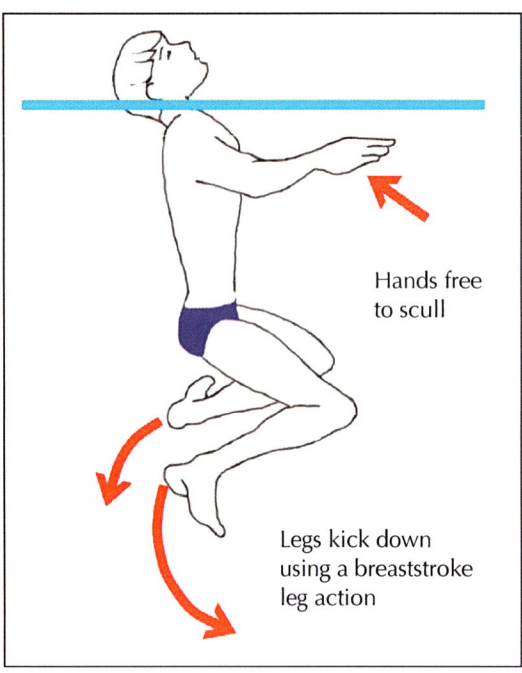

Hands free to scull

Legs kick down using a breaststroke leg action

Figure 9.1
Treading water with a breaststroke leg action

The hands add support by sculling hard. This leg action is strong because the movement is simultaneous. Each kick down raises the body up (action/reaction). As the legs recover, the body sinks a little. This causes a 'bobbing' effect.

The advantage of this style of treading water is that the strong leg action together with the use of the hands for sculling, keeps the head and shoulders high out of the water.

Other leg actions

There are two other leg actions which can be used when treading water.

An alternator leg action

This is similar to the breaststroke leg kick but the thighs are spread wider and each leg performs the breaststroke kicking movement alternately. The focus is on turning out the foot during this alternating breaststroke leg action so the inside of the lower leg can be used effectively to press out and down. For a more advanced practice, the hands can be held just above the water, relying on only the leg action to keep the body up.

A flutter kick leg action

The pupil performs a front crawl leg kick in a vertical position while still using their hands to scull. This is easy to teach, but if the hands stop sculling and are raised into the air, it becomes more difficult to support the body.

 When first teaching the skill:

- An initial demonstration by a skilled performer is often helpful.
- The pupils sit on the side with their feet in the water, practising each method. This allows them to see the shape they are making with their legs.
- The pupils start with two floats, one under each arm; then they gradually discard the floats.

SURFACE DIVING

Surface diving is used for survival and leads into underwater swimming.

There are two methods:

Head first surface dive

Look for:
• From the extended glide position, the arms being pulled strongly out and round.
• At the same time, the chin is tucked into the chest and the body is piked at the hips.
• The palms turn over and sweep forwards as the legs are pulled up. The weight of the unsupported legs takes the body down.

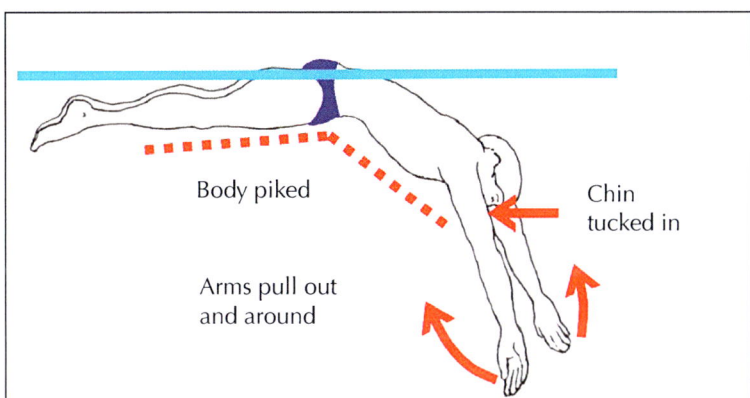

Figure 9.2a
Stage 1 of the head first surface dive

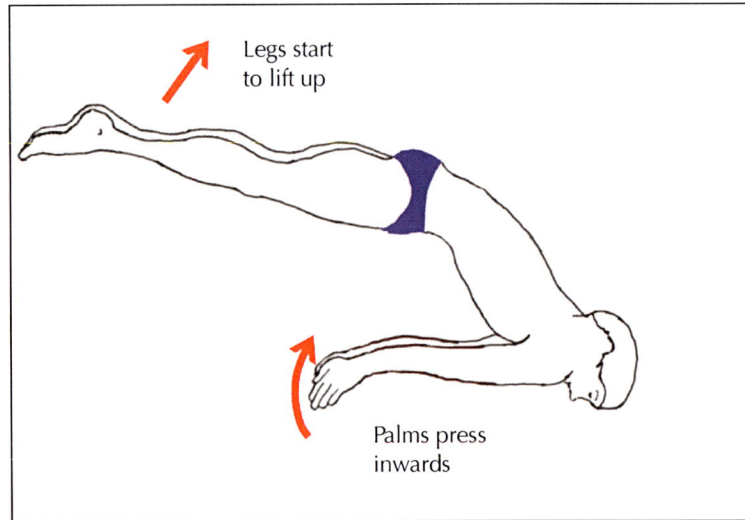

Figure 9.2b
Stage 2 of the head first surface dive

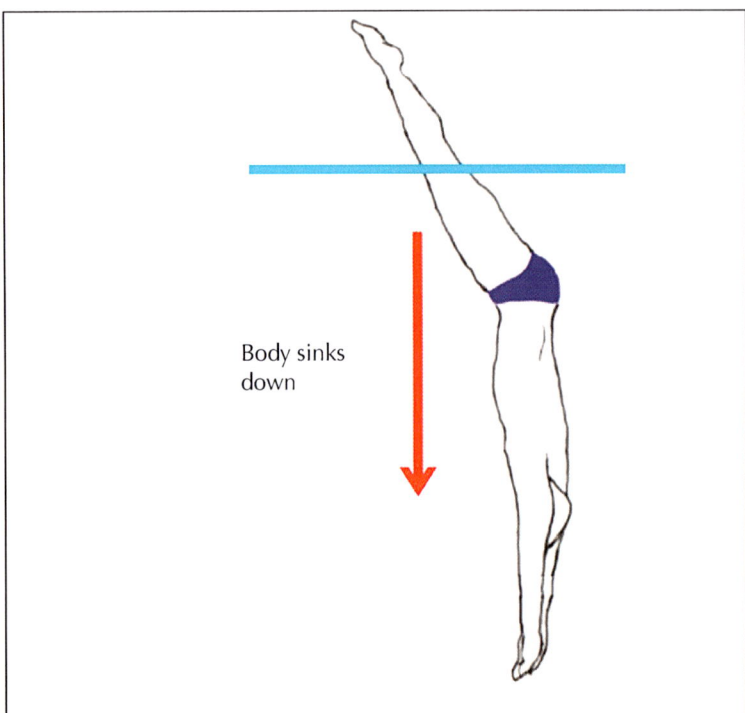

Figure 9.2c
Stage 3 of the head first surface dive

A progressive method to teach this skill is shown below:

1. Start with push and glide pulling the body into a long streamlined shape.
2. Mushroom tucks.
3. Mushroom tucks into a handstand.
4. Push and glide and pull the upper body into a pike leaving the legs stretched out on the surface.
5. Try the complete skill.

Feet first surface dive

From a treading water position, the legs are kicked strongly down, lifting the body out of the water and the arms are swung round above the head in a full stretch position. The legs come together and the body sinks in a vertical position.

To teach
Basically the pupils just have to try it. Emphasise the streamlined body stretching up with the arms coming together.

UNDERWATER SWIMMING

Swimming underwater improves confidence, is exciting and develops an excellent feel for the water. Teachers need to make this activity of value by teaching:

- How to control the breathing.
- Performing a variety of strokes.
- Ensuring the eyes are kept open.

To teach
1. Inhale first, sink down and from a strong push off with both arms extended in front of the head, swim breaststroke, breathing out gently through the nose and mouth.
2. As above, but instead of a breaststroke leg action, use a breaststroke arm action with a front crawl leg kick.

Extra interest can be achieved by:

- Having the pupils swim through hoops or partners' legs (individual or several pairs of legs making a 'tunnel'.
- Picking up objects from the pool bottom, (a ten pence coin is a great incentive).

SCULLING

We have already covered the basics of sculling in the backstroke chapter (Chapter 5) and the skill has been woven into the other three strokes. Sculling benefits all the strokes and helps the swimmer improve their feel for the water.

It is best practised by getting a swimmer to hold a pull buoy between the legs so the body is supported and sculling arms only. The skill can be performed in many different body positions, each one adding to the pupils' overall body awareness in water.

The benefits are:

- It teaches control.
- It stimulates interest.
- It adds fun to the lesson.

 Often boys find this difficult because their legs are heavy and they try to compensate by 'sitting'.

Types of sculls

- Travel: head first
- Body position: supine
- Hands: beneath hips
- Fingers: pointing towards ceiling

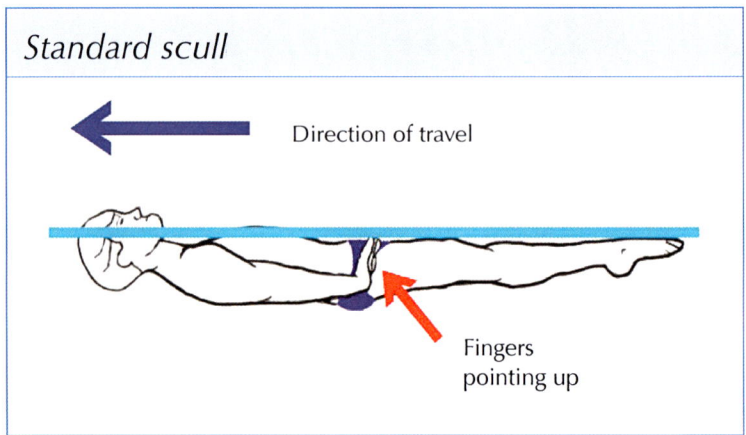

Figure 9.3
Standard scull

- Travel: feet first
- Body position: supine
- Hands: beneath hips
- Fingers: pointing towards floor

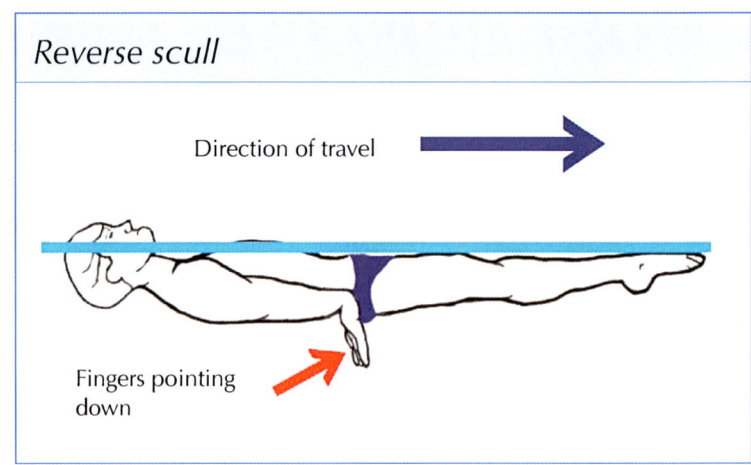

Figure 9.4
Reverse scull

336

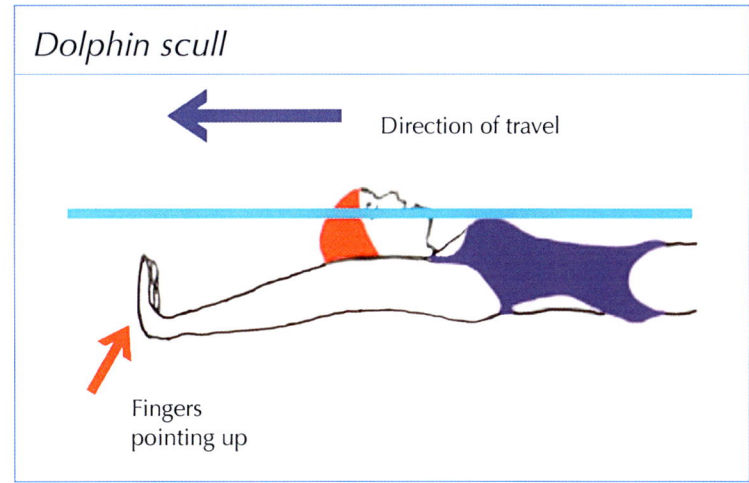

- Travel: head first
- Body position: supine
- Hands: stretched out behind head
- Fingers: pointing towards ceiling

Figure 9.5
Dolphin scull

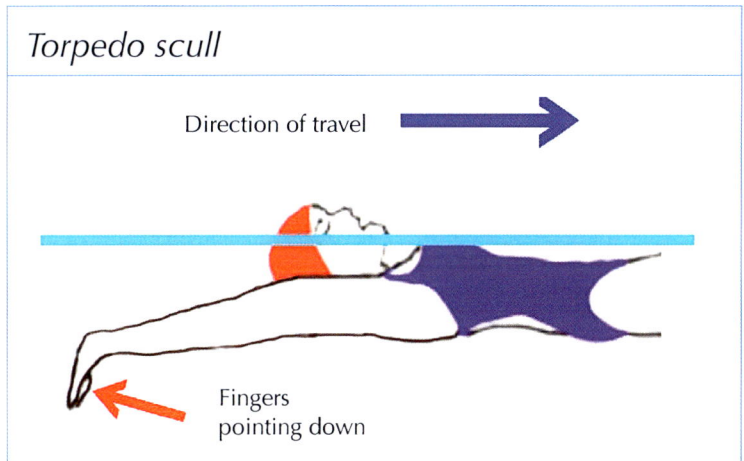

- Travel: feet first
- Body position: supine
- Hands: stretched out behind head
- Fingers: pointing towards floor

Figure 9.6
Torpedo scull

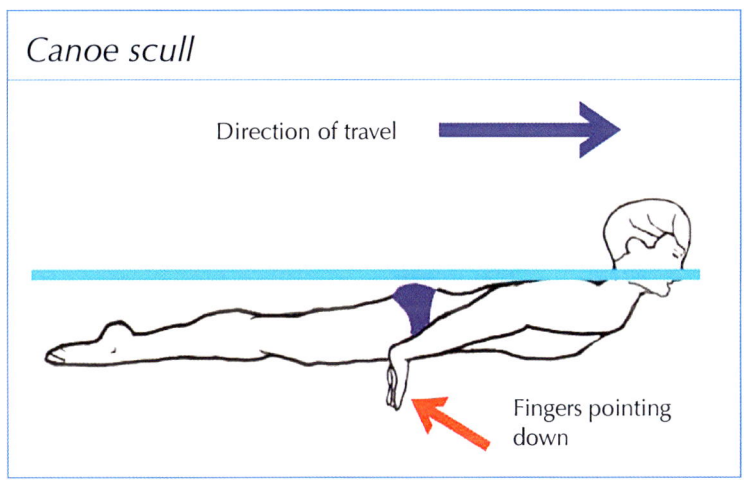

- Travel: head first
- Body position: prone
- Hands: stretched back down at the hips
- Fingers: pointing towards floor

Figure 9.7
Canoe scull

337

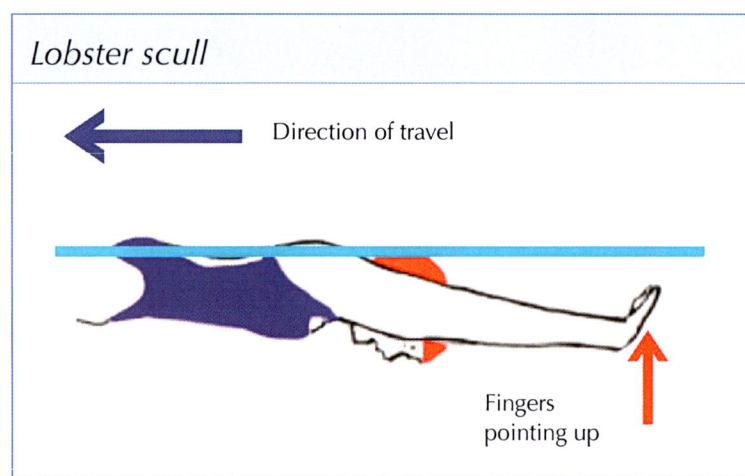

- Travel: feet first
- Body position: prone
- Hands: stretched out in front
- Fingers: pointing towards ceiling

Figure 9.8
Lobster scull

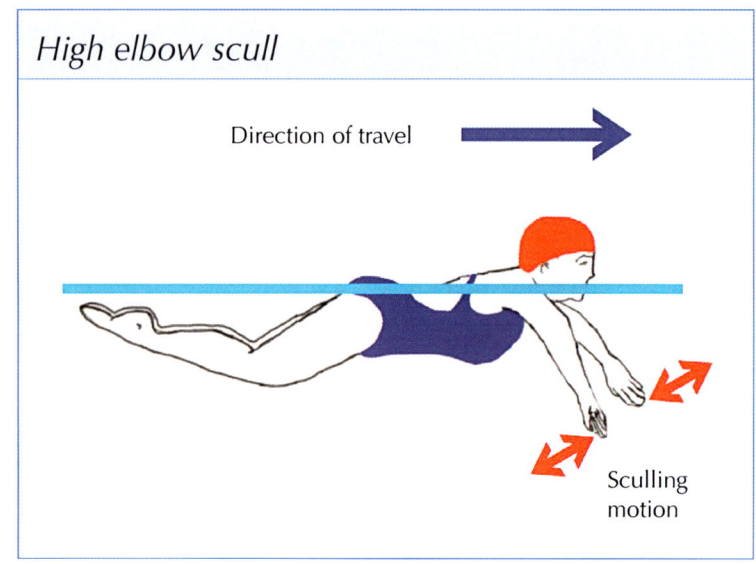

- Travel: head first
- Body position: prone
- Hands: under chin and below elbows
- Fingers: pointing towards floor

Figure 9.9
High elbow scull

Remember:

- The golden rule for sculling is that the body moves towards the direction the knuckles of the hand are facing.

- All of the sculls outlined above can be performed without a pull buoy using a gentle front crawl or backstroke kick to maintain a horizontal position.

- Sculling exercises can easily be integrated into combination practices involving kicking, pulling and full stroke.

Sculling can also be linked to somersaults. The body is tucked up tightly into a ball and the hands do:

- A backward sculling action to do a forward somersault.
- A forward sculling action to do a backward somersault.

In this instance, it often helps to call the scull 'skipping' comparing it to forward skipping, something that most children like to do.

This activity will also lead to tumble turns for competitive swimmers.

FLOATING

Types of floating

Standard float
The body lies flat in the water with the arms by the side.

Figure 9.10
A standard float on the back

Figure 9.11
A standard float on the front

Star float

The body lies flat on the surface of the water with the arms and legs apart in the shape of a star.

Figure 9.12
A star float on the back

Figure 9.13
A star float on the front

Pencil float

The body lies flat on the surface of the water with the arms and legs stretched out in line with the body. It is often fun to change from one shape to another. By pressing on the shoulder and hip, the body rolls round its longitudinal axis, first onto its side (as shown in Figure 9.16), then onto the front. This exercise is called a **log roll**.

Figure 9.14
A pencil float on the back

Figure 9.15
A pencil float on the front

Log roll

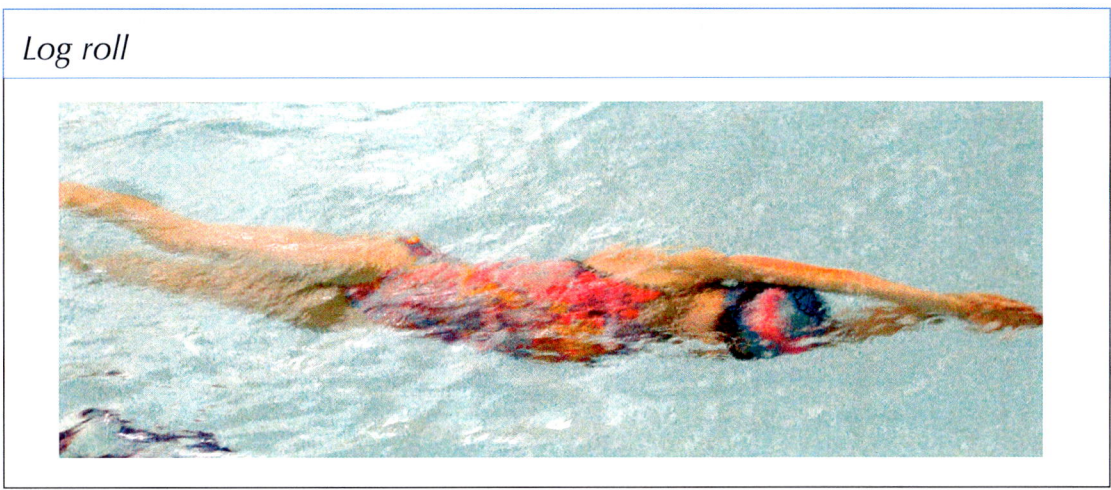

Figure 9.16
A log roll onto the side

Mushroom float

The body takes up a tuck position in the water. The higher the swimmer floats in the water, the more buoyant they are.

Figure 9.17
A mushroom float

ENTRIES

Types of entries

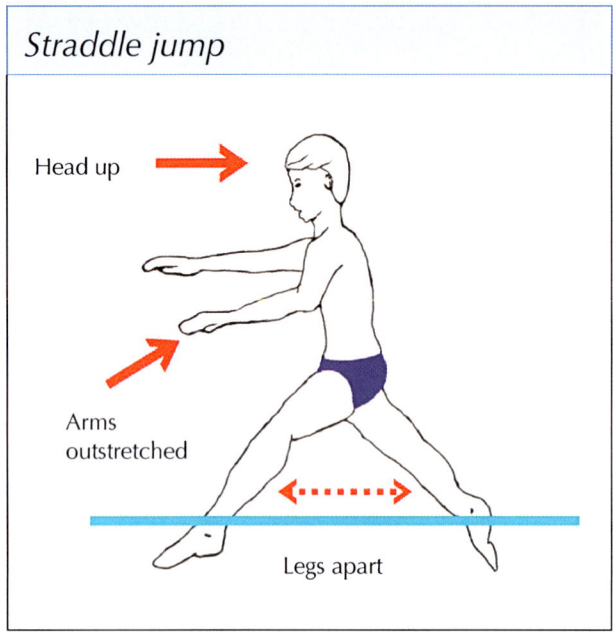

Straddle jump

Head up

Arms outstretched

Legs apart

From the side, the pupil steps out with one leg in front of the other, the arms outstretched, head up. The object is to keep as much of the upper body from going below the water on entry.

A good teaching point is . . . *'Can you keep your head dry?'*

Figure 9.18
A straddle jump entry

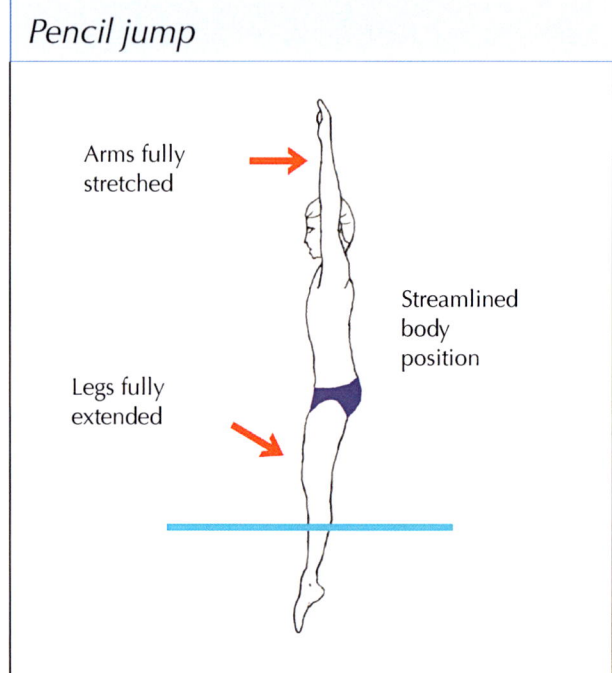

Pencil jump

Arms fully stretched

Streamlined body position

Legs fully extended

From the side, the pupil jumps with their body stretched hard, arms above the head. The streamlined position causes the body to descend quickly and deeply, so be careful that there is enough water depth. Also ensure that the pupils do not suffer from any ear problems.

Figure 9.19
A pencil jump entry

Tuck jump

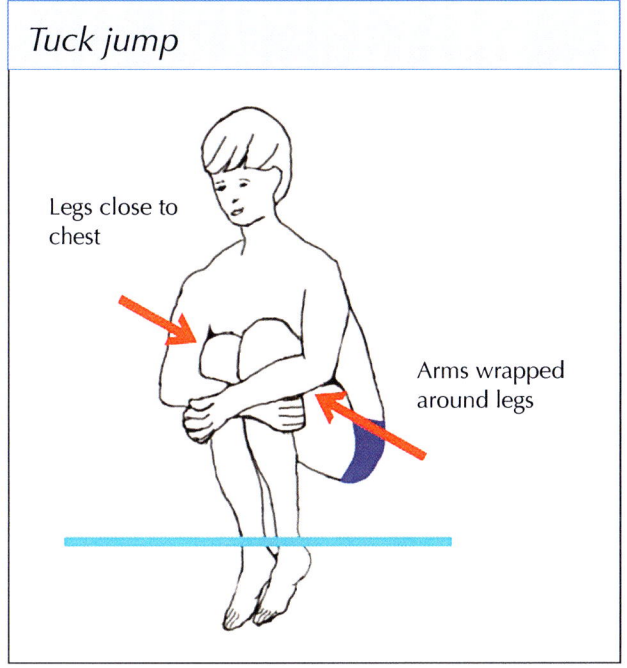

Legs close to chest

Arms wrapped around legs

From the side of the pool, the pupil jumps and tucks the legs close to the chest. This slows the descent as the landing is made with the body presenting a large surface area to the water.

Figure 9.20
A tuck jump entry

EXITS

These should not be ignored. With a deck level pool, exits are easy. With pools that have a deep overhang, it can be more difficult. Place both palms down flat on the side of the pool and give a strong breaststroke kick down. As the body lifts, straighten the elbows and climb out.

SOMERSAULTS

Forward somersault

Look for:
• From a front layout position, the knees coming up towards the chest and the head down towards the knees.
• The palms of the hands pressing down towards the bottom of the pool so the pupil rotates around in a forward tuck somersault.
• As the 360 degree rotation is near completion, the straightening out of the body to return to the layout position on the front.

343

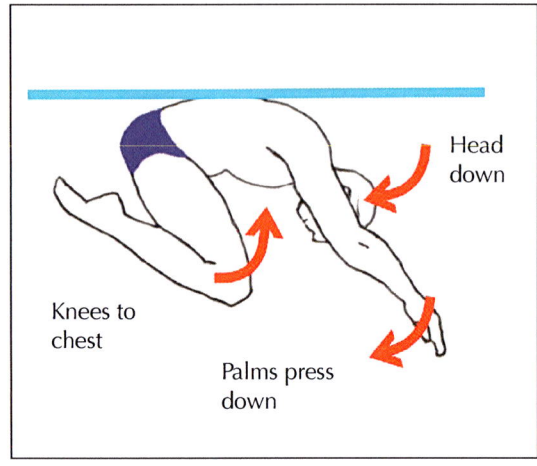

Figure 9.21a

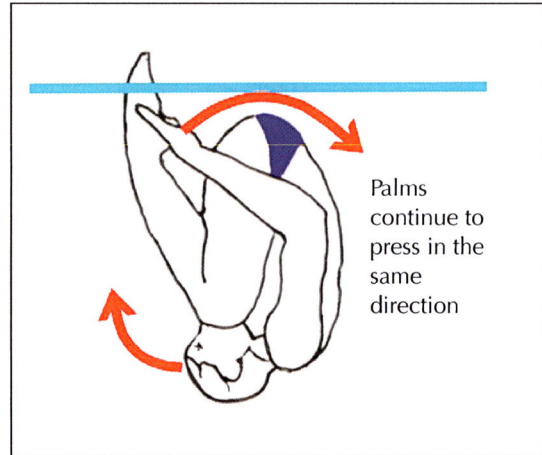

Figure 9.21b

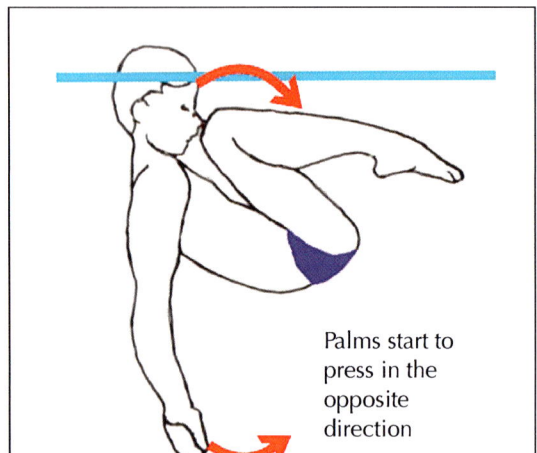

Figure 9.21c

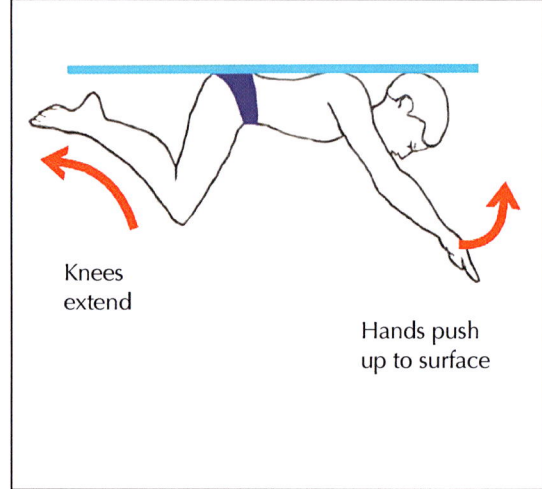

Figure 9.21d

Figure 9.21
Forward somersault

Backward somersault

> **Look for:**
>
> - From a layout position on the back, the knees coming up to the chest and the head down to the knees.
> - The palms of the hands pressing up towards the surface so the pupil rotates around in a backward tuck somersault.
> - As the 360 degree rotation is near completion, the straightening out of the body to return to the layout position on the back.

344

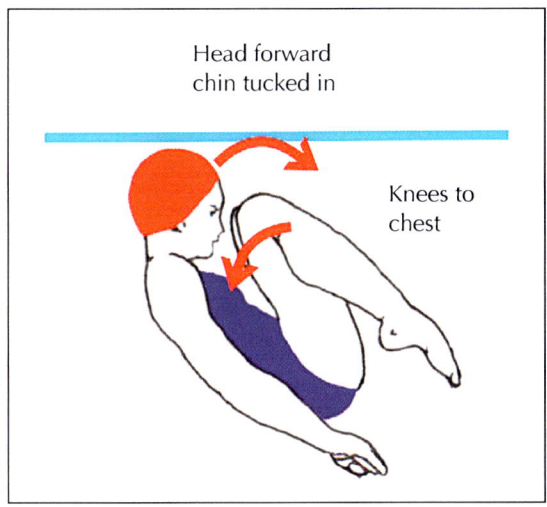

Figure 9.22a

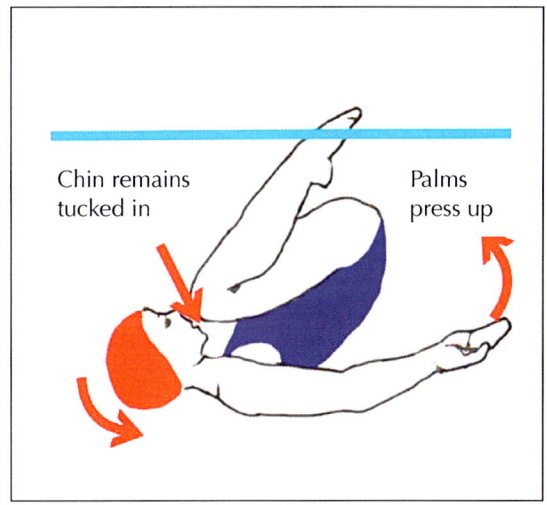

Figure 9.22b

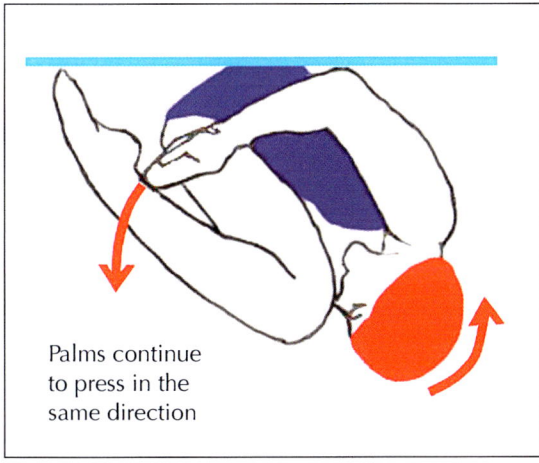

Figure 9.22c

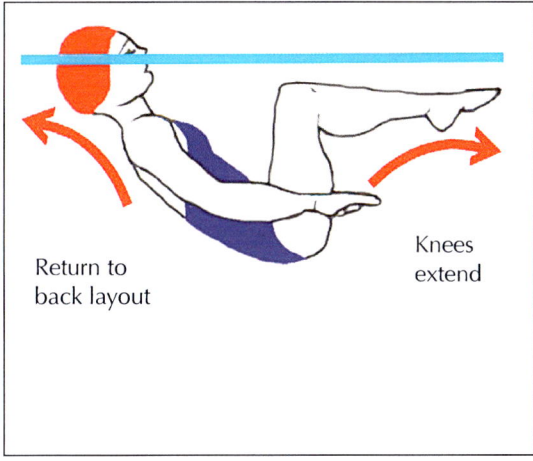

Figure 9.22d

Figure 9.22
Backward somersault

GAME ACTIVITIES AND PARTNER WORK

This can be very productive as the pupils practise skills in a fun activity.

Sculling in pairs or teams

Activity	Value of activity
In pairs, the swimmers lie flat on the water on their back with the second swimmer behind and in line with the first. Swimmer two tucks their feet under the arm pits of swimmer one. Both swimmers scull in tandem, moving either forwards or backwards. More swimmers can be added to the chain and competition can be introduced between teams.	• Stretches the body position. • The sculling work is hard. • It is also great fun.

Breaststroke 'train'

Activity	Value of activity
Swimmer one performs full stroke breaststroke while a partner holds onto their waist and performs just the leg action. Once again more people can be added to the chain to work together as a team.	• Encourages a lot of kicking and hard work for the leader.

Treasure hunting

Activity	Value of activity
Surface diving can be made great fun by assembling the class at one end of the pool. The teacher then throws lots of objects into the water to be picked up. On the starting signal, everyone swims around to find the objects and surface dives down to pick up as many as possible.	• A lot of practice on surface diving. • Encourages pupils to swim underwater with their eyes open.

Kick 'o' war

Activity	Value of activity
Working in pairs, two swimmers hold either end of the same float and kick as hard as they can to push their opponent to touch the side.	• Develops and strengthens the leg kick.

346

Blowing relay

Activity	Value of activity
Racing individually or in teams, swimming or walking across the pool while simultaneously blowing a ball or similar object.	• Encourages pupils to develop a forceful exhalation.

Counting fingers

Activity	Value of activity
Children are required to count the number of fingers shown on their partner's hands, which are underwater.	• Encourages pupils to open their eyes underwater.

Pigeon races

Activity	Value of activity
Children start sitting on the poolside. On 'go' they enter the water, swim to the opposite side and clamber out. The last person sitting again is eliminated. This game can be carried out as individuals or in team relay races.	• Encourages confident entries and exits.

Ring race

Activity	Value of activity
Lying supine, the contestants balance a diving ring or lightly weighted object on their tummy and continue by propelling themselves across the pool without losing the object, using any means of propulsion designated by the teacher.	• Encourages a more horizontal body position with a scull or leg action. • Can be carried out as an individual or as a relay team race.

Link tag

Activity	Value of activity
The game starts with one pupil as 'it' who proceeds to catch another pupil; they then join hands and so the line grows as pupils are caught.	• Promotes movement and confidence.

Wheelbarrow race

Activity	Value of activity
One pupil lies prone or supine with their arms extended above their head. Their partner supports their legs and pushes them across the pool.	• Promotes a good flat body position and confidence.

Float retrieve

Activity	Value of activity
A number of floating objects are thrown into the middle of the pool. Whoever collects the most is the winner.	• An individual competition requiring the use of propulsion and initiative with a limited use of limbs.

AT THE END OF THE LESSON

At the end of the lesson, when the 'graft' has been done,
Now is the time for an element of fun!
Floating and sculling and feeling the water,
Learning to make shapes, taller or shorter,
Ducking and diving, swimming through legs,
Seeking and finding those bright coloured pegs.
Treading water with a strong, steady beat,
Scull the hands round, the skill to complete.
Surface diving is great fun to do,
The different ways, number just two.
There's diving head first, eyes open wide,
Often done with a push from the side.
Or using the feet to lead the way,
The work is done, it's time to play!

Pat Parkes

FINAL THOUGHTS

On being a great SWIMMING TEACHER . . .

Your reading, theory, knowledge, practice and understanding will start you on your journey and take you so far.

The experience you gain along the way will take you a little further.

*An open mind, a willingness to try new things and a desire to continually do things better will take you to the end of your journey to becoming a **Great Swimming Teacher**.*

Good luck!
Colin Stripe and Patricia Parkes

Index